BERT
BACHARA

How To Do
Almost
Everything

SIMON AND SCHUSTER / NEW YORK

To Irma

THIRD PRINTING

SBN 671-20679-6
LIBRARY OF CONGRESS CATALOG CARD NUMBER: 76-129874
DESIGNED BY CARL WEISS
MANUFACTURED IN THE UNITED STATES OF AMERICA

CONTENTS

PART TWO / KITCHEN SNOOPING —QUICK COOKING HINTS

PREFACE

They say that anyone who ever wrote a book had to have a special motivation—and, in my case, there must have been as many as four, or maybe five, distinct ones. Here they are, although certainly not chronologically or in order of importance. There was the fact that some thousands of readers of my syndicated column wrote in, asking me, "Why don't you put all those great tips and hints in a book?" (Inasmuch as I do not have anywhere near as many relatives as the aforementioned thousands of readers, I accepted this as evidence of a fairly receptive market if I ever did write such a book.)

I have a very dear wife who has been deluded over the years into thinking her husband is a pretty good writer who could produce an immediate best seller. In consequence, I've had repeated reminders—like every morning, noon and night—in the form of the question: "When are you going to do The Book?" That brings me to another member of my family. I used to be well known as a columnist. I'm still fairly well known—but now, as a rule, it's for being Burt's father! And I couldn't be more proud of him, his wife, Angie, and our granddaughter Lea Nikki. The fact that Burt has done so beautifully as a composer, an entertainer and a fine gent has provided me with still a further motivation: after all, if I produce a great book, he may let me write the lyrics for one of his songs! But that probably won't work out, for he's blessed by having one of today's finest lyricists, Hal David, to work with.

At this stage, before I had definitely decided to do it, the final motivation occurred—in the form of a very simple and straightforward phone call. In it came the same old question: "Why don't you write a book on all those great tips and hints?" But this call differed from the others in that it came from Simon and Schuster—and they are now my Publishers! How about THAT?

—BERT BACHARACH

7

PART ONE

INSIDE
THE
HOUSE
AND
ALL
OUTDOORS

CLOTHES

AND

GROOMING

FOR MEN

☐ H A T S : Leather sweatbands in hats collect oil and soil. Occasionally wipe both sides well with a soapy cloth. . . . After hot days, turn the leather band of your hat inside out to dry it. . . . Keep perspiration from staining a hatband by rubbing a piece of paraffin over the inside of the leather sweatband, or put a strip of cellophane tape inside the leather sweatband of your hat.

> Brush hats even if they do not appear to need it. In the rain, the dust will turn to mud and stain the felt. . . . If the wind blows your hat into the mud, let it dry completely, then use a soft brush to wipe away dry mud crusts. . . . Never rub or dampen a felt hat that is spotted with soot. Cover the spots with dry salt and then remove with a stiff brush.

> Clean light-colored felt hats with a mixture of two tablespoons of cornmeal and one teaspoon of salt. Put it on with a soft cloth, rub off with a stiff brush.

> Use the small attachment of a vacuum cleaner to remove the dirt and dust that lodges in the creases of the bow on the band of your hat.

> Hat stores have special machines to steam hats. Achieve

a comparable effect at home and revive your bonnet by steaming it for a second or two over a teakettle. Then brush with the nap.

> When putting a seldom-worn hat on a shelf, turn up brim all the way round, and push dents out of crown. This will keep the hat in better shape for the next wearing.

> If storing a straw hat for the winter, wrap it in black or dark paper to keep it in the best shape. . . . It takes the pelts of five rabbits to supply enough fur felt for one hat—so put yours away in a box for the summer instead of letting it deteriorate open on a shelf.

> Did you ever think to ink your name and address on the inside of the leather band of your hat? If it's lost, or taken by mistake, there's the chance you'll get it back.

> Do not park your hat on a hook. You'll get longer service and it will look better if always placed on a flat surface.

> If your favorite hat seems a bit loose after a haircut, size it down by putting a small strip of adhesive tape inside the leather sweatband on either side of the temple. When hair thickens, remove the tape.

> When putting on your hat, hold brim front and back with fingers close to crown. Saves the shape.

☐ S H I R T S : Keep a seldom-worn dress shirt perfectly clean by enclosing in a large sheet of waxed paper. Seal the edges with a warm iron. This provides dustproof protection.

> If you take a wash-and-wear garment under the shower with you, it will get a thorough rinsing. It will drip-dry fastest if exposed to the air. Hanging in a humid, closed bathroom can almost double the drying time. Open window and door. But before putting on hanger, blot shirt well in a terry towel. It should be hung up to dry with all the buttons buttoned.

> A wash-and-wear shirt will be much dirtier at the collar and cuff lines than on the rest of the body. Pretreat these areas by rubbing in a paste of soap or detergent and a little water. Rub hard with thumb and forefinger to loosen the grease and dirt—then wash.

> If shirt front bulges and puffs out, hook a rubber band from a low shirt button to the top trouser button. It will stay flat and neat. . . . Tucking the tails of a dress shirt inside a pair of boxer shorts with a snug elastic band will keep your shirt front flat and smooth through an entire evening. . . . When you find the bosom of a formal shirt is shorter than you like, get the kind that has pleats running down to the bottom of the shirt.

> Put an indelible-ink mark on the collarbands of shirts with French cuffs. You won't have to unfold to know. . . . If no links are available for a French-cuffed shirt, bend a pair of paper clips to hold the cuffs temporarily.

> Instead of rolling sleeves in summer, fold them up neatly. They will be unmussed when turned down again.

> When you send sport shirts out to be laundered or cleaned, request that they be returned on hangers rather than folded. They'll be more sightly if uncreased.

> Shirt buttons sometimes take on a slight discoloration from laundering. You can usually remove this by rubbing the buttons with an ink eraser.

> To keep fresh for a lunch or dinner date when you will not be able to change your shirt, start out with French cuffs turned under instead of over. When reversed later to their regular fold, they'll be neat and clean.

> Pencil marks around the pocket of a shirt should be erased before washing, as the water will make the lead marks much harder to remove.

> If shirt sleeves are too long, it's best not to alter them at the shoulder or at midsleeve. Sleeve will fit better if cuff is taken off and then replaced after the sleeve is shortened.

> If a shirt has even the slightest snag or tear, have it repaired before putting it in the laundry. That way, the damage will not worsen.

> If you lose a button on the cuff of the shirt you are wearing, it can be held temporarily by your tie tack until you can have a new button sewn on.

> If your shirts are laundered at home, do not have the folds of the French cuffs pressed over. This grinds dirt into the creases. You can fold them neatly yourself when you don the shirt.

> Nothing is more uncomfortable in hot weather than a tight shirt collar. Put tight ones away for the winter—wear looser ones in the summer.

> A gain or loss of about seven pounds could mean that you need a different collar size for either comfort or appearance. . . . If you haven't had your collar size checked lately, it might be wise to have your men's store measure it. The average man's neck size grows about ½ inch every ten years, and that may be why collars no longer fit you.

> Avoid starch in collars—it definitely shortens the life-span of the shirt. . . . If a collar-attached shirt comes back from the laundry with too much starch, moisten the button-hole on the collar for easier handling. . . . When shirt collars have slots underneath for collar stays, it's best not to have these shirts starched. Starch will not distribute evenly through the many layers of fabric.

> Sometimes a shirt collar is wrinkled before you ever wear it, particularly from being packed while traveling. Try damp-ening the collar at night and pressing it against the flat inside wall of the bathtub; it will be neat and wearable the next morning. . . . If your shirt collar is slightly wrinkled, "iron" it for a few seconds over a hot (and clean) electric light bulb.

> Remove those little balls of fuzz from a shirt collar by going over the surface of the collar with a clean electric shaver. It will harm neither the fabric nor the shaver.

> When you put on a shirt, be sure the collar is turned down to the correct fold line in the back. If worn incorrectly, even for a few minutes, it will appear mussed and untidy for the rest of the day.

> To correct a shirt collar whose points curl upward, try (a) giving points a good stretch or (b) tying a smaller knot in your tie.

> Large pipe cleaners can be cut to size as extra collar

stays; or you can cut strips from the borders of that celluloid calendar you probably carry in your wallet. Hairpins or bobby pins will also do the trick. . . . Remove plastic collar stays before having a shirt laundered—extreme heat can fuse them.

□ SUITS/JACKETS: The neighborhood tailor can line the knees of homespun or tweed pants to keep them from getting baggy.

> On suits that are beyond repair, and too old even to give to charity, save the buttons. Any or all may come in handy when you lose buttons on a newer suit.

> When cuff edges of jackets show a slight sign of wear, a tailor can shorten sleeves a fraction of an inch to cover this up. (And 90 percent of men would look better in shorter sleeves.)

> Try wearing your belt buckle a little to the side, instead of centered. It's far more comfortable and your jacket will fit better.

> In brushing out cuffs and pockets of a suit, do not forget the inside seams on jackets and trousers. You'll find plenty of lint and dust there too.

> A suit has a better chance of recovering its shape when hung up overnight if everything is taken from the pockets— even the breast-pocket handkerchief.

> Make a practice of occasionally going over collar folds on jackets with a cloth dampened with cleaning fluid. This removes dust and dirt that can soil fresh shirt collars.

> Remove suits from wire hangers and put them on shoulder-shaped wooden hangers as soon as possible after dry cleaning or pressing.

> In getting a new suit fitted, put all the stuff in the pockets that you usually carry. This will ensure a proper fit after alteration.

> Hang up suits with pocket flaps flat and smooth. Otherwise the flaps can get sadly wrinkled and rumpled overnight.

> If you lose a button from one sleeve of a jacket and

haven't another to match, trim one from the other sleeve. Two buttons per sleeve are just as good style as three or four.

> There's humidity in the air year around, and it's the major cause of mussing of clothes. Give your suit a vigorous shake before putting it on a hanger—to readjust the fibers and remove wrinkles.

> If you get caught in the rain, see that your suit is thoroughly dry before you have it pressed. This will keep wrinkles from being pressed into the garment.

> Although hand pressing of suits is more expensive, it makes them look better and wear longer.

> When a jacket has to be touched up with an iron at home, wrap a terry towel around a rolling pin and insert in sleeves. They can then be pressed without acquiring creases.

> If you have a very loose button on a jacket and cannot have it stitched on at once, wrap a narrow strip of cellophane tape around the remaining threads; this will hold it safely until it can be fixed.

> How long since you wore that tuxedo that's hanging in your closet? Get it out, give it a good brushing, readjust it on the hanger—and give it a day's airing before putting it back in the closet.

> Don't be rude, men, but be firm when a hostess, or anyone else wants to pin a flower on the satin lapel of your dinner jacket. It will leave a hole that won't come out.

> It's a good idea to have a zipper closure put on an inside jacket pocket, to keep valuable papers and money from falling out and being lost.

> After you take your fall clothes out of garment bags, hang them on the shower rod of a steamed-up bathroom, and follow this with a good brushing. It will refresh them.

> When a summer suit is damp with perspiration, it's important to get it on a hanger as soon as you take it off. But do not hang away in a closet till it has dried out. Also, try to carry fewer gimcracks in your pockets in hot weather. Their bulk, plus humidity, can stretch your clothes out of shape.

> There isn't a suit or jacket that wouldn't look better, and keep looking better longer, if men would only learn not to keep stuffing their hands into the pockets!

☐ T I E S : If the end of a tie curls up, give it a little stretch. This will straighten the bias lining and loosen thread.

> Knit ties may stretch if hung up. They're better off rolled in a ball.

> The worst thing you can do with a good tie is to slide the knot and take the tie off over your head. Only an untied, hung-up tie can revive itself.

> Neckties will have a neatly pressed look if hung in the bathroom while you take a hot steamy shower.

> If you're tired of having ties hang haphazardly on an open rack, collecting dust, a cabinet about the same size as a bathroom medicine chest can be made or adapted to hold ties. Just put a bar across the top and fasten to your closet door.

> Ties often slide off smooth tie bars and end up on the floor. You can prevent this by circling the bar with a piece of cardboard or rough paper, joining the edges with cellophone tape. The tie bar will then be skidproof. . . . For an inexpensive and practical tie bar, put two cup hooks on the inside of the closet door and stretch a wide rubber band between them. The tie will not slide off.

> No matter how you love a certain tie, keep from wearing it on consecutive days. Like a suit or shoes, it needs a rest.

> Try to remember to knot ties a little less tightly on humid days, and there will be a better chance that wrinkles will come out and ties will regain their shape overnight.

> Do a really professional job of pressing your good ties by inserting a properly cut-to-fit piece of cardboard in the large end. This will prevent seam creases from showing through.

> Smart businessmen keep an extra tie of each color in their desk drawer at the office. Then, if the gravy splashes at lunch, they're okay.

> There are many ties that you probably will not wear during the summer. Put them all over the crossbar of a hanger, cover it with paper, and put it in a storage closet till next fall.

> When you take off your tie in the office, attach the tie tack or clip to the tie instead of leaving it loose, and avoid losing it.

> Many men have a habit of reaching up to feel if their tie knot is centered and their collar points smoothed down. Nothing contributes more to quicker soiling of tie knot and shirt collar. If you have the habit—break it.

> Use a tie clasp, rather than a tie tack (pin), with any of your ties of the satin type. The clasp will leave no mark or impression of any kind. . . . If you use a tie tack, try to pierce the tie in about the same general area each time to avoid having numerous pinholes in the fabric.

> When the large end of a tie comes out shorter than the small end, take the time to retie it properly—otherwise it will look badly wrinkled when next worn.

> If a tie shows perspiration stains at knotting area, allow to dry, then go over area with plain water. . . . . When something is spilled on a tie, take care to blot the spot rather than rubbing it. The latter usually shifts the weave of the fabric, embedding the spot even further. . . . You can remove water spots from silk ties by allowing them to dry, then rubbing briskly with another part of the tie. . . . If everything else fails in your effort to remove a stubborn spot from a good tie, try holding it over the steam from a boiling kettle for a few seconds, then rubbing gently with a clean cloth.

> In wearing a tie that is soiled at the knot, reverse the tying process. Start with the long end to the right rather than to the left. The soiled area will be covered.

☐ T R O U S E R S : After you've been caught outdoors in a shower, "finger-crease" your trousers. It may save a pressing bill.

> When the stitching of your trouser cuff breaks, repair it temporarily with a piece of plastic or masking tape.

> Did you know that there are slip-on trouser protectors to keep your trouser legs dry on a rainy day?

> When caught short of trouser hangers, put cuffs of trousers neatly across the top drawer of dresser, then close the drawer. It's much better than draping the pants over a wire hanger. . . . If you have to put trousers over the crossbar of a wire hanger, first cover the bar with a rolled-up shirt cardboard or a folded towel. This will prevent a cross crease and keep them from sliding to the floor.

> A circle of masking tape, with the sticky side out, will make a trouser bar skidproof. Tape provides enough friction to keep pants from sliding and does not leave a mark on fabric.

> On the inside of a closet door a towel rack will hold a pair of trousers in readiness for a hurried dress-up the next morning.

> If you have clamp trouser hangers, use them. The weight of the trousers, suspended from the cuffs, will stretch out most wrinkles.

> Be seated when pulling on pants. It can save you many backaches and even falls. . . . Try to remember to pull on trousers before putting on shoes—no stitching is indestructible.

> Trouser cuffs should be brushed out frequently. Grit left in them too long can damage fabric.

> If you carry a key chain in your trouser pocket, shift it to the opposite side every month or so to keep the friction from wearing out the cloth. . . . Carry your wallet in some pocket other than the one on your hip. It bulges the suit out of shape, and it's not good for the wallet to be sat upon dozens of times a day.

> Get a fabric-covered seat pad if you do a great deal of sitting at a desk. Friction of leather or plastic against suit will cause shine.

> Unbutton your coat and hitch up your pants when you sit down. The finest fabrics can stretch—and it's easier on the buttons too.

> If washable golf slacks have bad grass stains, most of

them can be removed by a good rubbing with soap or detergent before washing.

☐ AND A LOT OF OTHER THINGS: If a heavy overcoat is left hanging all summer, it will sag and stretch out of shape. Better to wrap it flat and seal package well.

> Most of clothes-closet shelves are pure chaos. Make order out of yours by segregating things in separate stacked boxes, with markings on the fronts to indicate contents. . . . If you have things stored in boxes on the top shelf of your closet, write down the contents on tags attached with long enough strings to have them hang down where you can read them.

> An absorbent mercerized-cotton undershirt will keep you cooler in humid weather. The V-neck style will look better with an open-neck shirt, and also create less bulk under the tie area.

> You can keep a wallet from slipping out of your pocket by wrapping a heavy rubber band around it. The rubber, which will catch against clothing, may save you a loss.

> A continually smoked pipe will become strong and smelly and if carried in a pocket will impregnate your clothes. . . . Cigar smokers should remember to blow ashes off their clothes, instead of rubbing, which makes a messy smudge.

> Toothpaste has been found to be an excellent cleaner for any of your cuff links, tie tacks and other jewelry. And a vinegar-dampened cloth will clean up the metallic buttons on your blazer, making them shine.

> Remember to occasionally wipe inside of leather belts with moistened cloth, to keep them clean and prevent them from discoloring trouser tops.

> Look over your wooden hangers. Use steel wool to smooth rough spots on the metal hooks; sandpaper and coat with lacquer any rough spots on the wood. This can prevent damage to clothes.

> If the neck hanger on your overcoat is broken, have it

fixed right away. Until you do, never hang it up by the neck. Put it on a hanger, or hang it by a shoulder of the coat—as the gals do with their fur coats.

> With all the new and popular wash-and-wear raincoats looking pretty much alike, letter your initials large on the inside of the yoke.

☐ H A I R   C A R E :   If you have to use a strange barber and want to avoid the chance of getting "scalped," tell him you want just a trim. It won't last as long as a regular haircut, but neither will there be a long period of reshaping your hair after a bad cut. . . . Before getting a haircut, give yourself a shampoo. It makes it easier for the barber to give you a neat and smooth trim.

☐ H A N D   C A R E :   An effective way to clean greasy hands is to wet them, rub about a tablespoon of granulated sugar into them, then rinse and finish job with ordinary soap.

> Tiny shavings of soap, rubbed into the fingernails and followed by a buffing, will give a masculine polish.

> A good way to clean the dirtiest fingernails is to dip nail brush in dry baking soda and scrub.

☐ S H A V I N G :   Immerse a pressure can in hot water for a minute to get the last blob of shaving cream.

> If you ever run out of shaving cream completely, get a fill-in shave—and a good one—with your wife's cold cream.

> After using the last razor blade, put the empty container in your pocket as a memory jogger to buy more. . . . Put the little screw top of an emptied tube of toothpaste or shave cream in your change pocket. It will remind you to buy a new one.

> The best time to shave, unless you have to go right out, is an hour or so after getting up. Face puffiness after sleep retards a good shave. . . . Go after the fine hair first and leave the coarse hair till last. That gives shaving cream a longer time to soften the tough areas of your beard. . . . Get a closer shave by cutting across your beard with diagonal strokes.

> For a smoother face, use a hot towel before shaving and a cold one afterward.

> Do not leave a blade in the razor in toilet kit. Remove it and wrap well with tissue paper to keep it from doing any damage.

> If there's no time to shave, a bright tie will divert attention from your five-o'clock shadow.

> If you cut yourself around the lip area while shaving, wet a piece of tissue and place it between gums and lip to stop the bleeding. . . . Fanning the face with a piece of cardboard or paper will stop bleeding from razor nicks. . . . If you cut yourself and have no styptic pencil, stop the bleeding by applying pressure to the cut with clean gauze.

> For electric shaves, it's best to have the face perfectly dry, so shave before showering. . . . Try shaving in front of an electric fan for smoother and faster job. . . . If you have no preshave conditioner, wash face thoroughly and shave when good and dry.

> Common errors in electric shaving are holding the razor too tightly, stretching the skin too taut, and digging and scraping with the shaver. Secret: be relaxed!

> If the little cleaning brush for the electric-shaver blades is lost, try using a pipe cleaner, folded double.

FOR WOMEN

□ CLOTHES CARE: When pinning a heavy piece of costume jewelry on clothing, hold a piece of felt beneath the fabric. Run pin through this added thickness, and it will save dresses from pin marks.

> For a snap fastener that does not stay closed, try tapping it with a hammer, right on the tip.

> Protect clothing from rust spots on wire coat hangers by covering spots with clear nail polish. . . . If you're using painted hangers for drip-dry garments, wrap the wood parts in aluminum foil to keep the clothes from being stained.

> To bring life to fur, spread it out flat and stroke gently with a thin stick. . . . Clean white fur or fake fur by rubbing with dry cornmeal. . . . Do not place mothballs on or in your fur coat. Some furs are allergic to them. . . . Beware of friction when wearing furs—it ages them more quickly than many other common causes.

> Lace will look nice longer if instead of being starched, it is dipped in water in which two lumps of sugar have been dissolved. Restore any velvet item by brushing well to remove dust and lint. Then steam on the wrong side with a steam iron, or by hanging in a steamy bathroom. Hang up to dry.

> Ladies should remove the metallic foil on a corsage before pinning it to their clothes, as the foil may leave a stain difficult to remove.

> Never pull a loose thread from clothing. Trim it off, carefully, close to the fabric. . . . If you have one button on your heavy-duty clothes that keeps coming loose from wear or strain, sew it on next time with dental floss. . . . When snipping a button off a garment, be careful not to cut the fabric. Best precaution is to slide the teeth of a comb under the button.

> Line sweater pockets with matching cotton material to prevent stretching and increase life of pocket. . . . The only way to keep angora from shedding is to put it in a freezer, wrapped in a plastic bag, before wearing it.

> Cellophane tape wrapped around the hand or a 3x5 card, with the sticky side out, will remove hair and lint from dark woolens quickly and efficiently. If using the card, slip hand under tape and use like a clothes brush.

> Run an ordinary lead pencil up and down a sticking zipper. The graphite will lubricate the parts and make the zipper run smoothly . . . For those hard-to-reach back zip-

pers, straighten out a wire hanger. Put hook into eye of zipper and pull up.

☐ G L O V E S : When washing leather gloves, use a hair shampoo or soap with lanolin to help restore the oil of the glove skins. . . . A few drops of olive oil added to the rinse will keep doeskin, pigskin and chamois gloves soft and pliant. . . . Roll gloves off hands after washing; do not pull them off, as pulling stretches glove fingers out of shape. . . . Washable leather gloves will dry softer if rolled for a minute in a moist terry towel after washing. . . . Push clothespins carefully into fingers of newly washed gloves to keep them from losing shape while drying.

> If leather gloves are to be stored, wrap in tissue rather than in plastic bags, so they can get required air.

> If it's hard to get a glove over a large ring, turn the stone to the inside of your palm.

> You can clean white kid gloves by pulling them on hands and dousing in alcohol. Or, rub with cloth dipped in skim milk —they will dry quickly without retaining an odor. . . . To remove spots from white kid gloves, slip gloves on hands and rub spots with an art gum eraser. . . . To dye white kid gloves, dip into strong black coffee. To make kid gloves look like new, rub with egg white after cleaning.

> Clean suede gloves by putting them on and rubbing hand with thick slice of stale bread, changing to another slice as the bread becomes soiled. To freshen suede gloves, rub with fine-grained side of an emery board.

☐ H A T S A N D V E I L S : Spots on a felt hat can usually be removed by light rubbing with a clean blotter. . . . Rain spots on a felt hat can be easily removed if they are brushed with a soft wad of tissue paper in a circular motion.

> Applying a thick paste of baking soda will remove perspiration stains from the band of a hat.

> To give a crisp shine to a straw hat, and a new look to the veil, use the hair spray that keeps your hair in place.

> You can stiffen a limp-looking hat veil if you drop it in beer, shake out vigorously, and lay it out on a towel to dry. . . . Or place waxed paper over a veil and run a hot iron over it; the veil is stiffened and freshened as the wax comes off on the veil. . . . Revive a wrinkled veil by "ironing" it back and forth over a hot light bulb.

> If a veil is torn, just put colorless nail polish on the torn ends and hold them together firmly for a few seconds; the tear is repaired and the polish will not show.

☐ JEWELRY: To string pearls or beads, dip the end of dental floss in colorless nail polish. After it dries, the dipped end forms a firm needle for stringing through beads. . . . Or, nylon fishing line is great for stringing beads—strong, flexible and stiff enough to use without a needle. . . . Or, a violin string is also excellent for stringing beads.

> When restringing beads, line them up in desired order on a strip of cellophane tape, then string with no scattered or lost beads.

> Dull rhinestone jewelry will shine if soaked in detergent for about 15 minutes and then rubbed with a flannel cloth. . . . If metal jewelry gets dull and dreary-looking, dunk it in a small glass of warm water and detergent. In a few minutes it will come out sparkling.

> A discarded mascara brush is a handy cleaner for getting into crevices on jewelry.

> A small piece of white chalk in the costume-jewelry box will keep the contents from tarnishing.

> Keep diamonds and other precious-gem rings sparkling by brushing with toothpaste; rinse in clean cold water. . . . To give diamonds a good cleaning, soak them for 30 minutes in a cup of hot sudsy water with a few drops of household ammonia. . . . For extra sparkle, drop diamond rings in seltzer, leave for 10 minutes and then shake dry.

> An expert advises taking care of your cultured pearls like this: 1) Wear them as often as possible and they will never get dull. 2) Wipe occasionally with soft damp cloth. 3) Have

them knotted and restrung at least once a year. . . . Don't store away pearls in drawer or jewel box without air for long periods. Whenever put away, wrap each piece in tissue or soft cloth.

> To clean pearl and amber beads, rub lightly with just a little olive oil. . . . Take off real or cultured pearls before using hair spray or perfume atomizer. Certain ingredients may affect the luster of the pearls.

> To get a tight ring off the finger, soak hand in ice-cold soapsuds. Then rub on more suds to let ring slip off.

> If you want to give a girl a ring as a surprise, and you do not know her size, slip one of her rings over a tapered cork and mark the place. A store can measure that.

> If a silver ring turns dull and dark, soak it in ½ cup of vinegar and 2 tablespoons baking soda for two hours. After the soaking, rub the ring with a towel. It will be as shiny and good as new.

> When a link chain is tangled, rub it between the palms of your hands and it will untangle itself.

☐ LINGERIE: Dust baby powder in lingerie drawers for sweetness and easy, smooth donning of undergarments in sticky weather. . . . Or give lingerie a freshener by adding a few drops of cologne to rinse water when doing hand washing.

> Black lingerie often has a tendency to turn brown after washing. To restore original color, use plenty of bluing in the rinse water.

> Curtail static electricity and excess clinging of nylon slips in cold weather by adding a small amount of liquid detergent or fabric softener to final rinse water.

> Dab an unexpected run with wet soap and it will stop there till it's time to change. . . . Or apply hair spray to stop a run.

> Run strips of cellophane tape along any rough edges of desk and chair to save stockings.

> Freezing will add life to nylons. Wet the stockings and put in a plastic bag. Place in the freezer or in freezing compartment of refrigerator. Take out after they are frozen and let thaw. Squeeze and hang up to dry.

> Nylon stockings will dry quicker if you blow through them as you would a balloon, after blotting with a towel. . . . Next time you wash hosiery, tie pairs together loosely before washing. They dry easily and there's no time wasted sorting out mates.

> A number of mateless stockings can achieve a common color and be matched if boiled slowly for about 15 minutes in enough water to cover stockings. Allow to cool in the pan, rinse and hang to dry.

IN GENERAL: CLOTHING TIPS (FOR MEN & WOMEN)

☐ S T A I N S : Here is a brief compendium of ways of removing spots from washable clothing.

> *Coffee:* cloth should be stretched over a bowl while boiling water is poured over stain from a height of two or three feet.

> *Grease* stains should be rubbed with a dry cake of soap, then washed with warm suds.

> *Liquor* spots should be soaked in cold water, then washed in hot soapy water.

> *Fruit* stains should be rubbed with glycerin and then treated like a coffee stain.

> If you get any *liquid* on clothes, don't use warm water— it sets the liquid into a stain, while cold water usually removes it.

> If you get *chewing gum* on clothes, hold an ice cube against the spot for a minute—and you should be able to lift the hardened gum right off.

> Try rubbing *lipstick* stains off washable clothes with petroleum jelly before washing them in hot suds.

> If there's *iron rust* on a garment, squeeze some lemon juice on the stain, then spread in the sun for a while and rinse.

□ STORAGE: Before spraying clothes with *mothproofing* when packing them away, also spray the box or garment bag they're to be put in, for extra protection. And don't forget to give your clothes closet a good wiping with a cloth dampened in turpentine. It will help prevent moth damage. . . . Lukewarm soapsuds rubbed across *plastic garment bags* will keep them clean. . . . *Closets* that are damp and dark encourage insects and mildew. Turn a lamp on inside your closet occasionally to help dry it out and your clothes will be safer. . . . Freshen your clothes closet after the humid summer by letting an electric fan run for a while, sitting on the floor of the closet. It's especially good if there are remaining odors of moth repellent. . . . Put leftover pieces of soap in bottom of *clothes hamper* to give it a fresh smell.

> Sweaters, or any *knitted apparel,* should be folded neatly and placed on a shelf or in a drawer, rather than being hung up. If left on hangers for any length of time, they may stretch out of shape. . . . When wrapping anything of *wool* for summer storage, use plenty of newspaper as a wrap. Moths hate it.

□ EYEGLASSES: Keep eyeglasses from fogging when going from outdoor cold to indoor heat by applying a thin film of soap on lenses and polishing as usual. Repeat every other day. . . . Eyeglass wearers who have to be out in driving rain can keep glasses clear if glasses are washed, dried and then rubbed on both sides with soap. Polish till all traces of soap disappear and they will be rainproof.

> To clean glasses without streaks, use a drop of vinegar on each lens—or a drop of gin or vodka.

> Sunglasses that are smudged with suntan oil can be

cleaned with rubbing alcohol, ginger ale, or spray-on window cleaner.

> If you are going on a trip, take along an extra pair of glasses and/or the prescription for new lenses. . . . A business card or slip of paper with name and address tucked inside the case might ensure their return if lost. Gold-foil tape is now available on which the name and address may be written and put on leather or plastic cases. . . . To adjust earpieces on frames of eyeglasses, heat them *carefully* over a toaster and then shape them to fit properly.

☐ HAIRBRUSHES & COMBS: Adhesive tape is good for cleaning the teeth of a comb. Press on—pull off. . . . Dip combs in alcohol solution after cleaning to completely remove all harmful bacteria.

> A good way to get loose hair out of a brush before washing is to use the notched end of an old safety razor (without the blade, of course).

> Soak hairbrushes in a mixture of six parts of water to one part clear ammonia for the best cleaning. . . . Or use equal parts of salt and flour. Rub mixture into brush, comb through bristles and shake vigorously. Mixture picks up all oil and dirt. . . . Or cornmeal may be sprinkled on the bristles, and a comb run through until both brush and comb are clean. Wash in suds and rinse well. Rinsing in an alum and water solution restores stiffness to hair brush bristles.

> Brushes and combs may also be washed in a sinkful of warm water to which a couple of tablespoons of baking soda are added. Soda's alkaline action cuts oils and grease. . . . Or clean your comb and brush with the same shampoo you use on your hair.

☐ SHOES AND RAINWEAR: After a night's rest, your feet are at their smallest. To ensure comfort, it's better not to buy new shoes first thing in the morning. . . . Too many shoe salesmen measure feet when the customer is sitting down. Shoes should be measured and fitted when the entire weight of the body is on the feet. That's when they're at their largest. . . . Never insist on getting the same size shoes you're wearing. Have your feet measured every time, and accept the size that the gadget indicates. . . . Even though new shoes fit properly and comfortably, don't press your luck. Wear them for intervals, rather than steadily, until they're well broken in.

> You can tell something about the quality of a new pair of shoes by carefully examining the insoles and lining. Be sure they're smooth and without ridges or projecting stitches.

> To keep the size marks in shoes legible for future reference, paint over them with clear nail polish when the shoes are new. . . . When you buy new shoes, coat the edge of the soles with colorless nail polish. It will help retain the finish and prevent scuffing. . . . To prevent slipping when wearing brand-new shoes, rough the soles up a bit with sandpaper. It will not affect the wear of the shoes. . . . You can get the stiffness out of shoe heels, and relieve friction against socks, by rubbing the heel lining with soap and flexing the counter.

> It takes 48 hours for a shoe to dry out properly after it has been wet by a rainstorm. . . . Apply saddle soap to rain-soaked shoes while they are still wet. Let them dry with the soap on them, and it will keep the leather from stiffening. . . . If your shoes get really wet on the inside, stuff them solidly with paper, to help dry them out and support the shape, until trees can be inserted. . . . Remove mud from leather shoes by first allowing them to dry, then rubbing vigorously with a dry cloth. . . . If dirt and mud are caked between the uppers and soles of shoes, try an old toothbrush to get them out. If they're too hard, use a wire brush. . . . Kerosene will soften leather shoes and bags that have been hardened by rainwater. When dried, they will take a good shine again.

> When polishing shoes, use a cotton-tipped swab stick dipped in the polish to get to hard-to-reach places between the uppers and the soles. . . . If winter shoes have been stored over the summer, it's wise to have them polished before wearing. Even if they look all right, they need the lubrication. . . . You can keep shoe polish in a can from caking and hardening by cutting a piece of aluminum foil slightly larger than the can, putting it on the can and then replacing the lid. The polish will stay moist. . . . Never apply polish to soiled

shoes. First use a dry cloth to remove dust or a bristle brush to remove mud and dirt.

> Waxed paper rubbed on white shoes after polish has dried will protect the shine and will keep polish from getting on dark clothing.

> When you need a shoeshine quickly, shine shoe with dry cloth, then add drops of water to the shoe and buff to a high gloss. . . . Or, for emergency shine, rub leather shoes with inner side of a banana skin. Wipe clean and polish with a woolen cloth.

> Nylon-hose friction builds up a magnetic attraction that will give your shoes a wonderful shine with either polish or water. . . . Benzine will remove accumulated polish from shoe tops. . . . Try using baby oil to polish shoes. Leave oil on for a few minutes, then polish with a soft cloth. Makes leather supple and shoes last longer. . . . Brown leather shoes or belts can be darkened by rubbing with milk to which a few drops of household ammonia have been added. As soon as dry, polish with a soft cloth. . . . An old sock serves as a good shoe-polish applicator, and the can can be stored in it, too. . . . If your youngsters scuff the toes of their shoes (and what kid doesn't?), brush several layers of shellac over the fronts when they're freshly polished. . . . Try applying shoe polish at night and leave the buffing till the next morning. The polish soaks into the leather and prolongs the life.

> Restore original luster to patent leather shoes by an application of thick soapsuds applied with a sponge. Clean surface by wiping with sponge squeezed nearly dry of clear water. Polish with soft cloth. . . . To remove spots from black patent leather dress shoes, use a solution of vinegar in water. . . . When patent leather slippers are badly scuffed, blacken them with any black shoe polish and cover with clear nail polish. They will shine like new, and you can polish them again simply by using polish remover and another coat of clear polish. . . . Orange juice can be used to make patent leather shine.

> You can remove most stains on suede shoes by rubbing with a piece of white bread. . . . Or suede can be cleaned with a soft sponge. Even suede brushes can rub away the nap

if rubbed too vigorously. . . . A steam iron will raise the nap on suede.

> A very bad scuff on a pair of shoes can be made more sightly if several layers of shellac are applied after the shoes are polished. . . . Apply a touch of India ink on scuffs on black shoes. It will cover them up and take a good polish.

> Tennis shoes wash fine in an automatic washer, and they are not harmed in dryer. . . . Give tennis shoes a treatment with white starch after each washing to keep them white. . . . When you've played your last round of golf for the season, give your golf shoes a good cleaning, put them on trees, lubricate well and store in shoe bags for the winter.

> Whiten white shoelaces by washing them with sour milk. . . . A knot tied at the end of shoelaces, after the shoes are laced, will prevent a child from unlacing them. . . . A pair of eyebrow tweezers is the best tool for untangling badly knotted shoelaces. . . . If you lose the tip of a shoelace, dip the end in colorless nail polish. When dry, it will be as stiff as the tip.

> Use lighter fluid to get tar stains off shoes. . . . People rarely think of cleaning shoe brushes, yet that will make them give you a much better shine. Give them an occasional soaking in warm suds to which a few drops of turpentine have been added.

> When doing any rough work around the house or garage, pull an old pair of socks over your shoes. It might save them from deep scratches. . . . If storing away heavy shoes for the summer, apply a thin coat of wax to the soles to avoid mildew. They're better off, too, if on a rack instead of the floor. . . . Thin lightweight innersoles in your shoes will keep your feet cooler in hot weather. They provide good insulation against steaming pavements. . . . Use shoe trees to prevent creases from becoming cracks, as well as to maintain the overall shape of the shoe.

> If you have a shoe shelf on the floor of the closet, cover it with strips cut from an old desk blotter. This will absorb moisture and prevent mildew. . . . Rubbing imitation leather or plastic with petroleum jelly will prevent cracking. . . . On

very icy days, a few strips of adhesive tape on the soles of shoes will help keep you upright.

> Cut off the toe parts of an old pair of socks and put them on the fronts of shoes when putting on rubbers or galoshes. Shoes will stay shiny. . . . Strips of adhesive tape fastened around inside tops of boots and galoshes will prevent rings around stockings. . . . Pulling on rubber boots over shoes is often a tough task. A couple of strips of cellophane tape over the rear edge of the heel of the shoe will make them slide on easier. Or, a folded piece of paper inserted above the heels will help.

> If rubbers and galoshes are stored away, stuff them with tissue paper to keep the rubber from cracking and splitting. . . . Or, before storing, apply a coat of self-polishing floor wax to retard drying and cracking of rubber.

> Keep galoshes clean and new-looking by sudsing them in the washing machine for a few minutes. Rinse thoroughly and dry in a warm—not hot—place. A coat of paste wax will preserve the rubber and keep galoshes shining. . . . The insides of galoshes or stadium boots, especially those with pile-type lining, should be washed with warm soap or detergent suds. Rinse by rubbing with a clean damp towel, and stuff with old dry towels, blot, and dry. . . . Clean the insides of rubbers and galoshes with a vacuum cleaner while they are dry. Accumulated dust and dirt can spoil shoeshines and soil trouser cuffs. . . . Clean plastic boots with a paste-type silver polish. . . . A mixture of kerosene and detergent on a cloth will remove scuff marks from those white or light-colored boots.

> To keep rubbers and overshoes from getting mixed up, fasten them together with spring-type clothespins, lettered with initials. . . . Or use a felt-tipped marking pen to put your initials on the inside of your rubbers or galoshes.

> If you're ever caught without rubbers or galoshes, create a temporary makeshift pair with two sheets of Saran Wrap and a couple of rubber bands. . . . Or, use two plastic bags.

> Put thin pieces of foam rubber in the toes of oversized

rubbers or galoshes. They will pad the extra space effectively, without harming the shoes.

☐ UMBRELLAS: A lost umbrella may find its way back if you write your name and address on a small slip of paper and seal it to the upper shaft with cellophane tape. . . . An old nylon stocking is good protection for storing an umbrella that does not have a cover. . . . Repair small damages to umbrellas with masking tape, matching, if possible. . . . Make an old umbrella look practically new again by brushing the fabric with a solution of ammonia and warm water.

☐ TOOTHBRUSHES AND PASTE: If a toothbrush is too stiff, soften by soaking in hot vinegar for a half hour, then washing in cold water. The brush will be much softer. . . . To make toothbrushes more readily identifiable, initial them with red nail polish. . . . A sprinkling of sodium bicarbonate on brush is a good substitute for toothpaste. Table salt will also do the job.

☐ WATCHES: Avoid placing a watch on a very cold surface for any length of time. It can injure certain timepieces. . . . Never shake or bang a watch to start it running. Not only will this not make it run, but it can damage the works. . . . If a watch crystal is loose enough to come out of the frame, put the crystal (only) in the refrigerator for an hour or so. This contracts it enough to fit easily back in place. On warming to room temperature, it will expand to fit snugly once again. . . . Experts say that some watches offer resistance when turned back to reset. And the movement shouldn't be forced. It's safer with all watches, though a bit more bother, to move them ahead.

> Always wind your watch one way, away from you. It saves wear and tear, and static electricity will not accumulate dust. . . . It is a good idea to occasionally wind a good watch that is not often used. Let it run for a while; dealers say this will keep it in better condition. . . . The best time to wind a watch is in the morning, and it must be wound fully. This tightens the spring and prepares the timepiece for a day's buffeting.

> If working where moisture might get at a wristwatch, wrap cellophane from a pack of cigarettes around it. It protects the watch and you can still see the time. . . . When putting on watch, hold hands a few inches above a table, or, even better, a soft bed. If the watch slips, most of the shock will be cushioned.

CHILDREN,
PETS
AND OTHER
HOBBIES

CHILD CARE

☐ BATHING AND HAIR WASHING: Putting cold cream on eyelids and brows will keep soap from getting into the eyes when a youngster's hair is being washed.

> When bathing a tiny baby in a large bathtub, use a soft-plastic latticework laundry basket for the utmost safety. . . . Wear an old cotton glove on your left hand when giving baby a bath. You will have a better grip on his soapy little body.

> Draping a towel over the top of the bathroom door will keep small children from locking themselves in.

> Weigh your baby on an ordinary bathroom scale by stepping on the scale while holding him, then by yourself. Deduct the latter weight from the former and you have the baby's weight. (Same system can be used for weighing laundry for the washing machine.)

☐ CLOTHES: When washing baby's rubber pants, add a little baby oil to the water. This helps to soften the rubber and prevent cracking and stiffness.

> Small woolen articles such as baby clothes and gloves will dry more quickly if they are pinned to a large turkish towel and the towel is hung on a clothesline.

> The good parts of a worn woolen blanket will make warm interlinings for a schoolchild's coat.

> Keeping diaper pins or needles in a bar of soap will make them slip through material easier.

> Put iron-on patches inside the knees of new jeans. They will wear longer, and the padding protects the child's knees as he plays.

☐ EATING: For careless young eaters, substitute a disposable sheet of aluminum foil for the place mat that would have to be washed after each meal. . . . An oblong of transparent plastic film under a child's place setting will protect your tablecloth.

> Use fringed terry cloth guest towels for napkins for children. They are extra large, are durable, and require no ironing.

> For the toddler who is inclined to throw his dish on the floor at mealtime, buy a plastic child's dish with a rubber suction cup on the bottom.

> Children's drinking glasses wrapped with several wide, colorful rubber bands are less likely to slip from hands. . . . Or, a strip of adhesive tape around a child's glass will make it easier to grip.

> If your child is bored by mashed potatoes, try adding a colorful *vegetable* dye before mashing. (Please pass the pink potatoes.) . . . For children who don't care for milk, add a few drops of vegetable coloring and serve with straws.

> Keep the bottom of the electric coffeepot in the baby's room as a bottle warmer for the 2 A.M. snack. Put the bottle in a couple of inches of water, plug in the cord and in two min-

utes the milk will be the right temperature for the little one's nightcap.

> Mothers of new babies can save themselves eyestrain if the ounces on the baby bottles are marked in red nail polish. This works particularly well on plastic bottles.

> To clean milk sediment out of baby bottles, break a slice of white bread into small pieces. Put them into the bottle and add a little water. Shake the bottle a few times and it will sparkle without brushing. You can clean several bottles at the same time by pouring the same mixture into each. . . . Soaking baby bottles in vinegar for several hours will remove traces of hard-water film.

> If youngsters carry lunch to school, here is a simple solution for packing a quick, hot meal. Fill a vacuum bottle with hot soup and add two wieners. Butter two hot dog rolls and pack them separately. At lunchtime, there will be hot soup and wieners for a nice appetizing meal.

> When you can't get the lid off the screw-type baby-food jar, punch a small hole in the top of the lid. This releases the air inside the jar and makes it easy to unscrew the lid.

□ MEDICINE / FIRST AID : You can get youngsters to take pills by crumbling the medicine and mixing with their favorite pudding. . . . If your children can't stand the taste of medicine, try mixing it with grape juice.

> When youngsters balk at cod-liver oil, first chill it in the refrigerator. Taste and odor will be reduced.

> Where the prescription calls for one teaspoon, pour it into a tablespoon. This saves many a spill.

> To protect small fry, put clear cellophane tape over unused wall sockets. It will not mar decor, and will prevent burns or shocks.

> Tack a cork to each end of the rocker on a child's chair to prevent tipping.

> Next time you have to examine or paint the youngster's

throat, use a small lollipop for a tongue depressor. It turns an uncomfortable maneuver into fun.

> Mark the hot-water faucet with red nail polish. It will help tots tell it from the cold one.

> To remove gum from a child's hair, saturate hair strands with a washcloth soaked in witch hazel. Olive oil applied to the scalp or the white of an egg will also remove chewing gum. . . . If the gum is on a child's face, start another piece, press it on the first piece and pull off.

> Write on the back of your child's birth certificate the name and date of each communicable disease. (They are hard to remember in later years.)

☐ PARTIES: An empty spool tied to the string of a child's balloon will make it easy for him to carry and will act as a weight.

> When wrapping a gift for a child, stick shiny pennies, a lollipop, etc., on the outside; it doubles the recipient's pleasure.

> Create a festive atmosphere at an outdoor party by hanging balloons, party favors, and strips of lollipops from a clothesline. . . . A bouquet of lollipops makes a welcome and attractive centerpiece for a children's party.

> Print the name of each guest on a paper cup or drinking glass with colored nail polish. Cups or glasses serve as place cards, and this eliminates mix-ups when they are refilled. After the party, use nail-polish remover on the glasses.

> For a child's birthday party, frost the cake to resemble a clock with the hour hand pointing to his age.

> Where the children are seated at a party, fasten a balloon to the back of each child's chair with his name written on it in nail polish.

> When your Halloween clowns, goblins and witches return from trick-and-treating, whisk away their makeup with baby oil—without need of rubbing. Saturate large cotton balls and wipe off.

☐ ROOM DECORATIONS: Decals placed on window shades in a child's room will give it added color.

> If one wall in a child's room is decorated with pegboard, it will allow clothes hooks, blackboards, etc., to be adjusted to the proper height as the child grows taller.

> To decorate a child's room, use an animal-shaped bath sponge. Dip it into a color to contrast with the wall color and apply it to the walls to form a pattern. This will give the effect of wallpaper.

☐ SHOES AND SOCKS: While cleaning and polishing children's sandals, slip your hand into a small plastic bag before you slip it inside the shoe. This way your hand will not be stained with polish.

> Spray your child's new sneakers with starch. The dirt will not become embedded and both dirt and starch can be brushed off. . . . An excellent cleaner for sneakers is a soapy scouring pad. . . . To make sneakers extra white, use lemon juice in the last rinse water; it bleaches out stains.

> Children's torn tennis sneakers can be gaily mended by the use of different-colored iron-on tape.

> When children's shoes are scuffed too badly to take polish, rub them with a raw potato and they will shine like new when polished.

> For an emergency repair of children's shoelaces, use a piece of twine coated with matching shoe polish.

> Baby shoes coated with clear nail polish will look new longer.

> Never be guided by the size of the last pair of shoes bought. A 10-year-old's feet, for example, can grow from one to three sizes every 12 to 16 weeks.

> If rubber boots are two to three sizes too large for a child, place a pair of woolen socks over shoes before putting on boots.

> Hand-me-down clothes make good sense, but never ex-

tend the practice to shoes. If not properly fitted, shoes can be a menace to foot health.

> Apply clear nail polish to the eyelets of shoes to keep the tongue and shoelaces from turning black from their contact with the metal.

> To get children's white socks clean, give them a soak in a warm solution of washing soda before you wash them. This loosens the dirt.

□ T O Y S :   If you live in a house, keep the children from running in and out to see what time it is by putting a clock, face out, at a window.

> Make sure toys are larger than your tot's fist. Anything smaller can be swallowed.

> Cover a cot mattress you don't use often with heavy denim and let your children use it for a gym mat. It saves the furniture.

> Sew a piece of canvas all the way around the edge of a beach umbrella to convert it into a tent for youngsters.

> Tacking a rubber stair tread on the seat of a child's swing will prevent splinters. It dries quickly after a rain.

> Sharpen crayons by dipping ends in hot water, then rolling them to a point between thumb and forefinger. . . . Use empty Band-Aid tins as containers for crayons to prevent breakage and crushing.

> To keep kids happy on rainy days, add a drop of glycerin to soap-bubble mixture and have colored bubbles.

> If plastic toys get out of shape, place them in hot water for a few minutes, then work them back to correct shape.

> Used toys can be cleaned with a moist cloth dipped in baking soda. . . . To clean stuffed toys, put them in a large paper bag and add a generous amount of cornmeal. Shake the bag vigorously and then gently brush off cornmeal.

> Shellac games made of cardboard and they will have a

longer life. Stop toys from rusting at the beach by spraying with shellac.

> To refreshen the face of a china doll, give it a coat of clear nail polish. . . . Give paper dolls a coat of clear nail polish to keep them from tearing easily.

> If the children like to write with ink, use liquid bluing instead. It can be washed without trouble from clothes and floor.

> Make a useful blackboard by cutting a piece of beaver-board or any smooth wallboard to the right size and painting with black paint.

> Use a useless hula hoop as a colorful wall frame for decorations in a child's room.

> Don't discard empty coffee cans. Paint them a bright color and use in room as trinket holders.

> An old piano bench makes a fine play table for children when used with low stools or chairs. It even has storage space for crayons, drawing paper, games and other articles.

> An orange crate can make a fine toy chest. Sand and paint the crate and decorate it with a few designs or decals. Attach coasters to the bottom of the crate. . . . An old army footlocker, painted in a bright color, is also a good toy chest.

> To prevent the cover of a toy box from falling on little fingers, nail a rubber bumper at each of the two front corners of the box.

> Drill holes in a wooden ruler so it will fit over the rings of a youngster's looseleaf school notebook. That way it will not be lost.

> Paste a long envelope inside each notebook to hold pencils and important papers for schoolchildren.

> Fasten baby's toys to ribbons and hang from high chair. He will learn to retrieve his own toys, and it saves bending.

> Give an old shower cap or plastic dish cover to your youngsters for an excellent rainy-day bicycle seat cover.

> Rubbing a child's hands with soap will make modeling clay easier to work with.

☐ TRAVEL TIPS: Tiny tots are more prone to carsickness in the back seat than they are in the front.

> To lessen the effect of motion sickness on children prior to traveling, put them on a high-carbohydrate, low-fat diet for a few days. Go easy on liquids just before the trip.

> When taking children motoring, pack a few oranges sliced and wrapped in foil. They'll quench thirst and prevent sickness. . . . Wrap bottled milk in tinfoil; it will keep cold.

> Crib mattresses are almost the size of the back-seat area of a compact car. Take along Junior's and let him romp on it.

PETS

☐ BIRDS: Be careful when using ammonia products in kitchen if you have pet birds; the fumes could be harmful.

> When spray-painting tarnished bird cages, be sure you use a nontoxic paint.

> Line the bottom of a birdcage with an adhesive-backed plastic material. It is washable and easy to keep clean. . . . Cover the bottom of a bird cage with 10-inch paper doilies. They are great time-savers when you're cleaning cage, and add attractiveness.

> Spilled birdseed can easily be picked up from the floor with a damp tissue.

> If your canary shies from his bath, put a few seeds on top of the water as a come-on. Put a little sand in the bottom before filling with water. Experts say the bird dislikes a slippery bottom to his bath.

> Birds can spread disease among themselves through their

birdhouses and feeders they use. It's essential to keep these havens clean with hot water and soapsuds.

☐ C A T S :   Never pick up a cat by the nape of the neck. Mother cats do it, but only to their babies. The proper method provides support for hindquarters.

> A mothball or two stuffed in the cushions of a sofa or chair will serve as "not welcome" sign to a cat.

> If your cat is being naughty on the rug, put slices of raw onion on the spot. The odor will discourage the practice.

> A piece of firewood nailed to a stand will serve as a scratching post instead of the furniture.

☐ D O G S :   If you have to wash your dog in a shower or tub, put a ball of steel wool in the drain opening; it will catch dog hairs and keep them from clogging the pipes.

> Dog's coats will be extra soft and shiny after a bath if you add two tablespoons of baking soda to both wash and rinse water. . . . After bathing a poodle at home, add a creme rinse to the bath water and the coat will be much easier to comb out.

> If dog encounters a skunk, don't try to scrub him with soap and water. A rub with vinegar will remove all odors. So will tomato juice.

> In bathing your dog, put cotton in each ear to keep out water, and a drop of castor oil in each eye to keep out soap. . . . Your dog may not be so unhappy about getting a bath if a rubber mat is put on the bottom of the basin or tub.

> After giving a dog a bath, use the blower of the vacuum cleaner for quick drying of the coat.

> Instead of giving pooch a regular bath in cold weather, rub baking soda in and out of his coat. It deodorizes as well as cleans.

> After snow falls, don't forget to wash your dog's feet with a baking soda solution if he's been walked on sidewalks

sprinkled with snow-melting chemicals. Soda soothes the burn-ing sensation which causes pet to lick his paws, and licking these chemicals can cause serious illness.

> If your dog is a constant "shedder," lubricate the coat with olive oil, coconut oil, or lanolin every 10 days or so. . . . Three egg yolks weekly will help canine have a healthier and shinier coat.

> Tar or chewing gum on a dog's coat can be removed by application of an ice cube to the spot. This hardens the sub-stance and makes it easy to remove.

> Use the small upholstery brush of a vacuum cleaner on the dog. Follow natural hair pattern, and remove all loose hair. Pooch will enjoy the massage too.

> Fleas do not like salt. Wash dog in salt water, or, if it is convenient, let him swim in the ocean. Keep salt around the crevices of doghouse to keep fleas away.

> To remove fleas from doghouse in summer, scrub dog-house regularly with a strong solution of washing soda—a cup-ful to a bucket of water.

> You can remove burrs from a dog's hair by working oil into the tangle with fingers. . . .Another good way to get stubborn burrs out of a dog's hair is to crush them with pliers. Collapsed burrs lose their holding power and can be combed out.

> Best way to remove tick from dog is to saturate a cotton-tipped stick with carbon tetrachloride (cleaning fluid) and touch it to the head of the tick. You can then pluck it out easily with tweezers. . . . Or, soak each tick with alcohol, and then pull from dog very gently.

> Veterinarians recommend that dogs' teeth be cleaned weekly with dry baking soda applied with a damp cloth.

> Pet owners should be extra careful to see that their dogs do not get a chicken or turkey bone, which can cause great suffering. Also resist the temptation to give candy and pastry to pets.

> Give a dog plenty of fresh, cool water in the summer, but

not ice water. . . . A dog's diet in the warm weather should contain a minimum of fats.

> To make dry dog foods more palatable to pet, mix bouillon cube with hot water and pour over the dry meal.

> If dog will not eat, to the degree of growing under-nourished, try feeding him some stale beer. It's been known to whet the appetite.

> Know how to give dog liquid medicine? Raise his head, pull out lower lip to form a pocket, pour in medicine and then hold jaws shut until he swallows. . . . Next time you have to give your dog a pill, put it in a blob of peanut butter—which he will gulp down fast.

> You can remove puppy stains from carpets by sponging the area with a solution of white vinegar and cold water. . . . Or, apply quinine water or club soda to the spots. . . . Or, quickly sprinkle baking soda on the spots, then add a little water and let stand until the bubbling stops. Sponge with fresh water. . . . Or, use a damp sponge run over a cake of brown soap and sprinkled with dry baking soda. Rinse off with a clean damp sponge to get rid of spot and odor.

> To remove pet hairs from upholstery, wipe with a damp chamois cloth.

> Cement a rubber jar ring to bottom of dog's feeding dish to make is skidproof.

> You can keep a new puppy quiet at night by parking a ticking alarm clock near his bed. Seems little dogs are afraid of silence and the ticking comforts them. . . . A new puppy who is lonesome for his mother will appreciate the warmth of a hot-water bag. Fill it with warm water and wrap a square of old blanket around it.

> Nail a strip of heavy-duty sandpaper on the part of the door where pooch plays and scratches. It protects the wood and buffs his nails at the same time.

> An old foam-rubber auto seat, cut down to size, makes perfect bedding for a doghouse. Ticks, etc., that may infest ordinary bedding will not stay in foam rubber.

> To cure a car-chasing dog, try tying a short chain to the collar. It will whip his legs when he tries to run.

HOBBIES

☐ A R T : Sunday painters will be able to get the balky caps off tubes of paint by holding them over a lighted match for a few seconds. Keep those metallic frozen-food pans. They're fine for paint mixing for amateur painters. . . . A plastic egg tray makes a fine palette for mixing small quantities of water paints. After cleaning brushes, rub on a small quantity of petroleum jelly to preserve them and keep them soft.

☐ B O O K S : To prevent cracking or peeling of imitation-leather and plastic book covers, apply a little petroleum jelly.

> A clean wide paintbrush is ideal for dusting the tops of books.

> Coat book covers with clear shellac; dust will wipe off easily. . . . To clean book covers, rub them briskly with a clean cloth wrung out in a solution of one part vinegar and two parts water. . . . Rub book covers with waxed paper and they will stay cleaner.

> To kill fungus that mildews books, wipe with cloth dipped in rubbing alcohol. . . . A piece of charcoal placed in a bookcase will absorb dampness and protect books from mildew. . . . Or, protect books from mildew in damp climates by keeping a small electric light burning continuously in the bookcase.

> Soiled or spotted page edges of a book can be cleaned with fine sandpaper around a curved sanding block. Sand lightly and carefully.

> Always see that books stand upright on shelves. Allowing them to lean can strain the bindings and eventually lead to crippled books. . . . Never build bookshelves over radiators

or in a spot exposed to strong sunlight. Pages will fade and
covers will warp. . . . Do not crowd your bookshelves. Bind-
ings may break apart from the pressure.

> Instead of turning down the corners of pages to mark
the place, make simple bookmarks by cutting the bottom cor-
ners off envelopes. Neat—and they make it easy to find your
place.

☐ P H O T O G R A P H Y : When mounting pictures in an
album, slip the negatives behind the print. . . . If picture-
album pages are sticking, separate them without ruining pictures by letting steam permeate the album; the pages will open
gently. . . . Use white liquid shoe polish to write on the black
pages of photo albums and scrapbooks. . . . Apply paste
with a pipe cleaner when mounting photos or stamps. A minimum of paste is used and smearing eliminated.

> Soiled photographs may be cleaned by rubbing with soft
bread. Another excellent method is to moisten a soft cloth with
warm water to which a few drops of ammonia have been
added. Wring the cloth very dry and lightly wipe photograph,
drying immediately after with a soft dry cloth.

> Keep home movie camera clean and free of dust. Wrap it
in an old stocking before putting in the case.

> When cleaning the lens, be sure to clean the lens cap as
well so it will not resmudge the lens. . . . Should camera have
a cloth shutter curtain, keep the lens covered when not in use.
Sunlight may focus through the lens and burn the nonmetal
material.

> Advice to home-movie-camera owners: Between shooting
sessions with 8mm or 16mm cameras, let spring motor run
down completely, to relieve tension on the spring and ensure
stronger spring motor for a long time.

> Photographers as well as their subjects should relax.
Tension on the camera end spoils many good pictures.

> Freezing weather congeals oil and can slow camera-
shutter speeds. Keep camera under outercoats where body
heat will keep it working smoothly.

> When photographing a very shiny item in sunlight, give it a light coat of hair spray to eliminate glare. When finished, wipe off.

> Glue a small piece of emery board or sandpaper to the bottom of photo-flash gun to rub base of bulb before using.

> Read instructions that come with roll of film. The number of helpful hints included will surprise you.

> Keep from forgetting what type of film is in camera by using cellophane tape to affix the film-box tab to the back of the camera.

> High humidity can cause undesirable changes in film. Don't store any packages in damp places. Film should be exposed and processed as soon as possible.

> When doing outdoor color shots, select a sky that is deep blue in color for best results.

> For leveling a photographic tripod, make ½″ to ¼-inch marks on the legs with colored nail polish.

> You can make a suitable home movie screen by placing a card table on edge with two legs extended to hold it up. If dark-colored, cover with a white cloth.

> Put a few dabs of luminous paint in strategic points in darkroom, for orientation in complete darkness.

☐ RECORDS / PHONOGRAPHS: In this day of high-fidelity recording, be careful how you handle records. Touch edges only; keep fingers off grooves.

> Ordinary rubbing alcohol is helpful in cleaning records. Wipe on with a piece of urethane foam to remove all dust, dirt and fingerprints. . . . Or, keep previous LP records clean with cool water and soap. It removes all dirt, grime and grease. To dry, place them in dish rack.

> Keep waxed paper between phonograph records to prevent scratching.

> To straighten records that have warped, place each record on a smooth surface, preferably glass, that has been cov-

ered with cloth. Weigh down with about eight heavy books and remove books after about one week. This usually does the trick.

> Many record players and radios will give better sound with less vibration if the set is placed on a heavy fiber mat, like those so often used under typewriters.

> The brush on the end of a typewriter eraser makes a handy gadget for cleaning a phonograph stylus.

☐ A N D A L O T O F O T H E R T H I N G S : Stamp collectors can easily remove wanted stamps by applying lighter fluid to the inside of the envelope behind the stamp.

> Wrap children's modeling clay in aluminum foil, which will keep it moist and pliable indefinitely.

> Nail polish is just the thing for patching the fabric of model planes.

> When you buy a game with separate directions, paste the directions on the cover of the box and it will always be handy for easy reference.

> Bowling pros advise dusting highly absorbent baby powder on hands to keep them dry for a smooth release of the ball.

> Discothèque dancers should dust baby powder on feet for cool dry comfort no matter how wild the dance.

☐ C A M P I N G : A good substitute for steel wool for cleaning pots and pans is a handful of broken eggshells.

> Pinecones are nature's instant cooking fire. Just toss a handful on campfire, and in minutes they are glowing just right for making biscuits, pancakes, cornbread, baked spuds, etc.

☐ F I S H I N G : Using worms? A way to pick up 200 lively ones fast is to mash up the hulls of 20 black walnuts in three gallons of water. Splash the magic liquid over a 2-foot-square area. Get ready! In 15 seconds, here come the worms; just pick them up.

> Sprinkle some coffee grounds on the ground to bring angleworms to the surface.

> Need live bait? Place a few punctured beer cans in shallow water. Soon there will be plenty of soft-shelled crayfish inside.

> Here's a near-sure way for fishermen to get lots of bait. Fill a soft-drink bottle with water, add a tablespoon of powdered mustard and sprinkle on ground. If there are any worms in the area, they will come up to investigate.

> A fine "chum" for fishermen is a batch of broken-up dried eggshells. Attracts fish like crazy.

> When you're transporting live minnows on a fishing trip, the best way to keep them alive is to pack them in a bucket of wet grass.

> Keep the hooks out of fingers and in tip-top condition for the fish. Just a dab of water-soluble glue on the tip of the point will form a protective covering to ensure hook-free hands. When the hook hits the water, the glue dissolves.

> Sandwich extra fishhooks between two strips of cellophane tape for safety; and do the same with kitchen matches to keep them dry and ready for use.

> To keep fishhooks from rusting when not in use, stick them in a cork and store the cork in a jar of baking soda.

> You can dye fishhook leaders by soaking them for a day in strong coffee or tea.

> Bait hooks for small fish with marshmallows; they are as effective as earthworms, if not more so.

> Wash fishing rod in fresh water after each fishing trip, especially after saltwater fishing.

> A used flashlight bulb makes a good bobber for a fishing line.

> Coat wooden fishing rods with automobile wax to protect finish.

> Make long-lasting repairs on split fishing rods (and loose grips on golf clubs and tennis rackets) by binding them with cellophane tape and using a coating of lacquer.

> Wind fishing line on old metal adhesive-tape spools. Snap cover back on—and the line will be safe and untangled.

> If fish have been out of water for some time, scale them easily by first dipping in boiling water.

> Fish by the barometer. When it's high, your luck should be good. When low or falling—not so hot.

> Scour out old skillets with dry baking soda after you've cooked the day's catch.

> To help find articles lost in the water, put a flashlight in a fruit jar, secure lid tightly and lower into water.

> A cheap clipboard is ideal for cleaning fish. The clamp holds tail tight.

> In a pinch, a nylon-mesh shopping bag will do double duty as a head net for a fishing trip.

> A stiff wire shoe brush is excellent for scaling fish.

> Ever catch a mess of fish and find yourself without ice, a fish box or the like? Just cover catch with grass that has been soaked in water, and keep the catch fresh for several hours.

> TV-dinner trays make fine dishes to hold assorted parts when you're making repairs on fishing (or hunting) gear. If tiny parts are involved, further insure against loss with this tip: Tape on a strip of clear tape, sticky side up. Tiny screws and springs stay put even when elbows bump 'em.

> You cannot scare away fish by talking in a boat. Conversation noises do not penetrate water.

> Keep a fishing hole in the ice from freezing over by pouring enough olive oil or glycerin on the water to form a thin film. It is good for days.

> If bugs are annoying during night fishing, attach a lantern to the end of an oar and fasten to the boat so that it

extends as far as possible over the water. Insects will be drawn to light and away from you.

☐ G O L F : Don't throw away worn winter gloves. With fingers cut off, they're good as golfing equipment.

> Wooden golf clubs will keep their luster and finish if occasionally rubbed with shoe polish.

> Small pieces of aluminum foil will clean rust, dirt and grime from golf clubs.

> It's hard to remember everything, but try to wind up with your weight on your right foot when taking a trap shot. It will keep you from swaying. . . . For better putting, shorten the backswing, keep club head closer to the ground, and concentrate on keeping the club face square to the hole.

> A small sack containing para nuggets or crystals (moth repellent) will prevent mildew accumulations on shoes and clothing in golf lockers.

> Clean club heads after a round of golf rather than before the next one. . . . To clean golf irons without fear of scratching, rub with a little dry baking soda applied with a damp sponge or cloth. The soda will even remove minor rust spots.

> Canvas bags can be cleaned before storing by scrubbing with damp, stiff bristles rubbed first over a cake of brown soap, then dipped in dry sal soda. Rinse with fresh water.

> If you wear a belt, try wearing the buckle at the back to avoid scratching your forearm on the backswing.

> Clean golf cleats after each round, before mud cakes too hard. A wire brush, carried in the golf bag, is the best gimmick to clean dirt from spiked shoes.

> Do not let mud dry on golf shoes. It can stain the leather permanently. Wipe the uppers well and use an old toothbrush on soles.

> Old golf balls can be brightened up if soaked in a quart of water to which three tablespoons of concentrated sal soda has been added.

> A clean airplane picks up 6 mph in speed over one that's dirty—and the same principle applies to golf balls. Keep them clean.

☐ H U N T I N G : Here's the fast way to get a dent out of a prized gunstock. Wet a rag and lay it over the dent. Then, with a hot iron, press down again and again over the dent. Steam will swell wood fibers; dent will swell right away.

> Now's a good time to sew buttons on the shoulders of favorite hunting shirts. They will keep the rifle sling from slipping off while you walk with both hands free.

> For quicker plucking of waterfowl, dissolve two table-spoons of detergent in a bucket of boiling water. Dunk bird, rinse in cold water and start plucking.

> Any sportsman worth his ammunition knows that two different-gauge shotgun shells fitted one inside the other make a perfect waterproof container for matches.

> When wearing rubber hunting boots, put cotton socks over woolen ones. They'll absorb moisture that condenses on rubber and keep the wool socks dry.

> Going on an extended hunting trip? You'll do better in a beard. Many animals are frightened by a clean-shaven face.

> If entering strange woods, and leaving your car on the road, note the number of the nearest telephone pole. If you come back on the road at a distant spot, you can tell by the numbers on the poles which direction will take you to the car.

> The most common hunting accidents are burns, snake-bites, and—believe it or not—fainting! Carry petroleum jelly, snakebite serum, and plenty of smelling salts.

☐ I C E S K A T E S : Store ice skates in plastic bags to keep them from rusting. Put petroleum jelly on ice-skate blades before storing them over the summer.

☐ S W I M M I N G : Rub tar off hands and feet with lard.

> Always rinse swimwear in clear fresh water after each trip to the beach. Sand, grit and salt can harm the fiber.

> Rub a little mineral or olive oil over lashes before swimming in a pool to keep chlorine in the water from stinging the eyes.

> Salt water and chlorinated water from swimming pools should be washed out of hair promptly.

GENERAL

HOUSEKEEPING

WASHING AND IRONING

☐ WASHING BRIGHT-COLORED
CLOTHES: When you're washing colored material, a
teaspoon of Epsom salts added to each gallon of water will
prevent even delicate shades from fading and running. . . .
Bleeding can also be prevented by addition of two or three
teaspoons of salt to the wash and rinse cycles of the machine.

☐ DARK-COLORED CLOTHES: When a lot of
coffee is left over, freeze into cubes and use to add to the
rinse water for dark garments. For some reason, this prevents
lint from sticking. . . . Another way of removing lint is to
add a half cup of vinegar to each gallon of the last rinse
water. This will also prevent dark cottons and linens from
graying. There will be no vinegar odor.

☐ GLOVES: Solid washable gloves should be washed
inside as well as outside.

> A little water softener added to soapy water is a great
help in cleaning washable gloves, especially white ones. Dirt
will also float away if gloves are soaked for 20 minutes.

> To wash white cotton gloves, keep them on when hand-
washing hosiery.

☐ HANDKERCHIEFS : If white handkerchiefs are discolored, try using a little cream of tartar in cold water.

☐ KNITWEAR : Put knitwear in a mesh bag or pillow-case before machine washing to prevent stretching or snag-ging. When washing heavy knits by hand, use the bathtub so suds will have room to circulate.

☐ RIBBONS : Clean ribbons, etc., by putting them in fruit jar half filled with a good cleaning fluid. Put top on, shake well, rinse fabric and hang in air to dry.

☐ SOCKS : Add ¼ cup of vinegar to last rinse water to soften colored socks that are grimy.

☐ SHIRTS : A good way to launder a shirt in an auto-matic washer is to button shirt front, then turn shirt inside out—thus holding sleeves on inside and keeping them from getting tangled.

> Never throw damp shirts into a laundry hamper; allow them to dry first.

> Ink spots from ball-point pens can be removed from shirts by a quick rinse with clear water and a wash in soap-suds. . . . You can get iodine stains off a shirt by sponging the spot with household ammonia and then washing. . . . If there are wine spots on a shirt or handkerchief, soak them with cold water, then rub the area with a cut lemon before washing. . . . Hair-dye stains on a shirt (don't scoff—millions of men use a touch-up) should be washed in suds with vinegar added. Bleach with hydrogen peroxide and relaunder. . . . Perspiration marks will come out of shirts if they're soaked in a solution of strong salt water.

> Sometimes, after a brief wearing, only the collar of a fresh shirt is soiled. Wash the collar part only, pressing it against a flat surface like the bathtub while it dries—and get more neat wear out of it.

☐ WASH-AND-WEAR : Wash-and-wear items should have fewer wrinkles if rinsed out in cool water.

> When laundering wash-and-wear clothes, do not allow them to soak too long, for after about 20 minutes they might start soaking up the dirty water.

☐ W O O L E N S : Use a bit of ammonia to soften water in which woolens and knitted garments are washed. Then rinse with cold water.

> When washing woolens, be sure the rinse water is the same temperature as the wash water. The change from warm to cold water shrinks them.

> When you wash out fine wool hose, just a smidgen of soap in the final rinse water will help keep them soft and resilient.

> If washing woolens to be stored away, dissolve a dozen mothballs in the last rinse water.

> Add a little vinegar to the last rinse water when washing heavy woolens, to eliminate any trace of perspiration. This will also give woolens new softness and sheen.

> A woolen sweater can be nicely washed in shampoo if proper washing soap or detergent is not available.

> After a sweater is washed it will not stretch if it is rinsed in a colander and the excess water is squeezed out.

> When washing those good sweaters, stitch buttonholes together first, so they won't stretch.

☐ A N D S O M E O T H E R T H I N G S : Before washing anything of corduroy, turn the garment inside out to prevent having a deposit of lint on the face of the material. A rinse with vinegar will also help discourage lint.

> Prevent white nylon from yellowing with a pre-wash soaking in baking soda solution.

> A faded white dress may be made perfectly white again by boiling in cream of tartar water.

> Restore body and sheen to polished cotton material by dissolving one half packet of plain gelatin in last rinse water.

> Add a cup of salt to rinse water to keep bluing from streaking clothes.

> When laundering clothes of heavy-textured cotton, turn garments wrong-side out to avoid snagging long threads.

☐ DYEING: Never dye anything that isn't washable—it's liable to shrink excessively. Do not dye woolens in the washer, as agitation could sharply increase shrinkage.

> Fabric should be wet before it is put in a dye bath. After dyeing cotton garments, save some of the dye to put in a Permastarch solution for their final bath. This produces a more permanent finish.

☐ BLANKETS: Hanging a washed blanket over two lines will distribute weight and hasten drying.

☐ CURTAINS AND DRAPERIES: Renew freshness of nylon or fiber-glass curtains by adding one half cup of powdered milk to the last rinse water.

> Add a few drops of vinegar to rinse water when laundering synthetic curtains or draperies. This reduces their static electricity.

☐ KITCHEN LINENS: Kitchen towels, dishcloths, and pot holders should be bleached occasionally to remove stains. Rinse well.

☐ PILLOWS: Place foam-rubber pillows in a cloth case before washing to prevent fraying. Dry them outdoors or in a natural way, not in the dryer.

☐ SHOWER CURTAINS: When washing plastic shower curtains (or tablecloths), add a few drops of vinegar to rinse water. It will cut down on their dust attraction. A cup of vinegar added to the rinse water will make them dry soft and pliable.

☐ T O W E L S :   So that they will be used and, eventually, worn out at the same time, fold washcloths into matching towels after laundering.

> Save a few lemon rinds to boil with soiled towels, to whiten them.

☐ S T A R C H :   Some fabrics don't take well to ordinary starch. For these, dissolve granulated sugar in water and use in place of starch.

> Tablecloths will stay unwrinkled longer if treated to a very thin starch bath. They will also resist soil and stains better. Worn tablecloths will resume their original crispness and firmness of weave if a small amount of starch is added to the last rinse.

> To keep heavily starched items from sticking to clothesline, place a piece of waxed paper on the line before pinning garments to it.

> Add tea to starch when laundering black or dark clothes to prevent light streaks from showing up.

> Hot starch penetrates better than cold starch and does not leave glazed spots on garments being ironed.

> If there are one or two garments left to be done, and the starch has run out, roll them in already starched clothes and they will absorb enough to have a fresh look when ironed.

> Add a teaspoon of salt to starch. It will give clothes a smooth beautiful finish and keep iron from sticking. . . . You can also prevent sticking by adding a little soap to the starch solution.

> If articles are to be stored, omit starch in the final laundering before they are put away; starch attracts silverfish.

☐ A N D   S O M E   O T H E R   T H I N G S :   Perspiration stains will come out of washable clothes if they're soaked in a strong saltwater solution. . . . Or, apply a thick paste of baking soda to the stained area and leave on for about 15 minutes. Then wash in the usual way.

> Remember to dry, brush off, and rub with suds any muddy clothes before putting them in the washing machine.

> Greasy or oily work clothes or overalls will get cleaner if soaked for about 15 minutes in hot water containing a half cup of household ammonia.

> Remove chewing gum from washable clothing by first softening with egg white, then laundering.

> Gravy stains on washable materials should be soaked in cold water to dissolve the starch before laundering.

> The safest, cheapest and easiest bleach is lemon juice. A mild preparation may be made with a cup of 15 percent alcohol, a drop or two of glycerin and the juice of a lemon.

> To remove mildew stains from white fabrics, moisten with a mixture of lemon juice and salt, then spread in sun to bleach.

> To prevent chapping hands when hanging clothes outdoors, wet hands with vinegar and dry them before going outside.

> Save tiny soap leftovers; tie them in a soft piece of flannel and dip into boiling water until they're soft. Then hold in cold water till firm—and you will have a good solid ball of soap.

> After laundering dark or bright-colored items by machine, be sure to clean out the washer by letting it run through one suds-and-rinse cycle, or the color residue may settle on subsequent loads.

> If washing machine is balky, it may just need cleaning. Run it through its regular cycle, minus laundry, with about three tablespoons of sal soda added to the water.

> Clothes sprinkled with hot water will be ready for ironing sooner than those sprinkled with cold water.

> Wax a clothesline with a candle to strengthen the rope and prolong its use.

> Dip clothespins and clotheslines in salt water to prevent their freezing to clothes. If clothespins are soaked, one treatment should last all winter.

> A foam-rubber mat under a noisy washing machine will absorb vibration and sound.

> If clothespins become dirty, boil them in a weak solution of bleach and water.

> Close a zipper before washing, to keep it in working condition through laundering.

☐ DRYING / IRONING : Hang colored clothes inside-out on the line to dry to prevent sun fading.

> Corduroy garments should never be wrung out after washing. Hang up soaking wet and they will need no ironing.

> With limited clothesline space and lots of clothes, put various things on hangers, which, when turned sideways, take up little room.

> Sunlight is still the best bleach, so for getting whites really white, the backyard clothesline beats the basement dryer.

> If clothes come out of the dryer wrinkled, it may be because they are overdried. Set control for shorter periods.

> Save wear and tear on buttons on clothes that bang around in dryer. Button the garment first, then turn it inside out and dry in machine.

> Try removing fuzz balls—pilling—from sweaters by brushing them with a dry sponge.

> Flat-dry sweaters and other knitwear on the bottom of the bathtub, after lining the tub with a terry towel.

> Clothes won't freeze on the line if salt is added to the rinse water.

> Check clothespins for splintered edges that might snag fabrics; either sandpaper or discard them.

> Know how to avoid wrinkles in ironing shirt collars? Start at the point of the collar and iron halfway back toward the center; then turn shirt and iron back from other collar point. Any fullness will be in back, with no wrinkles in front.

> If wash-and-wear apparel is "touched up" after laundering, iron on the wrong side to prevent surface shine.

> Always iron eyelet and embroidery on the wrong side and over a folded bath towel for a deeper, richer texture.

> Keep an ice cube wrapped in a thin cloth handy while ironing. It's fine for dampening small areas.

> To press a hair ribbon quickly, pull underneath an iron, keeping iron stationary.

> Remove wrinkles from a knitted dress by spreading the garment over a large, heavy bath towel that has been wrung out of warm water. Cover with another bath towel and leave it overnight. In the morning, wrinkles are gone.

> The hood of an electric hair dryer can be used for drying small items such as stockings, handkerchiefs, etc., in a hurry.

> To keep corduroy materials soft, turn them inside out and spray with starch before ironing.

> Pink edges of iron-on patches and tapes. They will adhere longer.

> A smooth stroke will help you iron clothes better. Short, stubby strokes tend to bunch clothing.

> Never iron over spots and stains in fabric. It will set them in material.

> You can remove gloss spots left after ironing by sponging material lightly with a moist cloth.

> When doing the ironing, keep a pencil, a note pad, and pins handy. When a missing button, frayed cuff, or ripped seam is noted, pin a reminder to the garment.

> Iron heavy cotton materials on the wrong side to prevent shine.

> Ironing linens is easier when they're done on a wide padded table rather than on the standard ironing board.

> Never iron terry towels. It flattens the loops and makes the surface harsh and less absorbent . . . Shake out wet towels before drying on a rack or line. Smooth just-dried towels

with the hands before folding and putting away. This removes wrinkles before they set.

> When a blanket is almost dry after washing, a light brushing with a whisk broom raises the nap. The nap should never be ironed, as this helps wear it out; press only the binding, and that with a warm iron.

> To avoid ironing draperies, hang them while they are damp and stretch edges and seams.

☐ IRONS AND IRONING BOARDS: Try using a nip-cap bottle to fill steam iron. There is no spilled water.

> Ordinary tap water may be used in a steam iron if one tablespoon of ammonia is used for each cup of water. Ammonia softens water and prevents addition or accumulation of hard particles and sediments in iron. Ammoniated water also makes for smoother, cleaner ironing.

> Wash scorch stains off the bottom of the iron with a cloth wrung out of sudsy water.

> A drapery hook stuck into the end of an ironing board makes a handy holder for the cord while you're ironing.

> Tack a small square of asbestos to the ironing board as a resting place for the iron, and for protection of the cover.

> Slip a dry cleaner's bag over a folded ironing board. It will keep the top and legs clean.

> A sheet of aluminum foil placed between the ironing board and covering pad reflects the heat and cuts down ironing time.

> A new ironing-board cover will fit better if dipped in hot water and allowed to dry before use.

> Striped denim is a perfect ironing-board cover. The stripes serve to line up the edges of jackets, skirt pleats, curtains, etc.

> An ironing board is handy to use when an extra work space is needed in kitchen. Be sure to cover the board with a plastic cloth.

> Faded and frayed heavy linen draperies can be used as ironing-board covers. They are firm enough to provide a good foundation, and the iron will glide over them smoothly.

☐ SCORCH MARKS: If you scorch a white garment while ironing, wet a cloth with hydrogen peroxide, place it over the spot, and run a hot iron over it. The scorch comes off almost instantly. (Do *not* do this with colored cloth.) Fruit stains can also be removed this way. . . . Or you may be able to bleach a scorched spot by moistening it and holding under a sunlamp until it regains its normal color.

> Household ammonia will take out most scorch stains.

> If cotton should scorch while being ironed, plunge it into cold water immediately and let it stand for 24 hours. The scorched areas will disappear.

CLEANING TOOLS

☐ BROOMS/VACUUM CLEANERS: Never pick up pins, needles or other sharp-pointed items with the vacuum cleaner, as they could damage the belt or the bag.

> Empty the vacuum cleaner on a dampened piece of paper to prevent the dust from flying.

> Heat may damage a vacuum cleaner if it is stored too near a furnace or radiator.

> To toughen a new broom and give it longer life, soak it in a hot, strong saltwater solution before using . . . To clean a broom in winter, give about ten sweeps with it in the snow.

☐ BRUSHES: An old shaving brush is ideal for dusting small and/or fragile pieces.

> Dampening the brush and dustpan will keep dust from scattering when you are cleaning up.

> Clean brushes by soaking them in a sal soda solution; use cool water to preserve the bounce of the bristles.

☐ DUST CLOTHS: Rid your house of a fire hazard either by throwing away all greasy, oily rags or by recleaning them by soaking overnight in a strong sal soda solution.

> Dry a chamois cloth in front of an electric fan and it will be soft and pliable. A stiff cloth can be softened by rinsing in 2 quarts of water with a tablespoon of olive oil.

> Keep a polish-impregnated cloth in an airtight plastic bag for a quick last-minute furniture polish. One wipe and a tabletop will gleam.

> Looking for a dust cloth that will pick up dust instead of spreading it? Soak a cloth for several hours in hot suds to which a few drops of turpentine have been added. Dry the cloth and use.

☐ MOPS/DUST MOPS: Dust mops can be thoroughly cleaned with a vacuum cleaner. . . . Or, to rejuvenate a badly soiled mop, soak it overnight in a bucket of water to which a half cup of washing soda has been added.

> Clean an oily mop by placing it in hot water to which a little washing powder and ammonia have been added.

> Rather than shake a mop out a window, put the head inside a large paper bag, choke the mouth of the bag around the handle and shake.

> When dusting a floor, spray a household air freshener on the dust mop. It will aid in picking up the dust and will leave the room pleasantly scented.

> Half an aluminum-foil plate makes a fine disposable dustpan.

> Wax a dustpan with no-rub liquid wax to keep dust from sticking to it.

☐ P A I L S : Use red nail polish to mark lines on the inside of a cleaning pail at quart levels as an easy guide for mixing cleaning solutions to proper strength.

☐ R U B B E R G L O V E S : When the right-hand work glove is showing wear, turn both gloves wrong-side out and wear the left glove on the right hand.

> Lengthen the life of rubber gloves by putting small pads of cotton in the tips of the fingers.

> A little cornstarch sprinkled inside rubber gloves will let them slip on more easily. They will also slip on easily if hand lotion is poured inside.

☐ R U S T A N D D I R T R E M O V A L : You can remove rust from utensils and tools by rubbing them with a cork dipped in olive oil. . . . Or you can rub off rust spots with a typewriter eraser. . . . Also, lemon juice and salt are a good combination for removing rust stains.

☐ S O A P P A D S : Cut scouring pads in half before using; one pad goes further without rusting.

> Small clay flowerpots make good containers for damp steel wool pads, to keep them from rusting between use. The porous clay absorbs all the moisture. . . . Or, keeping steel wool pads in a jar of soapy water will prevent them from rusting.

☐ S P O N G E S / D I S H C L O T H S : Cut a plastic sponge to fit bathroom and kitchen soap receptacles, and park the soap on the sponge to avoid the usual mess.

> Put plastic sponges through the washing machine and they will come out fresh and clean.

> Soak natural sponges used in housework in cold salt-water to give them new life.

> Banish sour odors from sponges and dishcloths by soaking them in a sweetening solution of baking soda.

☐ CAUTION: Never mix two or more cleaning substances. Such chemical mixtures may release an irritating gas.

FURNITURE

☐ ASHTRAYS: When cleaning ashtrays, wash them out with lemon oil, which quickly eliminates any odor. Wax the insides of metal ashtrays. They will clean more easily.

☐ BRASSWARE: Brass will need less polishing and will look brighter if rubbed with olive oil after each polishing.

> One of the best polishes for brass is Worcestershire sauce.

> A wipe with a dry cloth followed by a rub with lemon oil will keep brass bedsteads sparkling.

> Clean brass candlesticks, drawer pulls or any brass accessory by soaking them overnight in a solution of vinegar and salt; then scrub with a brush, wash in hot suds, rinse and dry.

> To tell whether furniture hardware is brass or brass-plated steel, use a magnet, which will cling to the steel.

☐ CHAIRS: Weather stripping glued to the bottom of a rocking chair will prevent floor from being scratched.

> To tighten cane chair seats that have sagged, soak them well with hot soapsuds and rinse them with hot water. Allow to dry before using them.

> If the rung of a chair keeps loosening after being fixed with glue, try Plastic Wood next time.

> You can keep chair legs from sliding on polished floors

by glueing a cut-to-size piece of foam rubber on the tip of each leg.

> If a caster keeps falling out of a chair, slot the top of the spindle with a hacksaw. Spread the cut slightly, then snap the caster back and it should stay secure. . . . Less trouble, though perhaps not so effective, is to wrap spindle in one or more layers of aluminum foil.

> To clean leather chair seats, rub each seat with half a lemon and then shine with a soft cloth.

☐ K N O B S : If a drawer-knob screw will not hold, bend a piece of soft wire into the hole. It acts as a shim for screw and will last for some time. . . . Or, fasten loose knobs on bureau drawers by cutting a small washer of sandpaper and threading it on the screw with the rough side toward the drawer. Then tighten the screw.

> Metal doorknobs and light-switch plates can be kept free of finger marks and grease if they are painted over with colorless nail polish.

> When a bureau drawer has lost handle or knobs, it can be opened with a suction cup or rubber plunger.

☐ L A M P S A N D L A M P S H A D E S : Foam plastic that is used in packing makes good nonscratch pads for lamp bases. . . . Or, pieces of old felt hats, pasted under lamps, vases, etc., will prevent scratching of furniture. Make them flat by pressing under wet cloth.

> Parchment lampshades can be brightened if rubbed with a soft cloth dampened with milk, then dried with a clean cloth.

> To best clean a pleated lampshade, rub with cheesecloth dipped in dry soapsuds.

☐ M I R R O R S : A little borax added to the water will both clean and shine mirrors in one operation. . . . Remove film from mirrors by wiping them with a cloth dampened with ammonia. Rub dry and polish with clean cloth. . . . Or, clean your mirrors with a dampened chamois to avoid getting water on the back, which might ruin the silver coating.

> To mend a mirror that has a scratch on the back, smooth a piece of aluminum foil the size of the scratch over the back of the mirror. Coat well with plain shellac and allow to dry. The mark will disappear.

> Check the heavy mirrors on your walls occasionally to see if weight and vibration have loosened the hooks.

> Hang a copper-backed, water-resistant mirror in your shower and do your shaving while bathing. A splash of warm water keeps the mirror from fogging. (No electric shaving—natch!)

☐ MUSICAL INSTRUMENTS RADIO/TV: Protect radio from sand on the beach by enclosing it in a loosely fitted clear-plastic bag. You can work the dials and hear it just as well.

> Make an old beat-up-looking portable radio look like new by covering it with self-adhering contact paper that blends with the room.

> If your radio is plagued with unexplained static, see if there's a loose lamp connection nearby.

> Get rid of sticky fingerprints on a TV screen with a solution of sal soda and a good rinse. . . . Clean your TV screen by rubbing on a bit of toothpaste with a damp cloth. Then wipe off with another clean, damp cloth.

> If your TV channel dial is blurry, try rubbing a white crayon over the numbers to restore them.

> Tip to color-TV owners: Never put a lamp, electric clock or other electrical appliance on top of a color set. It can upset the color balance.

> Many people use milk for cleaning piano keys. Yogurt has an even better effect.

> To protect piano felts against moth damage, suspend small bags of para nuggets (mothballs) or crystals inside the instrument.

> Have piano tuned at least twice a year. If notes give ringing sound, make sure the piano is standing straight. If that doesn't correct the sound, some article in the room may be causing a vibration.

☐ PICTURES: Use alcohol or ammonia water to clean up dusty glass picture frames. Polish with crumpled paper when dry.

> Beer does a fine job of cleaning gilt frames without tarnishing them. . . . Restore gilt picture frames to their original luster by rubbing with a sponge moistened in turpentine.

> Dust can seep into even a well-framed picture. Cover the joints in the back of the frame with plastic tape to keep them cleaner.

> Keep stored pictures and papers in good shape by enclosing them in waxed paper and sealing the edges with a warm iron.

> An occasional coating of paste wax on picture frames will make them easier to dust.

> Use two nails, spaced slightly apart, for hanging pictures; this will keep them straighter than a single nail. . . . A weighted string will help you hang straight pictures. Just line one side of the frame against the string. . . . Or, to keep pictures hanging straight, wind adhesive tape on each side of the center of the wire, leaving just enough bare wire to fit over the hook.

> When hanging paintings, keep them out of the direct sunlight, as they can fade.

> If small pictures are always crooked on the wall, keep them straight by attaching a small strip of double-faced cellophane tape to the back of the frame (at the bottom) and to the wall.

> Two-sided cellophane tape can be used to hang prints or posters on plaster walls. Apply tape wound around border of back of picture and press against the wall.

> Nylon fishing line is great for hanging pictures. When suspended from molding it is hardly visible.

> Next time any pictures are to be hung, do a "dry run" by cutting out paper the size and shape of the pictures and pinning them on the walls. That will let you decide without marring the plaster.

> Put a rubber-headed tack or thumbtack behind each lower corner of a heavy picture. This will allow air to pass freely behind the picture and will prevent the dark streaking where frame touches the wall.

> Line the backs of picture frames with strips of adhesive foam rubber to prevent marks on walls.

> If a picture nail gets loose in plaster, wrap gauze around the shank of the nail, dip into glue and replace in hole. Let it dry for a day before rehanging picture.

☐ P O L I S H I N G   W O O D : First warm the bottle of polish by standing it in a basin of hot water; it will penetrate the wood pores more quickly.

> Most alcohol stains will come off wooden furniture if rubbed with olive oil.

> Try a furniture polish of 3 parts olive oil, 1 part vinegar (like the base for French dressing). . . . Or, for a high polish on wood furniture, rub with equal parts of lemon oil and turpentine. Wipe off excess oil and polish with a dry woolen cloth or a lamb's-wool shoe buffer.

> Wax wood furniture with paste wax every six months or so, as it guards against water marks.

> Varnished surfaces will clean up if rubbed with a cloth dipped in cool tea. . . . To clean varnished wood without impairing the gloss, use one cup of vinegar added to one gallon of warm water.

> Never try to put wax on furniture that has been oiled.

> An easy way to clean and polish carved furniture is to dip an old toothbrush in furniture polish and rub in.

> Wipe furniture with cedar oil to give the room freshness.

> Walnut furniture can be cleaned and polished with boiled linseed oil.

☐ POLISHING LEATHER: Genuine-leather chairs or sofas should never be washed or oiled. Wash with milk and they will retain their natural oils and stay shiny. Or rub frequently with egg whites which have been beaten to a stiff consistency.

> A cleaning cloth dipped into denatured alcohol will remove mildew from leather.

> Leather-covered furniture can be cleaned if washed with a sponge dipped in chlorine bleach diluted with water. . . . Stale beer also does a good job. . . . Or, rub the seat with half a lemon and then shine with a dry cloth.

> Keep leather-covered furniture from cracking by polishing regularly with a cream made from 1 part vinegar and 2 parts linseed oil.

☐ POLISHING TABLES: Club soda will clean and give a high polish to *formica tops* of tables.

> When cleaning a *glass-topped* table, run a little lemon juice on the top to make it really sparkle. Then dry with paper or glasscloth. . . . Toothpaste rubbed on the glass tops of tables with a soft cloth will remove small scratches.

> If a plastic tabletop has lost its luster, rub in some toothpaste to make it shine like new. There will be no greasy oil finish. . . . Or, cover with paste wax and buff.

> Try rubbing with a lump of butter wrapped in a cloth to remove a white spot from a hot dish left on a polished table. . . . Spit and polish may be a military phrase, but take the first, add cigarette ashes and polish like crazy; it takes the ugly white rings off tables.

☐ OTHER THINGS ABOUT POLISHING: Use a sliced onion and a dry cloth to polish tin.

> A dab of petroleum jelly on a damp sponge brings out the natural luster of unpainted furniture.

> Plastic seat covers and cushions can be kept new looking by occasional sponging with a solution of sal soda.

> Clean plastic upholstery with a good cleaning wax to keep it looking its best.

> To clean wrought iron more easily, dampen a cloth in sweet oil, rub thoroughly and then polish with a dry woolen cloth. . . . A coat of liquid wax will keep wrought iron furniture and lamp stands from rusting.

> Dirt can be rubbed off metal furniture with steel wool.

> A bottle brush is a handy cleaner for patio furniture with hidden crevices.

☐ PORCELAIN/MARBLE/COPPER: A stubborn rust spot on porcelain from leaking faucets will come off if you saturate a paper towel with household bleach and leave it on the stain for a few hours.

> The best way to clean porcelain is with a flannel cloth sprinkled with salt. . . . Stubborn stains on plated or porcelain fixtures can frequently be rubbed away with a pencil eraser (but not a typewriter eraser).

> A cut lemon dipped in salt will clean stains from marble. Rub on, allow to stand a few minutes, then wash off with soap and water.

> To preserve the whiteness and polish of marble-topped tables, just apply a thin coat of clear paste wax and then rub off.

> Out of copper polish? Sprinkle a slice of lemon with baking soda and rub. Catsup also works like magic.

☐ SLIPCOVERS: If you have plastic slipcovers on your furniture, it's a good idea to remove them about every two months, or the finish may become dull and the upholstery may develop a musty smell.

> Put slipcovers back on while still slightly damp. They'll smooth out as they dry, fit better than if you ironed them. Only ruffles and pleats may need a bit of touching up.

□ S P O T S / S T A I N S / S C R A T C H E S : Butter will remove tar spots if no turpentine is available.

> Get alcohol stains off polished furniture by rubbing with olive oil.

> Turpentine will remove rust or grease stains from metal furniture.

> Remove lipstick stains from furniture, particularly light wood, by putting a little toothpaste on a soft cloth and gently rubbing it over the spots.

> Remove grease spills and stains from wooden surfaces by pouring salt on at once. This absorbs the grease and prevents staining.

> You can remove most white stains on mahogany furniture by spreading a thick coat of petroleum jelly over them and letting it stand for 48 hours. Then polish it off.

> A mixture of equal parts of linseed oil, turpentine and vinegar is an effective solution for covering small scratches on furniture. Apply with cotton-tipped sticks. . . . Or, rub surface furniture scratches with a cloth dampened in denatured alcohol.

> Cover nicks and scratches in wrought-iron furniture with a black crayon; wipe off the excess with paper tissue.

> Use liquid shoe polish for touching up scarred furniture: brown for walnut, cordovan for mahogany, and tan for maple. Good, too, for picture frames.

□ T A B L E S : If a table wobbles because of a short leg, put a small amount of Plastic Wood on waxed paper on the floor. Set the short leg on it and allow to dry. Then trim down with sharp knife and smooth with sandpaper.

☐ UMBRELLA STANDS: Put a large sponge in the bottom of an umbrella stand. It will absorb the water from wet umbrellas.

> Spray the inside of a wooden box with shellac and put it near the front door as a receptacle for rubbers, umbrellas, etc., in rainy weather. . . . Or, a large desk blotter just inside the door on a rainy day is a fine spot to park and dry out rubbers and galoshes.

☐ UPHOLSTERY: Do not use cleaning fluid on upholstery over foam rubber. It can affect the rubber.

> Upholstery should be cleaned every two years. Even if it does not show dirt, it will wear much better.

☐ VASES: Grapefruit rind will remove hard-water deposits from vases. Slice rind into the container and fill with water; let it stand for a day or two. Water and the juice of half a lemon is also effective.

> To remove slithery film from vases, wash them in a solution of two tablespoons of baking soda per quart of water. Swish the solution around in the vase, let stand for a few minutes and then rinse. . . . Vases dulled by a brown film can be made sparkling if you put a few pieces of finely chopped raw potato inside. Add half a cup of vinegar and shake well. Wash with warm suds and rinse.

> When glass vases become stained, pour in warm water, add some tea leaves, and let stand for a few hours. Then wash with soap and water.

> Keep silver vases and frames gleaming and tarnish-free longer by rubbing with furniture polish after cleaning.

> To clean deep vases, allow a solution of salt and vinegar to stand in them for an hour. Shake well, then wash and rinse.

> A solution of hot water and ammonia cuts grime and film on flower vases. . . . Strong vinegar will remove lime deposits and other stains from vases.

> Smooth the rough bottom of a vase so as not to scratch

furniture by dipping in a shallow dish of turpentine, then rubbing it across a piece of sandpaper.

> Any large-mouthed bottle can become an attractive flower container. Wash the bottle, paint it with a lacquer paint, and allow to dry completely. Decorate as you wish, perhaps by trimming with raffia, cementing the raffia as it is wound around the bottle.

> Mend a leaking vase by coating the inside with a thick layer of paraffin and allowing it to harden. It will last indefinitely and the vase will not leak.

> Top-heavy vases can be made steadier by weighing down with clean sand in the bottom.

> To arrange long-stemmed flowers in a wide-mouthed vase, put a crisscrossing of cellophane tape across the top of the vase to hold them in place.

> Cut out various-sized circles from a discarded desk blotter and use when needed under vases and flowerpots.

☐ AND SOME OTHER THINGS: Soiled plaster of Paris statuettes will take on a new look if they are dipped in a solution of starch and water, then buffed with a soft brush when thoroughly dry.

> Stain Plastic Wood to match furniture with colored waterproof drawing ink.

> Erase bird marks from canvas covers of outdoor furniture with a stiff bristled brush run over a cake of yellow soap and sprinkled with dry washing soda. Hose well to rinse.

HOME MAINTENANCE

☐ BATHROOM: A thin coat of clear nail polish applied over medicine-bottle labels will prevent ink from running when wet.

> Line shelves of medicine chest with strips of blotting paper. It will absorb spills. Pick a color to match bathroom decor.

> Put your next new shower curtain in front of the old one on the same hooks. The old one will get the wetting and soaping and the other will stay new-looking.

> Keep plastic curtains soft and pliable by adding drops of mineral oil to warm water when rinsing.

> To keep cloth shower curtains from mildewing in damp weather, soak them in a solution of salt water before hanging them. . . . Use baking soda to remove a small area of mildew on a shower curtain. For more extensive mildew stains, wash the curtain in hot suds, then rub stains with a lemon. Allow to dry in the sun.

> When plastic shower curtains have turned yellow, wash in washing machine with mild suds. Then tint with a package dye that does not require boiling. Use warm water for rinsing so curtains remain pliable. Tint will not rinse off when curtain is used.

> Old shower curtains make fine drop cloths for home painters.

> Get soap-and-water marks off glass shower doors by rubbing lightly with sponge dampened in undiluted vinegar. . . . To remove soapy film from shower door, use a wax floor cleaner, then polish with a dry cloth. Subsequent soap film will rinse off easily.

> Soak rubber sink or bath mat in a weak solution of bleach and water for a couple of hours to remove grime and stains.

> Use a damp, soap-filled steel wool pad to freshen a scummy shower mat made out of rubber.

> When enameled bathtubs and lavatories become yellow, rub with a solution of salt and turpentine to restore the whiteness.

> Cleaning or lighter fluid will usually remove the most stubborn dark stains from bathtub or sink porcelain.

> Get water-rust stains off the bathroom sink and tub by rubbing with borax, sprinkled with lemon; or rub with cream of tartar and a few drops of hydrogen peroxide.

> Dull chromium sink fixtures can be spruced up by rubbing with a small amount of kerosene on a damp cloth.

> Clean grimy porcelain tiles with steel wool dipped into glass cleaner diluted with water.

> Tile floors should not be waxed, as this will make them grimy. Clean with detergent and damp mop only.

> Linoleum-covered walls and floors will make a bathroom soundproof.

> Silver polish will remove crayon marks from linoleum or tile floors.

> Applying laundry starch and then wiping with a soft cloth will brighten discolored bathroom tiles.

> Nail-polish remover rubbed into tile will remove paint spatters.

> To wipe down kitchen and bathroom walls in a hurry, use a sponge mop and detergent.

> Give glazed wall tiles the sparkle of newness by wiping them with a sponge dipped in ammonia and water.

> Rust stains on tile will usually yield to kerosene, if they're not too old.

> Clean bathroom tiles with solution of sal soda. For the stubborn cracks, apply the sal dry with a stiff brush. . . . To remove extra-stubborn spots on tile, use steel wool dampened with a liquid wax.

> If shower doesn't have full force, check the head for clogged holes. It may need cleaning in hot soapy water. A removable shower head may also be cleaned by a soaking in vinegar.

> To improve appearance of an old bathtub, coat exposed sides with bathroom enamel.

> Make the shower safer: Install a towel bar vertically for support.

> Fill the bathtub with a couple of inches of cold water before running hot, to avoid steaming up the bathroom.

> After bathroom gets steamed up from shower, turn on the cold water full force to quickly clear up the steam.

> There'll be no "ring" in the bathtub if a spoonful of synthetic detergent is added to bathwater.

☐ AND A LOT OF OTHER THINGS: Go over fixtures with facial tissue. Paper picks up all lint and leaves the surfaces shining. . . . To remove rust on bathroom fixtures, try a little glycerin or olive oil on your cleaning rag.

> Get rid of grubby blobs of dried soap spatters by rubbing on dry washing soda with a cellulose sponge.

> Straw or wicker hampers and baskets should be shellacked to prevent mildew.

> Keep metal clothes hamper from getting a damp, musty smell by sponging out with a strong sal soda solution occasionally.

> Use cotton swabs to clean the holes in a toothbrush holder.

> A fine gadget for bathrooms is a self-adhering hook that sticks to tile. Attach it over the washstand as a safe receptacle for rings and watches.

> Test the accuracy of bathroom scales by weighing the next 5-pound bag of flour or sugar that comes into the house.

> Hot salt water poured down drains of tubs and sinks several times a week will keep them free of grease and disagreeable odors.

> If the bathroom sink drain gets clogged by matted hair, straighten out a paper clip, leaving a slight bend at one end. Use this to fish out the obstruction.

> Put strips of adhesive around bathroom bottles (shampoo, hair tonic, etc.) or drinking glass that you may have to

handle with wet hands, to make them skidproof. A rubber band will also do.

> Avoid mildew damage by being sure terry cloth towels or washcloths are fully dry before putting them in hamper or bag.

☐ B E D R O O M :   When blanket wears thin, encase it in a blanket cover for a lightweight comforter.

> An old hairbrush is ideal for taking fuzz off blankets. Using downward strokes, brush the blanket thoroughly while it is wet or after it dries.

> If blanket is short, sew strip of material to end that is tucked in at foot of bed.

> Fluff woolen blankets, or air feather pillows, by tumbling them in an automatic dryer for three or four minutes.

> Store woolen blankets in a dresser drawer that has been lined with aromatic red cedar closet lining.

> When lining bureau drawers, use several layers of paper. When a change is needed, slide out the top piece.

> A small magnet on the dressing table will help collect scattered hairpins and bobby pins.

> Tuck empty uncorked perfume bottle in a corner of a bureau drawer to provide long-lasting scent.

> When turning a mattress, turn side over side one time and end over end the next.

> Sew several short straps to the side of a mattress to make moving and turning easier.

> Latex-foam mattresses have one special advantage: they never have to be turned.

> It's better to air feather pillows out of direct strong sunlight, as the rays can draw out the natural oil and destroy feather resiliency.

> For cooler sleeping, open the bed covers a half hour before retiring and aim electric fan, at highest speed, at the

sheets. Sprinkle talcum powder inside pillowcases and all over sheets before hopping into bed.

> Lightly starching pillowcases prevents hair creams and oils from staining them.

> Inserting sachets under mattresses or in pillowcases will leave a pleasant aroma in bedding.

☐ C L O S E T S :   A little floor wax applied to thᵣ rods in clothes closets will permit hangers to slide back and forth readily.

> To keep sliding doors of closets and cabinets running smoothly, remove doors and apply a thin coat of shellac to the grooves and sliding parts. When dry, rub paste wax over the shellac.

> Don't use oil on squeaking closet-door hinges and run the risk of staining clothes; a rubbing with soap will do the job.

> Use large shower-curtain hooks over the clothes rod for hanging handbags in the closet; also belts and umbrellas.

> To make a dark closet brighter, paint the walls and ceiling with white enamel.

> If a light is needed in a closet that is not wired, hang a sportsman's battery lantern on a coat hook high inside the door. Infrequently used batteries will last longer. . . . Or hang a flashlight.

> Apartment dwellers, who have a real storage problem because of lack of space, often forget to use empty suitcases and hanging garment bags as receptacles.

> Aromatic red cedar closet lining can be installed economically in existing closets. Pieces can be nailed right over walls, no finishing is needed and the clothes are safe from moths. . . . When an old cedar chest or closet has lost its odor, partly restore it by rubbing the surface with sandpaper.

> A reader says that dried orange peel on clothes-closet shelves will keep moths away and provide a pleasant scent. . . . In Europe, people swear by a saucer of tobacco in a closet to keep moths away. Elsewhere, it is claimed that horse

chestnuts do the same job. . . . Keep moths away from clothes with small bags filled with cloves. Or, moths and silverfish will stay away from a closet if the floor is wiped with a cloth dampened in turpentine.

> If humid weather has left closets with mildew aroma, hang clothes out to air and scrub interior with a strong solution of one cup baking soda per pail of hot water. . . . You can remove musty clothes-closet odors by placing a pan of water, with household ammonia in it, in the closet overnight.

> Enamel on the interior of closets is not only decorative but practical. It keeps closets fresh and clean, and since it is washable, it is more economical than using shelf-lining paper.

> Tie a pretty ribbon around an unwrapped cake of toilet soap and hang in clothes closet to keep clothes smelling fresh.

> A venetian blind works wonderfully when hung in front of a doorless closet or cupboard. It also provides ventilation.

☐ DINING ROOM AND KITCHEN: Two card tables with tape wound around the adoining legs will provide a sizable buffet or dining table when required.

> Place squares of cellophane wrap under bowls of spillable foods on the buffet table to prevent tablecloth stains.

> At least once a month open the dining-room table and remove bread crumbs that may have dropped through the crack.

> Untangle the fringes of place mats, napkins, guest towels, etc., with a small wire brush.

> Slide a small braid rug under a stove or refrigerator that is too close to the floor to allow passage of a mop. Dust will stick to rug, which is easily cleaned.

☐ DOORS: Coat the edges of doors and areas around doorknobs with paste wax. The inevitable finger marks will be easier to remove.

> If a door has warped enough to scrape the floor, put a

piece of coarse sandpaper underneath and work the door back and forth. This should correct the condition.

> When a door sticks, apply pressure to open it only at the spot where it is sticking. Forcing other parts may strain the frame.

> To keep a door from rattling, stick a felt corn pad to the door's lower inside edge.

☐ FIREPLACES / FIRES: When removing ashes from fireplace, burn a piece of newspaper in one corner of the hearth; draft will draw the dust up the chimney.

> The fireplace will be easier to clean if a layer of aluminum foil is placed under grate.

> Get rid of smoky smell from the fireplace when finished using it for the season by swabbing its floor and sides with a solution of three tablespoons of sal soda in water. Do the same with the andirons and the rest of the fireplace equipment.

> There's no need to scrub the fireplace so often if you throw salt on the logs occasionally. This will reduce the soot by two thirds.

> For easy cleaning of the sooty brick around a fireplace, scrub it with a pailful of hot water to which a cup of washing soda has been added.

> Use a drinking straw as a taper when lighting a fire in the fireplace—it's safer than a short match.

> Start a fire in a fireplace easily by letting some tallow drip from a candle stub over the kindling. This works even with damp kindling.

> Small strips of old linoleum make good fire lighters and kindling for fireplaces.

☐ FLOORING: Never clean wood floors with plain water. Dilute turpentine or white vinegar in water and wipe with a soft cloth. Floors will be bright, colorful and clean.

> To remove water spots on finished wood floors, rub gently with cloth dampened in alcohol and wipe with oily cloth.

> Stubborn patches of dirt can be removed from a floor by rubbing with fine steel wool moistened with turpentine.

> Coffee stains on wood floors should be rubbed gently with steel wool and alcohol.

> A soft cotton floor mop barely dampened with mixture of three parts kerosene and one part paraffin oil is excellent for dry mopping.

> Rubber heel marks can be erased from hardwood floors with a light rubdown of steel wool.

> Dark streaks on a bare floor where furniture used to stand can be removed with a soapy cloth dipped in kerosene.

> It is better to wax a floor on a cold day than on a hot day. Wax takes longer to dry in humid weather.

> To straighten a warped piece of board, apply dry heat to the convex side.

> Fine powdered graphite will often eliminate floor squeaks; puff powder into floor crack. . . . Squeaky wood floors can often be quieted with heated liquid soap. Put it in an oilcan and squirt between the boards. . . . Another method of stopping squeaks in a board floor is to dip a knife blade in liquid glue and work blade in and out of creaking crack. Allow to dry.

> A paste of salt, alum and boiling water will serve as cement when poured into cracks in a floor.

> If heavy furniture must be moved on an uncarpeted floor, put flattened milk cartons under sides of legs. Waxed cartons allow the piece to slide and the floor will not be marred. . . . Or, slip old wool socks over legs of furniture when moving across floors to prevent scratching.

☐ INSECTICIDES / PEST & RODENT KILLERS: Cucumber peelings, cut into thin strips and placed near the haunts of crickets and ants, make a safe and effective deterrent.

> If ants are getting into the house, sprinkle the place of entry with baking soda or salt. . . . Or, cayenne pepper, lightly dusted on kitchen shelves should eliminate ants.

> Seal porch-step cracks with putty and paint over them for termite protection.

> Any kind of mint scattered about shelves will drive away mice.

> If there is no cheese around the house, try baiting mouse-traps with peanut butter. Mice love it. . . . Or, bait a mouse-trap with absorbent cotton. The mice will attempt to use it to line their nests.

> A strip of unpainted redwood molding around the walls of a room will discourage insects. They can't stand the odor.

> An area frequented by cockroaches can be painted with a mixture of lime, water, and a small quantity of salt, and insects will be gone in a few weeks.

> To rid an area of insects, sprinkle insect powder on a slice of raw potato and place in a corner where pests have been seen.

☐ LIGHTING: LAMPS / CANDLES / CHANDELIERS: Avoid the mistake of using a single lamp to light a reading area, leaving the rest of the room dark. The contrast between the dark and lighted areas will cause eyestrain and fatigue.

> Some people like to remove the necks of bottles to make the bottom sections into lamps or vases. To do this, saturate twine in kerosene; wrap it around where the break should be; set fire to the cord and, when it has burned, pour cold water on the spot. It will come apart cleanly without breaking the whole bottle.

> Coat fabric-covered lamp cords with colorless shellac to prevent fraying.

> Unsightly dark extension cords in a light-colored room will be less noticeable if painted with white-sidewall tire coating.

> For maximum illumination, use one large bulb, not several small ones. A 100-watt lamp gives 50% more light than four 25-watt bulbs.

> If a light bulb looks shadowy, replace it. An almost-worn bulb wastes power without supplying full light.

> A fluorescent tube and its switch will have a longer life if it isn't turned on and off too frequently. If leaving the room for short periods, it's better to keep the light on. . . . If a fluorescent tube has darkened, reverse the ends. This often works.

> Decorate lampshades with maps from an old atlas; this is particularly good in a boy's room. Glue map down tightly to shade and allow to dry; then lacquer the entire shade. Or, leftover pieces of wallpaper can be used instead of maps.

> Cleaning people often neglect light bulbs. See if yours need a dusting, or a wipe with a damp cloth. Makes a big difference to the eyes.

> Candles can be made drip-proof by a soaking in salt water. Use two tablespoons of salt for each candle and just enough water to cover. . . . They will burn with less smoke and drip if first dipped in soapsuds. . . . A thin coat of white shellac makes candles last longer and prevents excessive dripping of wax. . . . Or, chill candles twelve hours before using them at table; they will burn evenly and not drip.

> If certain candles are just for show, keep them from drooping by coating with clear shellac.

> Always trim candle wicks after burning. Never allow pieces of wick, matchsticks, or other foreign articles to stay in the cupped part of a candle.

> Keep candles clean and unbroken by storing them in empty cardboard tubes from paper towels, etc.

> Hold bottoms of candles in hot water for a second, then insert in candle holder, holding them for a moment till they are firm and steady. . . . Or, taper a candle to fit smoothly in holder by turning the end in steel wool held in your hand. . . . Or, a dab of modeling clay will hold candle firmly in a candlestick.

> A piece of aluminum foil wrapped around the base of a

candle being stuck in a decorative liquor bottle will keep the bottle from cracking from overheating.

> Large, square iron nuts make attractive, rustic-looking candle holders.

> To free silver candelabra from drip wax, set them in refrigerator until very cold. Then press the ball of the thumb against the wax and it will slide right off.

> Put ammonia and water in a large-necked jar and hold the jar below crystal drops on a chandelier. Dip them in the solution to clean.

☐ LINENS / TOWELS — STORING: Infrequently used linens, which might turn yellow, should be stored carefully. They'll stay white if put away in a pillow case "blued" to a deep color with laundry bluing. . . . Or, linens and towels will keep whiteness better if the inside of the closet is painted blue. . . . Or, cover linens with dark-blue paper. Avoid excess heat, and do not store in cedar chests, as the fumes might tend to yellow the linens.

> When washing a rarely used tablecloth, fold it wrong-side out for storing. If the creases become soiled, they will not show when the cloth is placed on the table.

> Store good table linens by rolling them in long mailing tubes. This will prevent soiling and unsightly creases.

> The Navy rolls its towels, instead of folding them on shelves. This doubles storage space.

> Fold good linens differently each time to prevent wear in the same places.

☐ ODOR REMOVAL: Remove scent from an empty perfume bottle by filling with rubbing alcohol. Let it stand overnight, then wash with warm water. . . . Or, deodorize jars and bottles by pouring a solution of water and dry mustard into them and letting them stand for several hours. . . . Or, fill with warm water and a tablespoon of baking soda and leave overnight.

> Changing a vacuum-bottle cork occasionally will keep the contents smelling fresher.

> To keep bureau drawers smelling fresh, lay scented flannel at bottom of each.

> Leaving opened packages of scented bath soap in a linen closet will keep bedding smelling sweet.

> Using a fan on the floor of a closet will push out the stale air and keep clothes smelling fresh.

> To get the smell of varnish or paint out of a china closet or dish cabinet, leave a sliced onion inside overnight. (The cabinet will not smell like onion.)

> A few pieces of activated charcoal in a storage cabinet will absorb all food odors.

> Lime (found in hardware stores) put in a few shallow pans will chase away dampness and odor in the basement. A small pan of lime, placed out of reach, will keep the air in a closet or room fresh. Replenish every few weeks.

> To rid a cutting board of odor from onion, garlic, etc., rub the surface with a slice of lime.

> Remove onion odor from a knife by holding it over a flame for 2 minutes; garlic and onion odor can also be removed if the knife blade is run through a raw potato. . . . Or remove odor from utensils by rubbing with celery.

> Remove fish or onion odors from a pan by rinsing with vinegar while the pan is still hot.

> To remove fish and cabbage odors from utensils, soak in a vinegar and soda water solution, then wash in sudsy water; rinse and dry.

> When washing dishes that have been used for fish, use a tablespoon of ammonia or vinegar in the water to make certain no fish odor remains.

> Perhaps the most effective way to rid dishes and silver and pans of fish odor is to drop a teaspoonful of dry mustard into the dishwater.

> A few mothballs in the garbage can twice a week will eliminate most odors and keep out insects.

> Grind a half lemon into the garbage-disposal unit to remove any unpleasant odors.

> A garbage pail will stay odorless if given an occasional ammonia bath.

> Get fish odors, or any other odors, off hands by washing them with soap, then with vinegar or salt, then soap again.

> Rub the hands with a little butter to remove fish or onion odors.

> Chill hands thoroughly before handling fish to prevent odor from clinging to them.

> Wash hands in cold water, rather than hot, to remove onion odor. . . . Or celery salt rubbed on hands after peeling onions, and before washing, will remove odor. . . . Or, rub hands with freshly mixed mustard; then rinse in cold water.

> Wear a washable scarf around the head when frying onions and keep the hair from absorbing cooking odors.

> Wash the hands with deodorant soap to kill onion smell at once.

> Remove unpleasant onion or garlic odor—and keep skin soft—by rubbing lime over hands and nails.

> Eliminate the nauseating odor of paint when doing the inside of the house by adding two teaspoons of vanilla extract per quart of paint.

> Fresh-paint odors will vanish if a tablespoon of ammonia is put in a large pan of water and left in the room overnight. Even a pail of plain water, left overnight, will eliminate paint odors.

> A couple of pieces of white bread in the refrigerator will absorb food odors, as will half a lemon or a small ball of child's modeling clay. Vanilla extract, poured on a piece of cotton, works too.

> To get rid of garlic odor, try leaving sprigs of parsley around the room.

> Dab a few drops of perfume on a light bulb. When the bulb is lighted and becomes warm, fragrance will spread through the room.

> Replace the smell of antiseptic cleanser with fresh perfumed fragrance by burning a little cologne in a saucer. If it is heated first, it burns better.

> If a room deodorant is not readily available, strike a match to effectively remove offensive odors.

> To get rid of unwelcome cooking odors, boil three teaspoonfuls of ground cloves in two cups of water for 15 minutes. . . . Or, pour cold tea into an atomizer and spray. . . . Or simply burn dried orange peel slowly on top of the stove.

> A pail of cold water placed at the kitchen door when onions are cooking will keep the odor from spreading through the house.

> Keep a ball of ordinary twine in bathroom and burn an inch every so often to absorb the bathroom odors.

> Keep a room from becoming stale with cigarette smoke during a party by putting a small bowl of vinegar in an inconspicuous place. (But make it really inconspicuous—or somebody might drink it!)

> Put a little household ammonia in a saucer and leave overnight to remove stale smoke odors.

> A paste made of baking soda and water will take the odor out of a carving or bread board.

> Sprinkle a little dry baking soda on the bottom of a bread box, cookie jar or any closed container when away from home on extended stays. It absorbs moisture that could cause mustiness.

> To remove odors from a lunch box, wash with plain soda water, rinse, then allow to dry in sun.

> If a metal teapot is seldom used, place a lump of sugar inside to eliminate musty odor.

> Automatic coffee makers sometimes retain odors. To remove them, fill with cold water and let stand for a day.

> Odors that cling to plastic tablecloths and mats and defy soap-and-water washings respond quickly to a soaking in a baking soda solution. . . . Also works for dishcloths, sponges, and towels.

> If old furniture has a musty odor, stick some cloves in a green apple and place in a drawer. This will freshen it.

> Odors can be driven away effectively if ammonia is rubbed into the spot immediately following the accident that causes the odor.

☐ R U G S : When removing furniture, be sure to lift it. Pushing heavy pieces across carpet may damage fibers.

> To remove marks left in carpeting by furniture, hold a hot steam iron two inches away from the rug; brush nap. . . . Or, go over marks with a vacuum cleaner. . . . Or, dampen with warm water, then rub with the edge of a coin. . . . Or, pour a little water into the marks and let stand overnight.

> Dull spots caused by weight of furniture can be brightened if you rub French chalk into them with a stiff brush and then remove the chalk with the vacuum cleaner. . . . Or, restore nap by placing damp chamois cloth, folded several times, over depression. After a few hours, nap should rise.

> If carpet corner should begin to curl, apply a hot iron to a damp cloth on both face and back of corner.

> To prevent carpet from curling at edge, sew an L-shaped cardboard on corner.

> A scatter rug will hold its ground if an old rubber bath mat is placed underneath. . . . Or, attach rubber inserts from jars under sides of scatter rugs. . . . The undersides may also be sprayed with a rubberized spray.

> Make rug feel thicker and plusher by placing a 1-inch foam-rubber undercoating beneath it.

> Carpet wear may be caused by an uneven floor. Use carpet cushion where this condition exists.

> Switch position of rugs occasionally to distribute the wear more evenly.

> Wool carpets and rugs will last longer if the air in a home is not too dry (a third of the natural content of wool is moisture). . . . Spray fiber rugs occasionally with water to keep them from drying out, but do not soak.

> If you must beat a carpet, don't hang it up. Place it on the grass nap down. Rug beating can break the backing of a rug.

> To speed drying of a wet spot on a rug, insert vacuum-cleaner tube under the carpet at the spot.

> Carry a large rug without having it buckle by rolling it diagonally.

> Don't store a rug on end unless it is rolled around a pole of some kind for support.

> Attach fringe to a small rug without sewing. Use masking tape, and the fringe can easily be removed for a change of color.

> If an apartment is small, matching floor covering throughout will give the impression of depth.

> If having the carpet cleaned, wash floors at least two days before carpet is reinstalled to avoid mildew.

> Add ammonia to a bucket of warm water and run a damp mop over rugs as you would wipe up a floor. This brightens color and removes dirt.

> After shampooing rug, brush and smooth nap in one direction with a soft brush or dry cloth. Then put heavy aluminum squares under all furniture legs and long triple layers of it under full length of chest and bureaus. This guards against marks and stains when carpet dries.

> Try sprinkling rugs with salt and then vacuuming. They will be brighter and cleaner, and salt helps destroy moths. . . . Or, wipe carpets or rugs with cloth or sponge that has been dipped in strong salt solution and wrung out. . . . Also try

cleaning rugs with a mixture of cornmeal and salt. Rub well into rug with a scrub brush, then remove mixture with vacuum cleaner.

> Dampen the brush on the carpet sweeper before using it and it will pick up raveling and lint without trouble. . . . Or, pick up lint and thread from rugs by brushing gently with a toothbrush.

> Use a diagonal stroke when vacuuming small rugs. This makes the rug less likely to wrinkle and become caught in the cleaner.

> When trying to remove a spot on carpeting, do not rub the stained area; *blot* with an absorbent material. . . . Many spots will come out of rugs if a little seltzer is poured on and allowed to soak. . . . Always begin at outer edges of rug, working toward center, to avoid spreading the soil. Wipe or pat lightly. Hard rubbing or brushing may injure the pile.

> Use ice cubes on gum to harden it—then try to peel off. If this does not remove it all, try a bit of egg white. . . . If other methods fail, gasoline will remove chewing gum from carpets and polished floors.

> Apply paste of milk and cornmeal to ink stain and allow to stand a few hours, then brush off. . . . Or, cover ink with table salt for a minute, then wash with vinegar.

> Cellophane tape will often remove crayon marks from carpet; press the sticky side against the spots.

> Dampen a slight cigarette burn spot with liquid bleach, then scrub with a brush in a circular motion and leave to dry.

> Blot up excess coffee, then rub the spot with a solution of detergent, vinegar and water.

> Use a thick paste of baking soda and water on grease. Apply to spot, allow to dry, then remove with a brush. . . . Or, sprinkle a little cream of tartar on the stain and let remain overnight. Then use vacuum cleaner to remove cream of tartar.

> Apply plenty of cold water to alcohol and mop with a clean dry cloth. Rub with nap. Repeat if necessary.

> Place a clean blotter on an oil spot and press with moderately hot iron; repeat if necessary.

> Mix one teaspoon of white vinegar with three teaspoons of lukewarm water. Apply to food stain with eyedropper and allow to stand for 15 minutes. Then blot with a clean cloth.

> Use food coloring as a cover-up for bleach stains on dark cotton rugs.

> Art-gum erasers will remove sooty footprints from light-colored carpeting.

☐ WALLS / WOODWORK / CEILING—CLEANING & REPAIR: To remove smoke and grease stains from woodwork, paint it with a solution of starch and water. After solution has dried, rub off with soft brush or clean cloth. . . . Or, to clean greasy woodwork quickly, especially around a stove, dip a cloth in turpentine and rub the woodwork lightly. . . . Or remove greasy finger smudges from woodwork by using an excellent cleaner made of a quart of warm water, a tablespoon of washing soda and a pinch of detergent. . . . Grease spots will come off a painted plaster wall if it's treated with a spray spot remover. Spray the spot, then dry with clean, soft cloth.

> Scratched woodwork can be repaired even when the scratches are very deep. Fill the scratches with a mixture of fine sawdust and spar varnish. After filler has hardened completely, smooth down with fine sandpaper.

> Use erasers to remove fingerprints from woodwork without discoloration.

> Paper stuck to a wood surface will come off if a few drops of oil are allowed to soak into it. Rub off gently with a soft cloth.

> To wash a shellacked wood-paneled wall, wipe it down with a cloth moistened in water that has a few drops of vinegar in it, then immediately wipe with a dry cloth.

> Large cracks in walls and wood furniture can be filled first with steel wool before a finishing off with plaster or Plastic Wood.

> Crayon marks on painted walls will come off easily if rubbed with lighter fluid. . . . Or, remove crayon writings from any painted surface by rubbing marks briskly with a dry turkish towel, turning towel surface often. It takes a while, but it works.

> To clean brown-stained wood of walls, use a cloth dampened in one part of water and one part lemon oil. This will maintain gloss and finish.

> Clean natural woodwork by moistening a cloth very lightly with a solution of water and a few drops of white vinegar.

> When washing walls, fold a washcloth and fasten it around your wrist with a rubber band. The cloth will keep water from running down your arm.

> Walls and woodwork should be washed from the bottom up. When water runs down on soiled surface, it leaves streaks that are difficult to remove.

> Wash walls with two ounces of powdered borax and one teaspoon of ammonia to two quarts of water.

> Vacuum cleaning walls in sooty areas is just as efficient as washing them. It can be done more frequently and, of course, does not affect paint as soap does.

☐ AND A LOT OF OTHER THINGS: Turn the thermostat down when vacuuming the house for an extended time. The warm air forced through the device raises the room temperature.

> Old flatirons make interesting bookends or doorstops if they are first enameled white and then decorated with colorful decals.

> Psychologically, the color blue makes a room feel cold. Red is a stimulating or cheering color to the lazy or melancholy, upsetting to the nervous or overactive.

> You can cover a cigarette hole in a bridge cloth by embroidering or appliquéing a design over it.

> Sheets of aluminum foil tacked on the wall behind a radiator will reflect more heat into the room.

> Brushing artificial flowers with absorbent powder will keep them free of dust.

> Dust artificial flowers and plants at least once a week and they will stay fresh indefinitely.

> Clean plastic flowers by putting ¼ cup of dry salt in a bag and dropping in the flowers; shake well and the flowers will be like new.

> The easiest way to keep artificial flowers clean is with an ordinary toothbrush, soap and water.

> To wash delicate flowers and/or porcelain birds, dip them in a solution of water and sudsless dishwashing detergent in a plastic bucket.

> Pour some common salt, then some water, in a container and arrange artificial flowers. When the salt solidifies, it will hold the flowers in position. . . . Or, artificial flowers can be kept in a fixed position in a vase or container if the stems are placed in sand and hot paraffin is poured over the sand. . . . And long-stemmed artificial flowers will stay as arranged if you place small balls of aluminum foil between the stems.

> Spray artificial flowers with hair spray to give them gloss and make them less vulnerable. . . . Or, spray dried-flower arrangements—such as milkweed—with hair spray to keep their fluff from falling.

> To get further use from old, soiled artificial flowers, shake off the dust and dip in or spray with gilt or bronze paint. They make a decorative winter bouquet themselves, or they can be added to dried arrangements. . . . Or, touch up dulled artificial flowers with colorless nail polish and restore their realistic appearance.

> Artificial flowers and leaves can be reshaped by dipping in boiling water for a few seconds, shaping and dipping immediately in cold water.

> To renew artificial fruits, wash quickly with mild suds, rinse and dry well, then rub a small amount of petroleum jelly

on your hands and gently coat the fruit with a thin film. The appearance will be natural and beautiful.

> Rubbing alcohol does an excellent job as a waxed-fruit cleaner, leaving a fine luster.

☐ W I N D O W S / S H A D E S : When cleaning venetian blinds, keep a spring-type clothespin handy. If phone or doorbell rings while you are working, slip the pin on the slat being cleaned so you'll know where to resume work.

> Art gum will remove smudges from venetian blind slats and taping.

> Clean venetian blinds by dumping them into a bathtub of hot water. Add detergent; then rinse them under the shower, let them dry in the tub—and they'll look like new. Add a cup of lemon juice to the detergent to keep them whiter. . . . Or, try cleaning venetian blinds with alcohol.

> You can dye the soiled and discolored tapes of venetian blinds with liquid shoe polish, which comes in a wide variety of colors.

> Replace a venetian blind cord by taping a new one to the end of the old one and pulling it through.

> You can protect bamboo blinds from mildew with a thin coat of clear shellac.

> Discarded turkish towels make excellent venetian blind dusters and are easy to wash.

> If you dust venetian blinds at least once a week, you'll never have to wash them.

> If the cords on traverse drapery rods are coated with a thin layer of petroleum jelly they will work more smoothly.

> Spray one of the liquid starches on tired, limp nylon curtains after they've been washed and hung on the line to dry. It will give them new life.

> Curtains will slip over curtain rods more easily and safely if you bind the end of the rods with cellophane tape.

> When placing curtains on stretchers, save your fingers by using a fork to press the curtains in place on the tiny spikes.

> Soiled curtains will brighten when washed if ½ cup of salt is added to the soaking water.

> Obsolete flat-type door keys make excellent weights for curtains or draperies. Just slip a key into the bottom hem and use the hole in the key to tack it in place.

> Small tears in window curtains can usually be mended with colorless nail polish.

> You can make window shades look like new, or give them an interesting pattern or color, by simply covering them with wallpaper.

> Prints are the latest thing in window shades. Make your own washable ones by cutting them from oilcloth to blend with your color scheme. Hem the bottom and insert stick, then tack onto a roller.

> A rough flannel cloth dipped in flour will do a quick job of cleaning dirty window shades. . . . A soft eraser may remove many spots and stains on shades.

> To tighten a window shade quickly, put the wide-pronged end in a keyhole and turn it until it is as tight as desired.

> Window shades drawn between dawn and dusk in the winter will keep a house warmer. The air pocket between window and shade is an insulator.

> To keep window shades from blowing when they are pulled down and the window is open, replace the ring on the bottom with a small suction cup, which can be stuck to the windowsill.

> Make window shades decorative by painting them with a plastic-based paint. They will be colorful and easily washable.

> Keep parchment shades clean by waxing them; it will make them easier to dust and adds a soft luster to the finish.

> A cool idea for summer heat: Use new "bottom-up" window shades, with the roller installed at the windowsill and the

shade pulling up toward the ceiling. They shut off the hot rays of the sun at the "living level" of the room, but invite fresh air to circulate from the top. Available in high-style cloth fabrics, they are both effective and uniquely attractive.

> A perfect mixture for window washing is a tablespoon of dishwashing detergent in two quarts of water. . . . For sparkling windowpanes, add two tablespoons of cornstarch to the wash water; or use equal parts of water and rubbing alcohol. . . . Or, spirits of ammonia, rubbed on glass and then polished with a dry cloth, is a fine way to wash windows.

> Windows will wash better with ½ cup of white vinegar in warm water. . . . Or, for a sparkling window job, wash them with a cloth soaked in vinegar, then polish with newspaper.

> To speed up window washing, use a solution of three tablespoons of washing soda per quart of warm water.

> A long-handled sponge dishmop is great for washing your outside windowpanes from inside the apartment.

> Don't throw away tissue paper even it it's too crumpled for wrapping purposes. It's great for shining washed windows or mirrors.

> Discarded nylon stockings used as cleaning rags will give mirrors and windows bright, lint-free shine.

> Use wet newspapers to wash windows and then polish dry with a dry newspaper for a bright shine.

> Rub the insides of windows with a sponge that has been dipped in alcohol, then polish with dry cloth or newspaper. This should keep windows free of ice and frost in even the coldest weather.

> To prevent the water from freezing when you're washing windows in cold weather, add a little vinegar or ammonia.

> Any leftover cola drink is good for taking greasy marks off windows.

> When you're polishing windows, rub horizontally on one side and vertically on the other side. If there are any streaks,

you will know which side they're on. (Useful procedure for washing car windows, too.)

> If there's moisture on the insides of windows, wipe from the bottom up. The windows will be cleaned.

> A dull, overcast day is best for washing house and car windows. Sunshine dries sudsy water so quickly that streaks may be left on the glass.

☐ SOME EXTRA TIPS FOR WINDOWS: Place a towel on the windowsill to keep drafts from coming under the window.

> In replacing a pane of glass, a good way to loosen the old one is to pass a red-hot poker slowly over the old putty.

> Before puttying windows, mix the putty with paint of the color you want. This saves painting later.

> A clean blackboard eraser is just great for getting a fine gleam on your windows.

> To avoid steamed-up windows in cold weather, wipe the windows with a cloth moistened with glycerin, leaving a little of the glycerin on the inside of the glass.

> There's a spray in a pressurized container that frosts glass windows. It allows full light to enter but ensures privacy. . . . Or, apply a coat of linseed oil paint to the window and stipple with a cheesecloth pad while it is still wet.

> To quiet rattling windows, secure a felt corn pad to the lower inside edge of the window. . . . Or, drive several rubber-headed tacks against the bottom edges of the lower sash. When the window is closed and locked, this will take up slack and prevent vibration.

> Polish windowsills with ordinary furniture wax. It will make them much easier to clean, and they won't show stains from the rain.

> Temporarily weatherproof a cracked windowpane by giving it a coat of fresh shellac.

> People forget the simple, effective way of loosening sticky windows. A vigorous snap of the window rope or chain will do it.

> Put a layer of gravel on top of window boxes to prevent rain from spattering dirt on windows.

> Each leaking window in the house wastes about 10 extra pounds of coal, or a comparable amount of oil, every 24 hours. See that they are sealed and weather-stripped.

> You may be able to keep pigeons away from windowsills by 1) sticking a strip of aluminum foil, with an inch or so of overhang, on the sill; 2) sprinkling the outside sills with moth crystals (this should move them elsewhere); 3) placing a rubber toy rodent or snake on the windowsill and fooling the pigeons completely.

> Aluminum window frames are hard to keep clean; try a cream silver polish.

☐ PAINTING AND PAPERING: An eyedropper filled with thinned-out spackle will fill small holes in a wall with efficiency and without air bubbles.

> You can fill tiny cracks that crisscross stucco walls by brushing into them a workable mixture of Swedish putty.

> To ensure clean hands for painting, dip them in paraffin wax before starting, and wash them clean when finished. Hands may also be rubbed with olive oil, petroleum jelly, or linseed oil and paint won't cling.

> Lighter fluid will remove paint from hands; baby oil on cotton will, too, and will keep skin soft. . . . Or, rub hands with a little cooking oil before scrubbing with soap and water. . . . Or, rub with a handful of sawdust mixed with turpentine, then quickly wash off with soap and water.

> When painting or gardening chores stain your hands, remove the marks with a cotton swab dipped in peroxide.

> If there is paint splattered around the house, or even on fingers, nail-polish remover will take it off.

> To remove paint stains from clothing, scrape off particles, steam and rub with soap. Equal parts of turpentine and ammonia will also remove paint from clothes.

> When painting a room, first wet windowpanes and mirrors and press newspaper against them to provide protection against stray paint splatters.

> A cloth dipped in hot strong vinegar should quickly remove paint splashes from mirrors and windows. If this fails, rub the glass gently with fine steel wool. . . . A copper penny does a good job of scraping dried paint from windowpanes without scratching the glass.

> To remove paint, mix two parts ammonia and one part turpentine. Apply with a brush. Leave a few minutes, then wipe off paint and varnish easily with a cloth.

> Glue a large paper plate to the bottom of the paint can to protect floors from drippings and to serve as a handy place to put down the brush. . . . Or, set the can in a large paper bag and roll the top down. It will catch all the drippings.

> Pull an old pair of socks on over shoes to keep them clean, and feet can be used to wipe up drippings.

> Add a teaspoon of oil of wintergreen, or a little of any insect repellent, such as camphor, to each gallon of paint to keep insects away until the paint dries.

> It is essential to let the undercoat of a wall dry completely before you apply the final coat of paint, to avoid cracks.

> To see how paint will look when dry on a wall, brush a little on a clean white blotter.

> Before painting a whitewashed surface, scrub down the area with a strong solution of washing soda.

> To keep white-painted surfaces glossy, wash them with milk and a minimum of soap.

> Make an efficient paint stirrer by grasping the two ends of a coat hanger and bending until they meet. The two rounded ends will break up the pigment better than a wooden paddle, and they can be bent to fit any can.

> Never allow turpentine to stand uncovered. Water condenses on it, and it becomes cloudy and loses its effectiveness.

> Tape a plastic bag around ceiling light fixtures to protect while painting. Cover all electrical outlets with masking tape to prevent paint from getting in and causing a short.

> A clean cloth dipped in turpentine and wiped over freshly painted enamel will remove some of the glare.

> Before using a new paintbrush, soak it for 12 hours in linseed oil. That makes it easier to clean.

> A tobacco can is just right for clean and soft paintbrushes. Put in enough turpentine to keep the bristles moist.

> If a painting job is incomplete and to be resumed in a day or so, wrap brush in waxed paper and there will be no need to wash it out. . . . A brush full of paint will not harden for a week or more if wrapped in aluminum foil.

> Old stiff and dry paintbrushes can be softened if boiled in vinegar, then cleaned with hot soapy water. . . . Or, clean paintbrushes with a mixture of 2 tablespoons of salt, ½ cup of kerosene and 1 quart of warm water. Soak brushes for about 2 hours, then wipe with a clean cloth.

> After paintbrushes have been cleaned, rub in a little petroleum jelly to preserve them.

> Loose bristles in a paintbrush leave a rough finish on the job. When a paintbrush is losing its bristles, apply nail polish at the base of the bristles—no more shedding.

> If loose bristles do come out of a brush and embed themselves in a freshly painted surface, remove them with eyebrow tweezers. An old pocket comb will also dislodge them.

> Moths love the taste of paintbrushes. Keep them covered and protected when not in use.

> Do not shake a can of paint. Stir carefully and well with a wooden paddle, to avoid streaking, uneven color and slow drying. Shaking water-thinned latex paints causes bubbles. . . . Good painters "box" paint as well as stirring it. That is, they pour it from one container to another to speed mixing process

and make sure pigment is completely blended with oil. . . .
For stirring small cans of paint, an old table fork will do the
best and quickest job.

> If the paint in a can is completely separated, drain off the
liquid from the top into another container. Stir thick mixture
in the bottom of the can, and add the liquid slowly while stirring.

> When mixing paint, remember that it will dry slightly
darker than the mix, so keep the color a bit light.

> Add a few drops of black paint to a can of white paint
and it will make the white paint whiter.

> To prevent splashes when you're stirring paint, wrap a
large piece of newspaper around the paint can so as to extend
its height, and fasten with a rubber band.

> For a small paint job, mix the proper color in a card-
board cream or milk container with the top cut off, and throw
it away when finished.

> Strain lumpy paint by cutting out a piece of old window
screen and dropping it into the can. As the screen settles, so
do the lumps.

> Save some of your wife's worn-out nylon stockings.
They're ideal to strain paint to remove lumps, scum, and
foreign matter.

> In mixing stains, use an old baby bottle. Ounce markings
make measuring simple, and the bottle can be shaken without
spilling.

> Drain sediment out of paint solvents or other thin liquids
by pouring out of a bottle corked with steel wool.

> To prevent paint spills, cover the rim of the paint can
with aluminum foil. This will also prevent paint from collecting
in the groove.

> It is important to keep paint-can rim clean so that lid will
fit tight. This way paint can be stored for longer periods without hardening.

> Before replacing the lid of a paint can, breathe lightly on

the paint to prevent formation of a film. . . . Another good way to preserve paint for later use is to float a few drops of paint thinner on the surface. . . . To preserve paint for longer periods, prevent a tough layer from forming on top by placing a piece of plastic wrap between the can and the lid. . . . Or, pour a layer of melted paraffin over the top of the paint.

> When a paint job is finished, place a rubber band around the can at the level of the remaining paint. Later, you can see from this what's left without opening the can.

> Keep empty nail-polish bottles for minute amounts of leftover paint. Fine for touching up scratches, etc., with the little brush inside.

> Keep the paint from dripping when you're painting a ceiling by cutting a rubber ball in half and making a slit in the center into which to slip the brush handle, with the concave side up. . . . Or, push a paper plate up the brush handle to catch the drippings.

> Paint a ceiling with a roller by walking up and down the room instead of climbing up and down a stepladder. Attach a broom handle to the handle of the roller.

> Work across the width of the ceiling, instead of the length; this helps in doubling back before the preceding lap has dried.

> To make a high ceiling look lower, paint it a darker color than the walls.

> To get a velvety finish on painted doors, sand surface between coats.

> When painting a door, coat the panels first, then the center rail, the top and bottom rails, the vertical stiles and finally the edges.

> To paint bottoms of doors without taking them off hinges, use an old toothbrush.

> A cellulose sponge makes a good "brush" for painting concrete floors. . . . Or, use a paint roller attached to a mop handle—to do the job in half the time without an aching back.

> Put sheets of waxed paper where one *must* walk until you're certain a newly painted floor is completely dry.

> When painting stairs, do every other step first, allow to dry, then do the others; that keeps the stairway open for traffic.

> Paint radiators when they are warm rather than cold or. hot. Moderate heat tends to bake on the paint. . . . Use flat wall paint or enamel rather than aluminum paint for better heat.

> To estimate the amount of paint needed for a radiator, measure the front area and multiply by seven.

> You can figure that a gallon of paint will cover 600 square feet for a first coat, about 900 square feet for a second coat.

> Light colors and pale tints appear farther away than they are, and tend to stretch walls. Bold, bright colors seem closer and appear to shrink the room. Use these principles to improve shape of room.

> Use strong colors for backgrounds to make home contemporary, despite period of furniture.

> A long narrow hall will appear wider if one wall is painted light and the other dark.

> Walls should be dusted with a clean, dry mop before painting.

> Remove outlet plates and paint them separately on a newspaper to keep them from sticking to the wall.

> When you're painting a wall, it's usually a good idea to begin at the upper left-hand corner and work to the right.

> Cardboards that come in laundered shirts make fine edgers for painting a baseboard. Slide one along the floor, close to the molding, to prevent smudging and splatters.

> Always sandpaper new unpainted furniture before painting. This removes unseen dirt and grease and provides a better base.

> To remove built-up wax on furniture, use turpentine and olive oil in warm water.

> For furniture touch-ups, mix oil paints to match color and apply with a matchstick.

> You can use regular fabric dyes to stain unpainted furniture. It's inexpensive, and there is a wider range of colors.

> It's unwise to do paint jobs on furniture in the basement. Many basements are so dusty that the finish, before it dries, will pick up a layer of dust.

> When painting a dresser, remove the drawers and set them with drawer fronts facing up. This will prevent the enamel from running.

> When painting a chair or table, hammer a small nail partway into the bottom of each leg. Then you can paint all the way to the bottom with no sticking to the floor.

> Paint the undersides of chairs and small tables first and then stand the piece upright and finish the job.

> For easier application, use a paint sprayer instead of a brush on reed and wicker furnishings.

> Remove knobs and hardware from furniture to be painted and insert matchsticks in screw holes to avoid filling them with paint.

> To paint furniture knobs, attach them with their screws to a cardboard box and the finishing job will be perfect.

> Try this formula to determine how many rolls of wallpaper will be needed to redecorate a room. Multiply the distance around the room (in feet) by the height of the room, then divide by 30. Deduct 2 rolls for every ordinary-sized opening such as windows and doors. The answer will equal the number of rolls needed. This allows for matching patterns, too.

> Before wallpapering, remove all picture hooks and insert toothpicks in holes, leaving ¼ inch extending. When paper is hung, these will stick through, showing exact spots for replacement of hooks.

> Repapering a wall? Put a thin coat of shellac over the old paper. That will keep marks from appearing on the new.

> When papering, place a dampened newspaper under and around article being worked on. Moistened paper will catch and settle most of the fine dust.

> After papering steamy rooms, such as bathroom or kitchen, paint all joints with clear varnish to prevent peeling.

> Washable wallpaper is practical for the bathroom, but it must be applied with a moisture-resistant or waterproof adhesive.

> Give wallpaper two coats of lacquer to increase the life of the paper.

> When covering walls with fabric, get out all the wrinkles by spraying with water.

> When finished papering, tack some of the leftover paper on an out-of-the-way wall of the attic or basement. If a patch is needed later, it will match perfectly. Left on the roll, it would be brighter than the paper on the wall.

> To prevent shelf paper from sticking to painted shelves, coat them with wax before laying down the paper.

> It's a good idea to keep your repapering data, such as room measurements and rolls needed, written on the back of a wall picture hung in the room.

> A paint roller soaked in hot water will help loosen wallpaper. For stubborn spots, apply a steam iron for just a few seconds. . . . Or, apply a solution of warm water and laundry starch; allow to set for 10 minutes; scrape off the wallpaper with a wide-bladed knife. . . . Or, spray boiling water on walls with a spray pump. Wet about 12 feet at a time, peeling off the original strips. . . . Or, spray with a mixture of 2 tablespoons of vinegar to 1 pint of water with vacuum-cleaner blower attachment. After 1 minute of soaking, the paper should come off.

> Clean soiled wallpaper with a cloth dipped in borax.

> Crayon marks on wallpaper will come off with a soap

eraser. Another approach is to scrape off as much as possible with a dull knife or spatula, then sponge lightly with cleaning fluid.

> Remove spots from wallpaper by covering them thickly with French chalk (from the drugstore) or fuller's earth (from art-supply store). Remove after 24 hours with a soft cloth. . . . Or, place a blotter over the spot and apply a warm (not too hot) iron.

> To remove grease or oil stains from wallpaper, apply a paste of powdered chalk and spirits of camphor. Let dry overnight and then brush off.

> Remove greasy hair-oil spots from wallpaper that has been leaned against by rubbing the spots with a cake of milk of magnesia. Leave overnight; dust off, and the grease goes with it. . . . Wet an ink spot or bloodstain on wallpaper with water and rub with white magnesia chalk.

☐ P L A S T E R I N G : For small plastering jobs, cut a 9-inch rubber ball in half. Mix the small bit of plaster needed in one half of the ball, and simply turn the ball inside out when the job is done. The plaster will fall out and the receptacle will be clean.

> To make a stickier plaster of Paris, stir in evaporated milk instead of water.

> Heat a nail before driving it into plaster and there will be less chance of the plaster's crumbling or chipping. Nails can be heated by dipping in hot water.

> To fill a nail hole in plaster wall, mix equal parts of salt and starch with just enough water to make a patching plaster. Fill hole and smooth the surface.

> Always let new plaster age for a few weeks before painting over it.

> When plastering cracks or small holes, apply plaster normally and then brush with a wet paintbrush. This removes excess plaster, and little or no sanding is needed.

> If you add plaster to water, instead of water to plaster, the mixture will have no lumps.

> Plaster often hardens so quickly that you haven't time to work on it with a trowel. You can slow the hardening by adding a little vinegar to the mix.

☐ VARNISHING: Furniture refinishers: plain vinegar is an excellent wood bleach.

> Varnishing is much easier if the can is placed in a pan of hot water while being used. The varnish dries faster, too.

> Dust specks will not cling to newly varnished furniture if suspended upside-down to dry.

> To remove old varnish, use 3 tablespoons of washing soda to one quart of water. Apply with rough cloth. . . . Remove old varnish from furniture or woodwork by scrubbing with a stiff bristled brush and a strong hot solution of washing soda. Loosened varnish can then be wiped off with old rags without the usual gumminess or odor.

> Use smooth, even strokes to apply varnish, straight strokes for shellac.

> Using orange shellac on dark woods and white shellac on light woods will give them a more natural finish.

☐ AND A LOT OF OTHER THINGS: Before painting or varnishing woodwork, rub petroleum jelly on hinges of doors. Any paint that gets on hinges may be wiped off easily.

> A warm iron pressed against cellophane tape will remove it from a wall without damaging paint.

> Never apply lacquer over paint, enamel or varnish. Lacquer acts as a paint remover.

> Finish painting an area once it is started. If the paint dries, the next strip may be a different shade.

> Model-airplane paint is perfect for any type of plastic.

> Line the roller pan with a sheet of aluminum foil, and throw it away when the job is done; no cleanup work on the pan.

> Add a few drops of food coloring to colorless nail polish for dabbing odds and ends with color. This saves buying a whole can of paint for only minor touch-ups.

> Speed up washing of walls by going over them with a paint roller dipped in sudsy water; rinse with a sponge dipped in clear water.

> Use a sweeping, fanlike motion to apply flat paint.

> To touch up nicks on enamel of kitchen appliances, use a cotton swab dipped in white paint. The swab works as an easy-to-use brush.

> When new paint flakes off walls, it is usually because there are too many coats under it. It is best to remove all old layers of paint right down to the plaster and start from scratch.

□ APPLIANCES: Keep an electric fan stable by setting it on a pad of foam rubber, cut 2 inches larger than base of fan. Keeps fan from traveling and cuts down noise. . . . Or stand on pad of newspapers.

> Stored electric fans should get a good oiling before being used. Then cover fan with large paper bag and allow to run for a few minutes. Bag will catch all oil splatters.

> Block drafts around air conditioner by applying rope calk. Just press it into cracks. . . . Or encase in plastic cover.

> Because static electricity attracts dirt and dust, the louvers of an air conditioner need frequent attention. Use a sponge wrung out almost dry.

> Plug an electric-appliance cord into appliance *first*, then into outlet.

> Protect the prongs on an electric appliance that is plugged in only when in use by inserting them in slits cut in a large cork. The plug will then be safe if stepped on or dropped.

> If a lamp cord is too long, wrap it tightly around a broom

handle for a day. This will cause the cord to spiral, thus shortening it.

> When sharpening knives, remember to run the blades across in only one direction.

☐ ELECTRICAL EQUIPMENT/WIRES: A couple of coats of white shellac will help prevent electric cords from getting frayed near the sockets.

> File the contact points of an electric plug occasionally, to prevent oxidation and ensure a steady flow of current to the appliance.

> Use a hammer claw to pare rubber insulation from wires.

☐ BASEMENT: Check on basement dampness by hanging a small mirror on the wall and watching for condensation on it in a few hours . . . Use the vacuum cleaner blower to help dry out a damp basement.

> If always banging head on a low overhang in the basement, tack up a latex foam bumper pad to soften the blow.

> Mix some fine white sand into enamel when painting cellar stairs to make the steps less skiddy . . . If cellar steps are dark, paint the bottom and top ones white for safety's sake.

☐ FLASHLIGHTS: Keep a flashlight from being turned on accidentally and burning out when in a drawer by sealing the switch in the "off" position with cellophane tape.

> Prolong the life of flashlight batteries by storing them in a cool place.

> When flashlight cells corrode and stick to the case, invert the case and pour in a solution of two tablespoons baking soda and ½ cup of water. Soak, then tap the case lightly, and the cells come out. Then dry case thoroughly.

☐ GLUING & PUTTY: Before regluing articles of wood, use hot vinegar to remove old glue.

> When gluing pieces of wood together, press a few shreds of steel wool between them. This prevents slipping and makes a better bond.

> Wrap a piece of modeling clay or florist's clay around a mended object to hold the pieces in place while glue dries. The clay is easily peeled off.

> When gluing chips of small pieces of china or furniture that cannot be clamped, hold the piece in place while the glue is drying with a strip of cellophane tape.

> To loosen excess glue after a pasting job, rub spots with cheesecloth dampened with alcohol.

> Use a small piece of candle, shaved to fit, as a stopper for a glue bottle. The glue won't stick to the wax. . . . Or, rub cold cream on the stopper of a bottle of glue before replacing it. This will keep it from sticking.

> When using putty, dip the putty knife into a solution of soap or detergent suds. The putty will stick where you want it, rather than to the blade of the knife.

> Soften up dry or hardened putty to a usable consistency simply by mixing well with a few drops of linseed oil.

□ HEATING: Test heating system in house by holding a lighted cigarette near the floor in the middle of any room. The smoke should drift slowly up or across the room. If it evaporates rapidly or gathers at one level, the heating system needs adjustment.

> If radiator is not working, remove the valve and boil in a quart of water to which one tablespoon of washing soda has been added.

> See that a radiator is perfectly clean; dust serves as an insulator.

□ LADDERS: Most home ladders are not built to hold much more than 300 pounds.

> Make a stepladder safer by gluing a piece of sandpaper on each step.

> To make handling a long ladder easier, paint a strip at the balance point, and always pick it up at the mark.

> Cover the top ends of a ladder with old socks, and nail a cheap rubber heel to the bottom of each leg. This will prevent the unsightly marking of walls and the marring of floors. . . . Or, put rubber strips cut from an old tire on the legs of ladder and at the top.

> If doing carpentry work on a ladder, tack a small metal jar cover on the top rung to hold nails and screws.

☐ L A M P C O R D S / F U S E S : To get an electric wire through a lamp base, tie thread to a bit of absorbent cotton and blow the cotton through. Tie thread end to strong twine, and then when this is through, tie twine to wire and pull.

> Electric cords wear out, in many cases from being too tightly coiled. This can break the fine wires and covering.

> Never run lamp cords over radiators or hot pipes, as this can cause a deterioration of the insulation and subsequent short circuits.

> Keep an old glove where extra electric bulbs are stored. It is handy for changing burned-out bulbs that are still hot.

> When brass switch plates get scratched and tarnished, cover them with one of the new sheet-plastic materials that are backed with adhesive. Just cut to fit and press on with hands.

> Remove a broken light bulb without cutting fingers. Push a large cork into the broken end and safely unscrew.

☐ P L U M B I N G : In summer, cold-water pipes sweat and drip; wrap the area with aluminum foil.

> You can temporarily stop small leaks in water pipes by wrapping an old leather belt around the pipe. Wrap with wire and tighten with pliers. Be sure to call a professional plumber.

> Keep plumbing up to par by pouring about ¼ pound of washing soda down the sink drain about once a week. Run hot water slowly until granules dissolve.

> Clean a clogged sink drain by dropping in a handful of baking soda followed by ½ glass of vinegar. . . . Or, when no plumber's suction cup is available, use half of a hollow rubber ball. Rapid pressing on the ball with the hand causes good suction.

> If a faucet drips and cannot be immediately repaired, put a sponge under the faucet. This quiets the drip and prevents rust spots in the sink. Or, tie a string to it long enough to reach the sink. The drops will then run silently down the string.

> To stop leak in hot-water storage tank, drive in a small wooden plug. It will soak up enough water to make a perfect seal.

☐ SANDPAPERING :   Sandpapering a discolored cork bulletin board will make it look like new.

> You can make a handy knife sharpener by pasting a strip of sandpaper on a wooden ruler; rub the knife back and forth over it.

> After sanding a surface, pull an old nylon stocking over your hand and rub it lightly over the wood. This will locate even the slightest rough spot.

> Sandpaper will be usable for a longer time, work better and resist cracking if the paper backing is dampened slightly. . . . Reinforce sandpaper strips against tearing by putting a few lengths of cellophane tape on back. . . . Wrap sandpaper around a block of wood.

> A handy sanding "block" to use along curved moldings or edges is made with an old pack of playing cards with a sheet of sandpaper wrapped around the edge of the deck. Thus the edge can be pressed against the edge to be sanded. Pressure will force individual cards to slip in or out until edge of deck matches contour of molding. Tight grip will then hold deck in this position so that it serves as a firm backing for the sandpaper.

☐ SCREWS :   If screws work loose, remove them, dip

them in glue and replace; they will hold tight. . . . Or, wind a few strands of steel wool around the threads of the screw.

> Remember this: "Left is loose and Right is tight."

> Difficulty loosening a tight screw? Try again after heating the edge of the screwdriver. . . . Or, put a few drops of peroxide on it and let soak for a few minutes.

> When a screw breaks off below the surface of wood, it is almost impossible to remove. Instead, drive it deeper with a nail punch, fill the hole with Plastic Wood and use a new screw.

> If you have no tool for a Phillips screw, adapt any screwdriver by grinding off the corners of the blade. . . . Or, try using a large new nail. It will often do the job if the screw isn't too tight.

> Instead of throwing away those transparent plastic toothbrush containers, use them as ideal holders for small nuts, bolts and screws.

> In using wood screws, dip the ends into a bit of shaving cream first. Acts as a lubricant.

> Prevent screws and bolts from working loose on items that get hard wear by loosening and dabbing a few drops of shellac or lacquer on threads. Tighten while coating is still tacky.

> Shellac the threads of a screw before using and this will prevent its rusting.

> You can keep a screwdriver from slipping, when used on a screw, by rubbing chalk on the blade.

> Never use a screwdriver on an object held in the hand. This is a very common cause of home accidents.

☐ S T U D S : Wall studs are practically all 16 inches apart, center to center. Find the studs in a wall with a compass, which will be attracted by the nails, thus showing the exact location.

☐ T H U M B T A C K S :   Keep stray thumbtacks on a cork. They are handy when needed, and easy to remove. Put a thimble over your finger when pushing tacks into place. It will save fingers from soreness and make the job much simpler.

☐ N A I L S / N U T S / C L A M P S :   Molded compartments in plastic ice trays are handy places to store screws, nuts and bolts.

> Keep stored nails and screws from rusting in a jar by adding some dry baking soda. . . . Or, nails will hold better and resist rust if first dipped in nail polish. . . . Or, to keep nails from rusting, store them in a coffee can and spray with kerosene or light oil.

> When driving a nail through plastic, heat point of nail over flame first, then hammer it quickly. It will not split plastic.

> Before driving a nail into wood, push it through a cake of soap. This may keep the wood from splitting. . . . Or, prevent splitting by blunting the point of a nail before driving it. Hold nail upside down on firm surface and tap point lightly with hammer. The blunted point will then shear through the fibers instead of spreading them apart.

> Save bruised fingers when hammering nails by using an old comb to hold them in place.

> Nails driven in at a slight angle will solidly hold two pieces of wood.

> To prevent nuts from freezing on bolts through rusting, dip threads of bolts in shellac first. They will always come apart.

> You can often easily loosen a rusted bolt or nut by applying a cloth soaked in any carbonated beverage.

☐ T O O L S :   Lengths of rubber tubing slipped over a pliers handle will give a sure, comfortable grip.

> Several mothballs in a toolbox will absorb moisture and prevent tools from rusting. . . . Use a pail of dry, clean sand as a storage place for small tools. This will retard rust. . . .

Keep a piece of charcoal in toolbox to absorb moisture and prevent rust. . . . A quick rubbing with an emery cloth will remove rust stains from tools.

> Improvise a funnel by cutting the tip off a cone-shaped paper cup.

> Keep insulating tape handy when doing electrical repairs; wind a couple of feet of it around the grip of the screwdriver.

> If the handle of a hammer is loose, tighten it by soaking in engine oil for a few hours. This swells the wood.

> Never use a good hammer to blunt a nail point or hammer masonry, etc.

> Force a piece of garden hose over the handle of a screwdriver for a better grip and fewer blisters.

> Tape the teeth of pliers to avoid scratching and marring a surface.

> Keep the wooden handles of tools from warping by occasionally wiping or soaking them with linseed oil.

> Wrenches should be cleaned with kerosene. Greasy tools slip.

> When using a yardstick for marking or cutting, coat the underside of the stick with soap to keep it in place.

> Before using a wrench on a plated surface, wrap adhesive tape around object to avoid scratching.

> Suction cups will adhere better to a flat surface if the inside rims are rubbed with wet soap.

> A slip-on pencil eraser will protect the points of scissors in a drawer—and your fingers.

□ W O O D : Keep plywood from splitting by putting a strip of cellophane tape at the point where you plan to start sawing.

> If you drill through metal or hard wood, first affix a small piece of masking tape to the spot. It will keep the drill from slipping.

> To draw an accurate line on wood, use a knife rather than a pencil.

> Unfinished wood in drawers often absorbs moisture and swells, causing sticking. Before sanding down, see if a lighted bulb left in the drawer for a while will not shrink the wood. . . . Or, sand down the high spots and apply a layer of very fluid hot paste wax. The wax provides lubrication and keeps out moisure.

> You can make a fine carving board by driving long nails through a good piece of lumber from the bottom. Nails will hold a roast or ham for carving. Rubber feet on the bottom will keep board from slipping.

☐ AND A LOT OF OTHER THINGS: A pipe cleaner wedged into the end of an oilcan spout is an excellent aid in lubricating hard-to-reach places. . . . Or, use an atomizer.

> To fasten a pencil sharpener or similar appliance securely to a table, place a piece of sandpaper with the rough side out to the underside of the table before tightening screw.

> Measure areas and distances more easily. Attach a small clip suction cup to the end of a tapeline.

> Shellac on the ends of a rope keeps it from unraveling.

> Installing any mineral-wool insulation? Leftovers can be used as garden mulch.

> Use the cabinet of an old console radio by adding shelves; slick it up with fresh paint and you've made a bookcase or writing case.

> Don't throw away an old bicycle inner tube. Cut it up into various widths and you'll have powerful, lasting rubber bands for many uses around the house and workbench.

> Store oily polishing cloths in empty coffee tins.

> Save plastic vegetable bags. When a particularly dirty job comes along, slip them on over work gloves and/or use the bags as mittens, with an elastic band over each wrist.

> Rub the worn edge of a rubber squeegee over a sheet of fine sandpaper on a flat surface. This restores the square edges and exposes fresh rubber.

> Callus preventer: When tackling an unaccustomed work job, protect hands by placing a thin piece of foam rubber in the palm of work gloves.

> For household gluing jobs, where heavy clamps are not needed, use a trouser hanger until pieces adhere.

> Small fragile articles can be protected when mailed by packing between two ordinary household sponges.

> To locate a gas leak, cover pipe with soapy water, bubbles will reveal the seepage.

> You'll be able to hear phone ring when in the basement if you put a metal pan on the floor and the phone atop it.

> If tiny particles of steel wool stick to fingers, use a magnet to remove them.

> Stretch life of awnings. After rain, lower the awnings until they are thoroughly dry; this will retard mildew and rot that results from moisture.

> Coat the bottoms of cork coasters with colorless nail polish to keep water from soaking through them.

> Sprinkle talcum powder on plastic materials to prevent their sticking when folded and stored.

> It's easy to oil a door lock: dip key in oil, insert in lock and turn several times.

HOLIDAY HINTS

☐ CHRISTMAS ORNAMENTS AND DECO-RATIONS: If the hanging hooks of ornaments are missing, paper clips are a good substitute.

> Make a Christmas frame for hall mirror by taping cards around it. . . . Or, hang cards over the slats of a venetian blind and staple them to long ribbons as wall-to-wall festoons or in the shape of a Christmas tree as a wall decoration.

> Remember that acorns make attractive decorations. Be sure to spray them with shellac, which acts as a preservative.

> Use clear lacquer in an aerosol can to brighten up old Christmas-tree ornaments. It will make them glossier and less fragile.

> Door decorations: Shape a wire coat hanger into a circle. Attach long sprigs of evergreen with thin copper wire, fasten a few bright ornaments and hang it on the door.

> If ornaments have become chipped in packing, red nail polish is a quick fixative, even on ornaments of different colors. It is more effective than a blank spot on an ornament.

> Let the kids make some of their own ornaments by cutting forms from cardboard and covering with aluminum foil. A paper cup, inverted, makes a fine silver bell.

> Start saving empty egg cartons for storing Christmas-tree ornaments.

> Make modeling dough for kids to turn into Christmas-tree ornaments by combining 2 cups baking soda, 1 cup water. Stirring constantly, boil until thick. Dough can be formed into balls and rolled in glitter, with piece of string or wire pressed into each for hanging when dough has dried.

> Make snowy coating for the Christmas tree by filling any spray gun with a strong baking soda solution and spraying it over the tree. . . . Or, make suds snow for Christmas decorations by using a big handful of packaged soap or detergent and a little water. Whip with a rotary beater and put on trees, windows, mirrors, wreaths, etc. When dry it will look like real snow, and will stiffen and last for weeks. Also use it to finger-paint names on Christmas balls.

> Don't throw out used light bulbs. Cover with paper and paint and decorate your Christmas tree with them.

> Make Christmas-tree stocking of a mesh orange or onion

bag. Cut it in a stocking shape. Fasten sides together with tape. Glue a strip of cotton at the top and fill it with goodies. Attach a small length of ribbon as a hanger, and hang it on the tree.

> If possible, stand Christmas tree in a container of water. It will keep it from drying out, reducing the chance of fire and retarding falling needles.

> If you get resin on your hands from installing the tree, wet them, sprinkle them with dry baking soda, rub together and rinse. The resin will be gone. (This also works for pine pitch.)

☐ GIFT WRAPPING: With a split-lip glue bottle, write the name of the recipient of the gift on his package; then, while the glue is wet, sprinkle glitter or Christmas snow over the glue. This extra touch will add a sparkling personal note to any present.

> If and when you run out of gift wrap, and it usually occurs, use household aluminum foil, decorated with colorful ribbons or tape.

> Wrapping paper and paper ribbon can be reused if the wrinkles and creases are wiped with a damp sponge on the wrong side and the papers and ribbons are then ironed.

> Bring double pleasure in wrapping youngsters' packages by adding to the outside a candy cane, a few bright pennies, a posy or tiny corsage for a girl, a chocolate cigar for a boy.

> Gift wrapping is simplified, and made neater-looking, with the new double-faced cellophane tape. Put between folds of paper, it doesn't show.

> Wrap an oversize Christmas gift with a holiday paper tablecloth instead of pasted-together smaller sheets.

☐ PARTY ITEMS: Keep birthday-cake candles refrigerated a day before using and they will glow evenly, burn slower.

> You can make party balloons stick to the ceiling by rubbing them against hair. The static electricity does it.

> Easter baskets, etc., will stay clean and fresh until next year if they are heat-sealed in transparent plastic freezer bags.

> Let paper napkins serve as place cards. Put each guest's initials on his napkin with plastic tape.

> Flameproof Halloween costumes and decorations by dipping into a solution of 7 ounces of borax and 3 ounces of boric acid in 3 quarts of water.

> For a festive holiday fire, soak some pine cones in a quart of water in which a cup of baking soda has been dissolved. Allow to dry a few days and the cones will make the fire burn with a golden glow.

> Colorful ice in a punch bowl: fill a clean balloon with tinted water and freeze. When frozen, peel off the balloon and the ice ball will be ready to use.

> Make gift-enclosure cards from last year's Christmas cards. Cut out any verse or picture that will allow enough space to write in your name and name of person to receive gift.

OUTSIDE

THE

HOUSE

GARDENING

☐ FERTILIZER: Don't throw away ashes from wood fires; they are perfect fertilizers for rosebushes.

> Used tea leaves make excellent fertilizer and stimulate the growth of plants and shrubs. They also act as an insecticide.

> If you do not have a spreader for fertilizer, an old colander or flour sifter will do the job.

> A good tonic for ferns is to "water" them once a week with tea.

☐ FLOWERS: It is best to cut a rose just when the buds turn soft.

> Use a sharp knife to cut the stems of fresh flowers; household scissors tend to crush the stems.

> Stalks of chrysanthemums and woody branches should be broken off and the ends smashed.

> Split the branch ends of cut flowers before putting them in water to prolong their life.

> To keep flowers fresh longer, cut a piece off each stem and plunge the stems into warm, then cold, water before arranging. The stems expand and take up more water. . . . Or, cut stems of fresh flowers a little bit each day to prolong their life. . . . Or, if you cut the stems on the diagonal, with a knife, and dip in salt, they will stay fresh for a whole week.

> Cut flowers will last longer if not crowded in the vase.

> One or two tiny blobs of wax dropped into the centers of freshly cut tulips will prevent their opening wide. . . . Or, drop a copper penny in the water.

> Remove leaves below the waterline, as decaying vegetable matter poisons the water.

> Short-stemmed flowers stay fresh longer if placed in a bowl of well-watered sand.

> Mix two ounces of glycerin to the water in a vase of autumn leaves to keep them from drying out.

> A little sugar added to water that holds cut chrysanthemums will help them stay fresh longer.

> Some thick stems on cut flowers or leaves develop an unpleasant odor after a day or so in water. Retard this decay by putting a piece of activated charcoal in the vase.

> Carnations will last longer if placed in water containing a little boric acid.

> Before arranging flowers, sprinkle a little cleansing powder into the vase to lengthen their life.

> Aspirin tablets, pennies or ice cubes in water are all said to lengthen the lives of fresh-cut flowers. . . . Or, add a teaspoon each of vinegar and sugar to each pint of water used. . . . Or, some weak tea may be added. . . . Or, flowers stay fresh longer if a teaspoon of salt or a thin slice of soap is added to the water in the vase.

> Rosebuds will open faster if a lump of sugar is placed in the water.

> Put short-stemmed buds and flowers in drinking straws and arrange them among taller flowers. Be sure the water is

high enough to fill the straws so the water will reach the cut ends of the flowers. The straws can be bent any way.

> To keep flowers fresh, change the water daily and scrub the vase with suds. Keep the flowers away from drafts or heat.

> The constant heat on the top of a TV set will wilt flowers.

> Hot, hot water will miraculously revive wilting flowers.

> If you have poor luck with cut flowers, try giving your vases a good wash with hot detergent suds to remove any bacteria that may be wilting the flowers.

> A teaspoonful of any household detergent added to a quart of water will revive wilted cut flowers.

> Wilting flowers can be revived and made to last longer if laid in a basin so that the water covers the entire stem.

> To revive cut flowers, put in a dark place for about an hour.

> Keep flowers, and even candles, off the dinner table. The scent disturbs the taste buds.

> If you have the occasion to tint white flowers, try standing their stems in food coloring or commercial floral dye.

> The lives of cut flowers may be shortened by refrigeration overnight.

> Fresh fruits and vegetables give off an ethylene gas harmful to flowers. Do not put fresh flowers on the same table with a fruit bowl containing apples, pears, or bananas.

> The tight buds of gladiolas will seldom open. If not removed, they will cause the top of the flower to droop.

> Many people feel that marigolds' magnificent colors and profuse flowering do not compensate for their overpowering, distasteful smell. A teaspoonful of sugar in a vase of marigolds will help to eliminate this.

> For an unusual touch, add a little food coloring to the water in which you are arranging cut flowers.

> Wrap flower bulbs in aluminum foil for winter storage to prevent their drying out.

> The small-sized lattice-weave plastic baskets in which berries are packed can be turned upside down and used as holders in deep flower vases.

☐ GARDEN HINTS: Don't give up gardening because there's no sun in an area. Baneberry, ferns, lily of the valley, and trillium will thrive in the shade. If there's just a bit of sun, anemones, primroses, foxglove and monkshood will flourish.

> A canvas hose soaker is the best way to water flower beds, as it lets water seep directly into the soil without waste. The least effective way to water is to stand and spray the bed with a hose, as the water wets the flowers and foliage, and for some plants this is an invitation to disease.

> Wear spiked golf shoes for outdoor work on soft ground, such as raking leaves. This makes for safer footing, and it works out the shoes in the off season.

> To attract birds to an outdoor birdbath, drop in a few colored marbles.

> Ivy grown in water does best in earthenware containers which exclude light.

> If the cuffs of work pants are cut off, there will be no grass cuttings, dirt, fertilizer, etc., in the washing machine.

> A large, heavy clay flowerpot can be made to serve as an outdoor grill. Fill with sand to the proper cooking level for a bed of charcoal; then fit the opening with heavy wire mesh for a grate. If you want ventilation holes for a better draft, a star drill can make them neatly and easily.

> Don't throw away an old hot-water bottle when it starts to leak. Fill with rags or sawdust and use as a knee rest for gardening or housework.

> Use a moisture-resistant pencil for marking garden stakes for permanent identification.

> Color has a definite effect on growing things. Under red glass, lettuce grows four times as quickly as under direct sun-

light, while blue glass stunts the plants. Beans flourish under red or white glass and die under green or blue.

> Grubby fingernails from gardening or puttering can be cleaned if you wet your hands and sprinkle a dampened nail brush with dry baking soda and scrub.

> Put a few navy beans or grains of corn in a small paper bag and blow it up. Tie the top and attach the bag to a stick in the garden. The slightest breeze will cause it to make noise, and it should keep birds away.

> Fasten wire to dried orange halves and hang them from trees for a bird feeder.

☐ G R A S S : Don't mow new grass until it's at least 2½ inches high, and never mow any grass less than 1½ inches high.

> In most parts of the country it is wise to sow bare spots in the lawn in February or March.

> If you have no lawn roller to press seeds into the soil, put down a wide board and walk on it.

> Salted boiling water will kill grass or weeds growing between sections of a cement walk or patio.

> To keep grass from growing between bricks in a wall, sprinkle the spaces with salt or a cheap motor oil.

> Next time you sow grass on your lawn, color the seeds with bluing. The birds find it unappetizing, and it doesn't hurt the seeds.

> Prevent the soil of a newly seeded slope from washing away by covering with burlap, staked down. Remove the cover when the grass pierces the mesh.

> When sprinkling the lawn or garden, wet the soil to a depth of at least four inches. This is equivalent to one inch of water, which you can gauge by placing an empty can near the sprinkler.

> Don't sprinkle your lawn every day. It makes the crabgrass flourish, but doesn't do the lawn grass much good.

□ PLANTS: Keep house plants dusted and washed, as dust shades the leaves and deprives plants of much-needed light.

> Sponge leaves of house plants with milk to remove dust and give the foliage luster.

> Green plants will have a brighter color if their leaves are washed with a little beer once a week.

> A few drops of mineral oil and a little water on a cotton ball will give plants a healthy luster.

> Add a few drops of castor oil to the dirt around plants to make the leaves greener.

> Indoor rubber plants, etc., will be sleek and attractive with a light application on a wad of cotton of petroleum jelly to the outside of the leaves only. It keeps dust off and makes them shine.

> Ferns will stay beautiful longer if you place a raw oyster at the base.

> To beautify house plants from ivy to rubber plants, whisk baby oil on the leaves.

> Buy planters deep enough to accommodate your clay-potted house-plant collection. Planted depth should be at least two inches more than the tallest clay pot going into it.

> Plant 8 to 10 orange, lemon, or grapefruit seeds about ½ inch down in the soil in a 4-inch pot. They will produce a lovely 7-inch citrus bush in a year.

> If you plant a peach pit one inch deep in a pot of soil, it will grow with long, thin willow-like leaves, tropical in appearance.

> Start avocado pits in water first and, when planting, be sure to keep the point up.

> Put Dutch flower bulbs and soil mixture in a small clay pot on the bottom shelf of the refrigerator this fall. Keep pots covered with small plastic bags and shade from the light with

brown wrapping paper. Remove from the refrigerator when stems sprout, in about 10 weeks.

> Moisten a sponge, sprinkle it with parsley and place it near a window; it will soon become a clump of foliage.

> Start small plants growing in a paper cup. Later, plant the entire thing, cup and all; the cup will decompose.

> Use cottage cheese or sour cream containers, or milk cartons split lengthwise, to start flower or vegetable seeds indoors for springtime planting.

> Place the top of a pineapple in a jar of water, with the bottom of the foliage in the water, till roots begin to sprout. Transplant it to a flowerpot.

> A tiny splint made of toothpicks and tape will often save the broken stem of a household plant.

> To keep from crushing the stems of fragile plants, tie them carefully with pipe cleaners.

> Narrow strips cut from plastic bags will neatly tie indoor plants to poles for support.

> Before sinking posts in the ground, cover the parts that will be buried with at least two coatings of creosote to prevent oxidation and decay.

> A small sliding curtain rod can be placed in the soil and tied to a sagging plant. As the plant grows, the rod can be extended.

> Hold a plant to a stick with a snap clothespin while you are tying it with soft twine.

> Water house plants regularly but do not let the soil get soggy. Aerate the soil from time to time with a fork.

> Give house plants a daily "thumb test." If the topsoil feels moist, delay watering, for overwatering is the cause of most houseplant failures.

> Keep a shallow pan of water near house plants to eliminate dryness from the heating system.

> Use ice cubes to water plants; the slow melting prevents saturation of roots.

> In wetting down house plants, use lukewarm water. A plant can be injured by too-hot or too-cold water, so let water stand until it reaches room temperature before watering plants.

> If a watering can drips when used on house plants, rub moistened soap under the lip of the spout.

> The chlorine in the water, in some sections, is sometimes harmful to indoor plants. Boil, then cool the water before using on plants.

> Water plants with the water in which eggs have been boiled, as it furnishes needed minerals. . . . Or, mix 3 or 4 crushed eggshells into a quart of water.

> When watering your plants, add a little milk at least once a week, especially in cold weather.

> Stale club soda is good for watering plants. Chemicals which remain add vigor and color to greenery.

> Scoop up some clean snow next time, and bring it in the house to melt. Use the water for house plants, for there are wonderful minerals in snow.

> A few drops of ammonia added to each quart of water with which plants are watered will improve the color of the foliage and increase the growth. . . . Or, a few drops of castor oil added to the soil of a plant will keep it greener and improve its blossoms.

> Try pouring some cool soapsuds over indoor plants to remove aphids (plant lice). Let a bit of the soapy water trickle into the soil.

> Place a dish of water under house plants for weekends away. . . . Or, a well-soaked sponge will keep a plant watered for a few days. Just put it on the soil. A cardboard collar around each plant will help it retain moisture.

> If you will be away from home for more than a few days, cut a strip of cloth 2 inches wide and 2 feet long, or, a couple

of feet of cotton clothesline. Put one end in a pail of water set a little higher than the potted plant, and bury the other end in the soil. This will be good for about a week.

> For longer absences, place all house plants in the bathtub, on thickly folded newspapers, in several inches of water. They will absorb moisture as needed and will stay fresh and healthy. . . . Or, stand plants on bricks submerged in water in the tub. The bricks absorb water to keep the plants moist.

> If your space is limited, you can still enjoy the natural beauty of living plants by selecting professionally grown combinations of 3 or 4 house plants contained in a single large clay pot.

> Keep plants away from gas appliances. Any slight leakage may damage or kill them.

> Save coffee grounds for feeding geraniums.

> You can achieve "living curtains" for summer by suspending clay-pot hanging planters containing small flowering and foliage plants from curtain rods.

> Most house plants will fare best when the room temperature is kept below 70 degrees during the daytime.

> In winter, set house plants in the bathtub once or twice a month and give the leaves a refreshing clear-water spray with a watering can.

> To keep house plants growing straight, it is a good idea to give them a quarter turn each day or so to receive an even supply of light. . . . If plants keep leaning toward the light, try putting sheets of aluminum foil behind them. The foil serves as a reflector and keeps plants growing straight.

> Philodendron is the longest-lasting live plant for home or office. It thrives in subdued light with little care.

> Oil dishes that hold potted plants to prevent lime and other chemical stains.

> Put camphor balls around the plants in your garden. The odor will keep marauding woodchucks and rabbits away.

> Plants absorb sound waves. A thick row of them in front of your home will deaden street noises.

> A shoehorn makes a great trowel for transplanting small plants or loosening soil in flowerpots.

> Empty milk cartons, rinsed well and with the tops cut off, make fine covers for tender plants on cold nights.

☐ POISON IVY AND DANDELIONS: Gasoline will eliminate dandelions.

> Be careful if you try to get rid of poison ivy by burning it, as the smoke can act as a carrier.

> To clear away poison ivy, spray the overgrown area with a solution of a gallon of soapy water and 3 pounds of salt. A few dousings will kill the stuff.

> Any tools used to dig out poison ivy should be washed promptly, to prevent spreading the poison; use several changes of thick hot suds.

☐ POTS AND WINDOW BOXES: A discarded casserole holder may be used to make an attractive flowerpot.

> You can make an attractive disposable flower container by cutting the top off an empty waxed milk carton and covering the outside with aluminum foil.

> To waterproof flowerpots, dip them into melted paraffin so that it sinks into the pores.

> An old piano bench can be converted into an attractive plant holder. Remove the lid and line the inside with zinc or copper to make it waterproof.

> To paint a flowerpot neatly, place it upside down over a large tin can. Rotate the can as you paint, and leave until thoroughly dry.

> Cementing a rubber jar ring to the base of a flowerpot will eliminate unsightly marks that the pot might leave on a windowsill.

> To make attractive covers for flowerpots, pin around them strips of wallpaper to match the walls, or use pieces of drapery or slipcover material to match other items in the room. Renew when necessary. . . . Or, cover tin cans with colorful self-adhesive plastic.

> Add color to window boxes by covering the soil with colored sand. It will keep loose dirt from overflowing the sides as well.

> Line the interior of a metal or brass planter with aluminum foil before filling with soil. This keeps the container from rusting through.

> To improve drainage in a flowerpot or window box, place a few pebbles in the bottom of the pot. . . . Or, a piece of burlap cut in a circle to fit the inside of the bottom of a flowerpot affords good drainage and keeps the soil from going out of the hole along with the water.

> Whitewash the insides of flower boxes before putting in soil and plants. This will preserve the box and discourage insects.

> Clay pots, because they're made from the good earth, keep the roots of all house plants 10 to 15 degrees cooler than synthetic containers, a particularly important factor for plants that prefer cooler temperatures.

> When a white or greenish crust forms on the outside of a clay pot, the porous pot is leaching out excess salts. Scrub off the accumulation with cold water once a month to keep the pot porous and allow life-giving air to reach the roots of the plant.

□ TOOLS: Never kink a hose to shut off the water flow. It weakens the hose. Try to avoid, also, shutting off the flow at the nozzle end for anything other than very short periods.

> Don't throw away a leaky old galvanized pail. Nail it to a garage or cellar wall with the open end facing out, and use it as a holder around which to coil a garden hose.

> Store a hose out of the sun and keep it wiped free of oil and it will give longer service.

> Keep wooden handles of tools from warping by oc-
casinally wiping or soaking them with linseed oil.

> Soak garden tools in hot suds to remove hardened earth
and dirt. Dry well and give a light coating of paste wax to
avoid rust and keep earth from sticking to them. . . . Or,
tools will last longer if, when the day's gardening is done, they
are plunged into a bucket of sand mixed with oil to scrape
off the soil and coat the tools with a light film of grease; this
prevents rusting and will keep the tool edges sharp.

> To keep metal garden tools rust-free, wrap them in clear
plastic.

> Clean rust from garden tools before storing by soaking
them in kerosene and rubbing with steel wool. . . . Or, rub
them with a cork dipped in olive oil.

> Paint initials on wooden-handled tools with red nail
polish. Fellow gardeners are not so liable to mistake the tools
for theirs.

> Keep small garden or household tools handy and easy to
locate in the pockets of a shoe bag nailed to a garage or cellar
door.

> Garden tools will be easy to spot in the grass if the
handles are covered with bright-colored plastic tape, prefer-
ably red or yellow.

> Keep lawn mower in top condition by wiping the blades
with an oily cloth after each use.

> Mark the handle of your spade in feet and half feet from
the top of the blade. That will tell you how deep you have
gone when you're digging holes.

> Do not leave the garden hose dirty and twisted through
the winter. Give it a good soapy sudsing, rinse, then coil it
evenly and hang it on the wall of the garage or basement.

> Before storing garden implements for the winter, go
over the metal parts with steel wool and apply a thin coat of
shellac.

> To clean garden sprayer before retiring it for the season,

wash all parts in a solution of 3 tablespoons of washing soda per quart of warm water.

> Store a power lawn mower in a plastic dry cleaner's bag.

☐ TREES AND SHRUBS: Don't plant trees or heavy vines too close to your house. Roots, in time, can penetrate foundation walls and pipe water into the basement.

> Exhaust fumes may be the culprit if shrubs beside your driveway aren't showing signs of life this year.

> You can give a tree a healthy green glow by watering the earth at the base of the tree with beer.

☐ WEEDS: Fall is the best time to kill weeds.

> When weeding the lawn, carry along a small screw-top jar of grass seed with several holes punched in the top of the jar. When you uproot a weed, shake a few seeds into the spot.

> Use an apple corer to dig out small weeds. It gets down under the roots without disturbing nearby plants.

OUTDOOR CARE

☐ GARAGE: Do not ruin clothes by hanging them on bare nails in garage or workshop; use a nail driven through a long cork instead. Or slip an old spool on the nail.

> Keep bats, mice, and sparrows out of the garage and attic by tying bags of moth crystals from the rafters.

> Get grease marks off the garage floor by sprinkling them with concentrated sal soda and lightly dampening with water. Let stand overnight, and then scrub and hose spots away.

> Orange crates are indispensable for providing extra

cabinets in workshop. Just sand and paint the crates and nail to wall.

☐ WORKROOM TOOLS: A split length of narrow rubber hose makes a fine protection for a saw blade.

> Store circular saw blades safely in the envelopes of an old record album.

> Keep grinding wheel in the workshop in best shape by occasionally grinding a cake of soap with the spinning wheel. This fills the abrasive pores and keeps it from clogging with metal particles.

> Hold a saw at about a 45-degree angle for crosscutting and at 60 degrees for ripsawing. Use a crosscut saw for cutting with the grain.

> Coat both sides of a saw blade with soap for much smoother cutting.

> To clean the messy head of a soldering iron, insert it while hot in a wad of steel wool and twist it.

> After using a workshop tool, wipe the cutting edge on paraffin to prevent rusting.

> Crusty residue that clings to the tools for barbecue cooking are banished when they're scrubbed with a damp brush sprinkled with dry washing soda.

☐ AND A LOT OF OTHER THINGS: Electric-light sockets outdoors, left empty, can be kept clean and dry by insertion of a burned-out fuse or plug.

> Use petroleum jelly to keep outdoor light bulbs from corroding at bases and "freezing" in sockets. Put a light cover of the lubricant on metal threads of bulbs.

> Keep steel screws from rusting and freezing in wood, when used outdoors, by first dipping the screws in a thick paste of powdered graphite and linseed oil.

> A couple of handfuls of coarse salt will keep gravel or stone driveway free of weeds and also control the dust.

> Simultaneously sweep and wash driveway or porch by using heavy rubber bands to attach a garden hose to a push broom. Place hose parallel to handle with nozzle facing down. This arrangement makes a hard job easier.

> A leather flap hung over an exposed outdoor lock will prevent weather damage and help keep it from freezing.

> To remove motor oil from driveway, allow sawdust to absorb oil for several hours. This should get most of it off.

> The best temperatures for exterior painting are between 50 and 80 degrees.

> Avoid painting in direct sun. It is a good idea to paint the south side of the house in the morning, then the west, north and east, so that the surface is shaded and not too hot.

> Empty cans can be placed under the feet of a ladder to act like snowshoes and keep it from sinking into soft earth.

> It's hard to get tar off cement or a brick walk. When the sun has softened it, put on a little carbon tetrachloride and scrape it up with the lip of an open tin can. Rub remaining stains with steel wool.

> Before sinking a post in the ground, soak the part to be embedded with at least two coats of creosote and avoid oxidation and decay.

> A new instant rust preventive that comes in a spray can can be applied to garden furniture or other metal possessions to inhibit rusting.

> Dental floss is excellent for repairs on outdoor materials. It works wonders on canvas, leather and heavy cloth. . . . When repairing canvas awnings, etc., first soak the fabric well and rub soap in. The needle will slip through the canvas easily.

> Rub a snow shovel with a candle stub or paraffin to prevent snow from sticking to it. . . . You can keep the shovel from rusting by wiping after use with a cloth dipped in kerosene.

> To make reflecting house numbers, cut the numbers out

of cardboard, paste crumpled aluminum foil over them, and varnish the surface to weatherproof.

THE OFFICE

□ G L U E : Coat the cork or stopper of a glue bottle with petroleum jelly to keep it from sticking, or rub oil or paraffin around the rim of a newly opened bottle. Hardened glue can be removed if first softened with vinegar.

> A pipe cleaner is fine for applying glue to small surfaces. It's rigid yet flexible enough to get around corners.

□ M A I L / S T A M P S / P A C K A G E S : Wet paper and mold it around breakables to be mailed. The paper will dry like stiff packing and prevent breakage. . . . Or, use popcorn as an insulator. It's light and won't boost the postage cost. . . . Or, wrap in latex-foam sheeting before packing. It's among the best shock absorbers.

> When wrapping a package for parcel post, be sure that the contents will not shift or rattle. Post offices are pretty strict about that, and it may be sent back for rewrapping.

> Before wrapping a package, first dampen the string. It will not slip and, when dry, will be taut.

> Rub a bit of furniture polish on a soft cloth and pass it lightly over the address on the package to be mailed. This will keep it legible in any weather and with the roughest handling. . . . Or, apply a coat of colorless nail polish or a strip of cellophane tape over the address.

> To address a package in big, bold letters, dip a cotton-tipped swab in ink. This makes an easy-to-use and disposable brush. . . . Or, use a kitchen match dipped in ink.

> Play safe when mailing parcels by inserting return ad-

dress *inside* package. If wrapping is torn or address obliterated, the P.O. will know how to return it.

> Save a few of those large string-clasp envelopes for the day when you want to mail a magazine or newspaper. Slit the sides, roll tight and tie.

> A bit of colorless nail polish will make a balky envelope flap stick tightly.

> You can get gummed FIRST CLASS, AIRMAIL and SPECIAL DELIVERY labels at the post office for free.

> When you have a lot of envelopes to seal or stamps to affix, use an ice cube in a saucer as a moistener.

> There's a way to seal an envelope so that it cannot be steamed open: use the white of an egg.

> To get an uncanceled stamp off an envelope, dip the corner of the envelope in boiling water for a few minutes and the stamp will slide right off, usually leaving glue enough to make it stick again when dry.

> Postage stamps that are stuck together can be separated more easily if you place them in the refrigerator for a time. . . . Or, put them under a piece of thin paper and run a hot iron over the paper very lightly. The stamps will then pull apart easily.

> Double-faced cellophane tape can be used to affix stamps that have lost their glue. Put a piece on the back of the stamp and stick to envelope. . . Or, moisten the back of stamp without glue and rub it over the glue side of an envelope flap.

☐ P A P E R : Remove cellophane tape from paper or cardboard without tearing it by heating the tape with the point of an iron. It will pull off easily and safely.

> To thumb through thicknesses of paper, moisten thumb with glycerin and rub it into skin before you start.

> Here's how to cut a long strip of paper lengthwise. Roll the paper evenly and stick a pin through all the folds at the proper point; unroll the paper and the pinholes will make the

straight line to be cut. You can narrow a window shade in the same way.

> Mildew, in many cases, can be removed from valuable papers and book pages if you dust with cornstarch and allow the powder to remain several days before brushing off.

> When you're stapling papers together, it will be a more permanent job if you bind the edges with cellophane tape and staple through that.

☐ P E N / I N K :   If a ball-point pen gets balky, try holding the writing end in a closed hand to warm the hardened ink. You may also hold the point in boiling water for a minute or so.

> A mistake, when you're writing with ink, can be deleted with household bleach. Dip a matchstick or toothpick in the bleach and erase with it.

> If you add a little vinegar to ink that has thickened, it will dilute it to a better writing consistency.

> Don't blot signatures on legal documents. Natural drying will lengthen the ink's life.

☐ P E N C I L S / E R A S E R S :   When using a pencil on a sloping surface, avoid the annoyance of having it roll away from you by pushing a thumbtack part way into the side.

> To revive the cutting edges of a pencil sharpener, hold a piece of sandpaper against the cutter and slowly turn in reverse.

> In using a mechanical pencil sharpener, handle pencils gently. Pressing the tip in too hard can waste twice as much wood as is necessary to get a sharp point.

> Tape a small emery board to your desk and use it to keep erasers clean.

> Extra lighter flints can be carried in the lead compartment of your automatic pencil.

☐ T Y P E W R I T E R   T I P S :   To do typing late at night, put a foam-rubber pad under the machine. It will make even a "noiseless" more noiseless.

> When you're inserting several sheets of paper and carbon in the typewriter, slip the flap of an envelope over the leading edge of sheets. It will keep them even.

> You can clean clogged letters on typewriter keys by pressing on a strip of adhesive tape and then lifting it off.

> A pipe cleaner, bent into the proper shape, makes a dandy gimmick for cleaning the hard-to-get-at places inside a typewriter.

> Nail-polish remover will clean typewriter type. It will not harm the metal and dries quickly. . . . Or, a cotton swab dipped in ammonia also makes an effective type cleaner.

> Keep a pair of rubber gloves in a desk drawer. Comes in handy when changing typewriter ribbons.

☐ AND A LOT OF OTHER THINGS: A dark-green desk blotter atop desk or table will eliminate the glare from light on a highly polished surface.

> Newspapers make good substitutes when no ink blotter is available. For best absorption, use the nonprinted margin.

> If you've struggled to find and raise the cut edge of a roll of cellophane tape, put a paper clip on the edge next time before putting it away; or stick on a button.

> It isn't necessary to empty and turn over a desk drawer to get it clean. Brush all dust and dirt into a small pile, press a small piece of cellophane tape over it, and lift all the dirt out.

> Want to make a copy of something in the newspaper? Hold waxed paper over it and rub hard with rounded stick. Then place waxed paper over a blank sheet and repeat the process.

> Put all birthdays and anniversaries on the proper pages of new desk calendar now to avoid embarrassing forgetfulness later.

> Before removing a rolled calendar or something similar from the tube in which it is mailed, hold the open end of the tube over steam from a boiling tea kettle to moisten the paper. This will permit the article to lie flat.

> Recondition your briefcase by giving it an even coat of good furniture wax; let dry and then rub with soft cloth. It improves appearance and makes leather stormproof.

> If home and office keys are similar, file a notch in the top of one. You'll be able to pick out the right one even in the dark.

CARS AND DRIVING

☐ A U T O C A R E :   Batteries need more attention in winter than in summer. Check water, etc., frequently.

> If your bumper catches on another, try putting a heavy board or log directly behind the front wheels. When you back up, it will probably raise the front enough to clear the other bumper.

> You can sometimes fix a small dent on your car body by forcing a plumber's plunger against the spot. The suction can restore the original shape.

> On hot days and heavy traffic—try shifting to neutral, when you're stopped, and moderately racing the engine for about 30 seconds. This will help prevent overheating.

> If your car is over a year old, don't buy retouching paint the same color as the model. White turns yellow, blue fades, etc. Try to match the present color.

> Worn spots on the finish of your car can be touched up with shoe polish. Rub in with soft cloth, then cover with auto wax.

> Have your car waxed periodically. This protects body from rain, snow, chemicals, road dirt, etc.

> If the hood doesn't look as shiny as the rest of your car, apply a coat of aluminum paint to the underside. It will deflect motor heat, which causes wax and polish to melt.

> Pieces of old carpet make good pads for polishing cars.

> In summer, don't wax the hood of your car too thoroughly, as the sun's glare reflected off it can be a driving hazard.

> To keep your car's chrome fittings from getting weatherbeaten, give them a good cleaning and apply a thin coat of clear lacquer.

> Try glass wax in polishing the nickel and chrome of your car, to preserve lustrous finish. . . . Or, a coating of furniture wax will keep chromium plating looking bright.

> You can remove rust from chrome with tinfoil by dampening the foil with water and rubbing over the rust spots.

> Remove water and stain spots from the chrome on your car with plain old lemon juice.

> A length of garden hose nailed to each side wall of the garage will serve as a good bumper to protect the finish of the car doors. . . . Or, save wear and tear on fenders by suspending a ball from the center of the garage ceiling and line the radiator ornament up with it when entering.

> If a narrow garage poses an in-and-out problem, protect your car by rigging an old mirror to the back wall that will let you see both sides.

> Heat will cause gasoline to evaporate more rapidly. Park your car in the shade where possible and save money.

> Guard against evaporation in the gas tank. The fuller it is, the less space for evaporation.

> You get more miles per gallon driving at 20–30 mph. . . . Motorists can save gas by avoiding fast starts. A quick getaway uses two thirds more fuel than a steady smooth start.

> If you're running short of gas, do not speed up to get to a station quicker. Slow down to about 25 mph to conserve your gas to the utmost.

> Keep handle locks on cars from freezing by slipping a finger of a rubber glove or strips of cellophane tape over it in bad weather. This keeps moisture from collecting. . . . Or, a little lubricating oil or graphite in the locks of your car will keep any moisture in there from freezing.

> Never fill your radiator to the top during winter. Leave room for expansion of antifreeze.

> If you get tar on your car, soak spots with linseed oil. When softened, wipe clean with soft cloth dampened in the oil. . . . Or, ordinary cooking lard may remove tar spots from the body of your car. Just rub on with a soft cloth and, after a few seconds, rub off. . . . Or, a mixture of one cup of kerosene to a gallon of water will also remove tar spots.

> To rid the car chrome of road tar or grease, rub with a damp rag dipped in a little dry baking soda. It won't scratch chrome surface.

> Cut a piece of old linoleum to fit the floor of the trunk. Keep it waxed and heavy articles will slide in and out easily.

> Ever hit a skunk with your car? Makes big trouble. Dissolve a cupful of dried mustard in a bucket of water. Use a mop to slosh down wheels, underbody, anywhere the scent may be. Repeat if necessary.

> If your automobile has safety belts, scrub them with soap and water frequently to keep them from soiling your clothes.

> Wax license plates to keep them as bright as the body of the car.

> Experts say a clean car is safer in winter, as road tests have proved that a dirty car is more difficult to see in winter darkness.

> Put a little olive oil in the water when washing your car.

> As with clothes, get spots out of car upholstery as soon as possible, before they "set."

> To remove spots from plastic car upholstery, wipe with a solution of 1 tablespoon of washing soda in 1 quart of water.

> When cleaning the inside of your car with fluids or solvents, do the job outdoors and with the car doors open.

> Do not wipe dust or dirt from a car with a *dry* cloth before washing the car. May scratch finish.

> Baking soda cleans spatter and traffic grime from windshields, headlights, chrome and enamel. Wipe with soda sprinkled into a damp sponge or dissolved (3 tablespoons per quart) in warm water. Rinse with clear water.

☐ DRIVING TIPS: Men who do a lot of driving claim that a straight board against the back of the driver's seat keeps them from getting a tired back.

> For driving safety in winter, keep one ventilator window open at all times.

> Experts claim that you see only half as much while driving at 70 mph as you do at 40, and blame the cut-down vision for many accidents.

> In rainy weather, the rhythm of your windshield wiper can act as a soporific and make you drowsy, so vary its speed once in a while.

> Because of the oil film on many roads, a light drizzle can make driving more hazardous than a heavy downpour. The latter can wash the film away.

> To avoid drowsiness on long drives, change stations on the car radio occasionally. And, during night driving, change the brightness of the dashboard lights once in a while.

> For expressway driving at night, darken the dashboard, as it will improve your vision.

> If you use toll roads and bridges, cellophane-tape a few coins to some unexposed yet handy part of the car.

> When touring, keep a couple of dimes stashed safely away for the times you will have to use a highway phone booth, miles away from anywhere.

> A truck driver writes: "On a long, tiring drive, if you're getting sleepy, buy a cola drink. Put a teaspoon of salt in it

and drink it down. You will be wide awake for the next few hours."

☐ E M E R G E N C Y   M E A S U R E S :   Keep a box of baking soda in the glove compartment of the car as an effective emergency extinguisher for an engine fire. Should a fire occur, turn off the ignition and toss the soda on the engine. Soda also smothers a blaze should a fire start in a seat cushion or floor mat. . . . Keep a sprinkling of soda in the ashtrays. It will prevent cigarettes from smoldering in the car.

> Keep a roll of reflector tape in your car. If a headlight burns out, paste strips over the lens as a safety measure.

> The signal for "help needed" if your car is stalled on the road is just to raise the hood—and, as an extra, tie something white to the door handle on the driver's side. Lock yourself in and sit tight. Troopers will spot your signal.

> Toss a couple of milk cartons in the trunk. If you're ever stuck on the road at night, each will make a fine flare, burning almost 15 minutes.

> Carry a pot holder in the car. If you have to remove radiator cap or other parts affected by overheating, you will be able to avoid burns.

> Composition shingles will get your car out of an icy rut as quickly as sand or ashes, and they certainly are much easier and cleaner to carry in your car trunk.

> An old piece of carpet in the trunk can help you get your car off icy and slippery spots this winter. Just put it under the rear wheels. (This is also effective in soft sand.)

> When a tire blows, few drivers know just what to do. Experts say you should never slam on the brakes. Keep complete control of the car by 1) maintaining a firm grip on the wheel, 2) leaving car in gear, and 3) applying the brakes gently.

> If your car needs water, and no bucket is available, one of those big hubcaps will serve as an emergency pail.

> Note your blood type on your registration or driver's license in case of accident.

> If you have to stop on the road at night, keep the turn light on as a blinker.

> To protect your car, see that it is towed away only in neutral and never at a speed exceeding 30 mph.

> Keep a stout rubber band in the glove compartment of your car. If you get stalled at night, it can serve as a third hand to hold a flashlight.

☐ STAY-CLEAN TIPS: Keep an old pair of socks in the glove compartment of your car to pull over hands and sleeves when changing tires, etc.

> Tuck an old window shade in the trunk of your car. Unrolled, it will make a good mat for tire changing and keep you clean.

> Keep a container of soapy water and another of clean water in the glove compartment of your car when touring for the time you will have to change a tire, etc.

> If you've been tinkering with the car and want to get rid of oil stains from hands and from under nails without using a harsh cleanser, try scrubbing with a damp nail brush sprinkled with baking soda. . . . Or, soak fingers in lemon juice for about 15 minutes.

> A pad of foam rubber glued at the base of the auto's gas pedal will protect the shoes of women drivers from heel scuffs.

> After cleaning car batteries, be sure to swish your hands in a baking soda solution or rub them with dry soda to get rid of battery acid. If it's not removed, you can get a bad burn.

> There's nothing much handier than a roll of paper toweling in your glove compartment.

☐ TIRES: If you do not have snow tires or chains, you will get better traction in snow by deflating the tires a little.

> When motoring through lots of snow, check the bolts on your tires for rust.

> Rotating the five tires on a car regularly (the spare, too) will add as much as 10,000 miles of wear. The right rear tire gets 38 percent of the wear; the left front only 14 percent.

> Don't neglect the spare when you put air in your tires.

> When you use a jack, block the tire diagonally opposite the one jacked up.

> No matter how good the treads on your tires, they're only as strong as the sidewalls, so avoid hitting and scraping curbs when parking.

> Did you know that new tires are better off for a break-in like a car, and should be driven about 1,000 miles at normal speed?

> When touring, try to let your tires cool down a bit before inflating them. Hot rubber tends to expand and let too much air in, and the pressure will be too high when the tire cools.

> Use long screen-door springs to tighten loose tire chains. Fasten them to the chains across the diameter of the wheel.

> When changing a tire to a new rim, smear a soapy solution on the "bead," or inner edge, of the tires as lubrication and it will slip onto the rim with little effort.

> Do not use steel wool or harsh scouring powder to remove curb markings on white-walled tires. They can scratch the surface. Instead, apply washing soda with a wet brush, then rinse. Or, a scrub with soap and water may do the job.

> Automobile tires can be kept cleaner if a few drops of lemon juice are added to the soap solution.

☐ TRIPS — TIPS: Before packing the trunk of the car with heavy luggage, try a "dry run" with the empty bags— and make a diagram so you'll know which pieces to fit where.

> In packing the luggage compartment of your car for a trip, put the jack and wrench in last. That way you won't have to unpack the whole trunk to get at them if needed.

> Before going on a motor trip, mark the route on road maps with an ink-dipped cotton swab. Cities and road markings will still be visible.

> If you're driving through Canada and have an accident, your car can be impounded by the police if you can't prove you carry liability insurance.

☐ WINDSHIELDS AND WINDOWS: Sometimes your car visor doesn't provide enough shade. Extend it by slipping a large manila envelope (folded to fit and secured by a rubber band) over the unhinged end.

> Do not throw away that old shower curtain. Put in the car trunk and use it to cover the windshield on a frosty night.

> If it's snowing or looks like snow, put sheets of newspaper over the windshield when parking your car. . . . In cold times, place a shirt cardboard under the windshield wiper when parking the car to prevent a frosted or snow-covered windshield.

> To make your windshield wiper give longer wear, turn it on at slowest speed and only after the windshield is thoroughly wet. This way dust and dirt will not harm the rubber blades.

> Among the many reasons for not driving too close to the car in front is the fact that your windshield and you will be collecting dust, fumes and oil particles.

> A small worn whisk broom kept in the glove compartment of the car will come in handy for brushing snow or mud off a windshield.

> Rub the blades of your windshield wipers with moistened baking soda and then rinse before driving in the rain. It will provide clearer vision and add life and wear to the wipers.

> If windshield wipers do not do a proper job, rub the blades with a sandpaper block to clean and smooth them.

> A cut onion rubbed on the windshield or the tobacco from a cigarette butt will keep the glass from fogging or frost-

ing. . . . Or, moist salt rubbed on the windshield, inside or out, will help keep it from frosting or icing.

> Before bad weather sets in, remember to stash a clean blackboard eraser in the glove compartment of your car. It can't be beat for cleaning steamed windows.

> Keep a sponge in a closed jar of ammonia water in your car, to use on the windshield whenever it gets too dirty.

> To clean the window in your convertible top, use a soft cloth moistened with water. Removing road dust with a dry cloth will damage the plastic.

> If insects are difficult to remove from your car's windshield, use a small amount of baking powder on a damp cloth. Then wipe with a clean, dry cloth.

> Tree sap on the windshield can best be removed with a liquid glass cleaner.

> Linen is the best material for cleaning the windshield and windows of cars. The older the linen, the better it will function.

> Never wipe car windows with the same cloth used to clean the car. The cloth usually has wax on it and will dirty the glass instead of cleaning it.

> If country driving leaves road scum on your windshield, it can be removed easily with a rag moistened with cola drink.

> A cellulose sponge is fine for getting fog and steam off car windows.

☐ AND A LOT OF OTHER HINTS: Many drivers carry an extra ignition key in the pocket of their wallets. People often mislay keys, but rarely their money.

> In buying a used car, check these clues to hard wear: rattling doors, worn upholstery near the handles, and the condition of the paint where the driver's arm has rested on the open window.

> Never leave spare keys in the glove compartment. It's the first place thieves look.

> A good way to tell if a used car has the original paint job is to check the rubber on the windshield. If there is any paint on it, the car has been touched up.

> Drop a business card down a side window of your car. It it's stolen and thoroughly camouflaged, you'll still be able to show that it's yours.

> A bumper jack is a tire-changing tool only. If it is necessary to work under the car, place supports under the car structure.

> Tools rust fast in many auto trunks. To prevent this, give jack handles and all metal tools a coat of paint two or three times a year.

> Steel wool is handy for making a loose auto tail pipe that rattles fit snugly. But first saturate the wool with rust preventive or it will rust and disintegrate.

> Paint license-plate frames with luminous paint and you'll find your car much more easily in a big dark parking lot. . . . Or, tie a bright-colored ribbon to the extended radio aerial.

> That new driver's license will stay clean if you encase it in self-sealing transparent Saran Wrap.

> If you suspect your car has an oil leak, spread newspapers on the garage floor under the front end and run the engine for several minutes at a slow speed (comparable to 20–25 mph). Any oil leak will show on the paper.

> When you carry an umbrella in your car trunk, protect it by covering with two heavy cardboard mailing tubes.

> If your auto is air-conditioned, carry along a spray deodorant to eliminate tobacco odor.

> When you park your car in the hot sun, leave vents open to keep the inside from becoming unbearable. However, close all windows tightly. An inch or two left open at the top to permit circulation of air is an invitation to sneak thieves who "fish" with a wire loop. The loop catches on the door latch and the thief merely pulls up and opens the car door.

TRAVEL

☐ L U G G A G E : Look for even, close stitching in the binding. Loose threads or skipped stitches indicate poor workmanship.

> A darkened, worn-looking piece of leather luggage can be lightened by sponging with the juice of half a lemon in a glass of water.

> To darken light-tan leather articles, rub the leather lightly and uniformly with an ammonia-dampened cloth.

> You can hide worn spots on leather luggage by applying matching shoe polish and covering spots with two thin coats of clear shellac.

> Luggage, belts, etc., can be kept new-looking and clean by a rubbing with egg whites beaten stiff.

> To clean soft pieces of luggage, such as the popular cotton-canvas carryalls, use dense suds to shampoo the surface. Work quickly, with overlapping strokes, and rinse as job progresses.

> Try to avoid storing leather luggage in a hot attic, where the leather will dry out.

> Leather must "breathe." Do not store in plastic bags.

> If luggage must be stored in the basement or any place where it might be damp, use boards to keep it off the floor. This will prevent mildew.

> When suitcases are cluttering up closets and storeroom, see if many of the pieces cannot be nested within one another. But put paper around the inside ones, to avoid damage to linings from the hardware.

> Lock luggage when checking it. That's not only for protection against pilferage; it also keeps the catches from snapping open under rough handling.

> Use bright-colored plastic tape to make an identifying mark on each end of your luggage. You will be able to point it out in even the biggest pile.

> If you're traveling with fabric luggage, hotel porters won't even bother to paste on those colorful stickers. They fall right off again.

> A surefire way to keep bottles from leaking in luggage is to dip the tops in melted paraffin.

> Remove destination luggage tags after each stop. Leaving them on may result in misdirection when they're checked at another airport or station.

> A broken handle on a suitcase can be replaced with a dog collar. Slip through loops and buckle to size.

> Plastic luggage and toilet articles and plastic-lined kits rate a soap-and-water washing between trips.

> Using paste wax on luggage locks will keep them looking bright.

☐ AIR TRAVEL TIPS: Wear heaviest shoes while traveling by air. They will take up too much room in luggage.

> Do not carry anything aboard a plane that won't fit under the seat. Many things are not permitted on the overhead rack, and there may not be room on the floor for such things and feet too!

> On a long plane trip, get two large bound magazines from the stewardess and put one behind your back, the other under you. May spare you an aching back.

> It's good to know the weight of your baggage before taking a foreign flight. Most luggage is too large to fit on a bathroom scale. Weigh yourself empty-handed, then holding bag or bags. The difference will tell you whether you'll be charged for excess.

> Whatever beverage or food is served aboard planes, tuck napkin under your chin securely; it will save clothes from spots and stains.

☐ C A M E R A S :   Register a foreign camera with the U.S. Customs Service before taking it out of the country and avoid difficulty bringing it back.

☐ C L O T H I N G :   Laundry tricks: Wash handkerchiefs in a washbowl with soap and water, rinse without wringing. Then "paste" the wet handkerchiefs against a tile wall, mirror, or side of the bathtub. They will dry smooth and ready to fold.

> Soiled laundry, rolled tight, will serve as good shoe trees on the way home.

> While not infallible, a little talcum powder will take most spots off clothing. Rub in—and brush off.

> To use a travel iron, improvise an ironing board by inverting a dresser drawer and covering it with a bath towel.

> When packing to leave a hotel, take a second look at the back of the bathroom door. That's where most things are inadvertently left.

> Travelers can insure their valuables while vacationing away from home with a short-term floater policy. Ask travel agent.

> Take little clothing for a trip. Have a lot of things that will "mix-and-match." This provides a maximum of changes with a minimum of garments.

> Carry along a dark handkerchief or sleepshade to shut out bright light in planes and hotel rooms.

> When packing suits, remove belts from the trousers. They'll take less space that way, and the trousers will fold more neatly.

> Cut a small piece of cellulose sponge to pocket size, and

use it for brushing clothes, rubbing spots off, or cleaning shoes.

> The fewer loose units there are, the easier it is to pack. Use tissue paper or plastic bags to wrap handkerchiefs, underwear or socks together.

> You're not completely out of luck if you forget to pack a shoehorn. The narrow end of a silk tie will do the trick.

> Nothing is harder to find in a strange country than shoelaces; take spares.

> There are new fold-up skirt or pants hangers in the stores that are great for traveling. Take up no space, and keep clothes in better shape.

☐ FOREIGN TRAVEL : To quoted rate in many European hotels, add 10 percent tax and 15 percent service charge per day. Add another 10 percent on whole bill. In other words, a $10 room actually costs $13.75.

> Soap is still not abundant in European hotels, so if you do not want to bother packing wet cakes of soap, use a tube of shaving cream instead. It will get you just as clean and is easier to carry.

> If the water in a foreign country disagrees with you, chances are the ice in drinks will, too.

> When buying anything out of the country, be sure to get, and retain, a receipt—no matter how trivial or inexpensive the item. It might be just the one thing a Customs officer would question.

☐ GIFTS : A nice idea when you're giving a gift to a friend taking a trip: gift-wrap it in a colorful road map.

☐ PACKING : When putting a suit on a hanger to go in a suitcase, do not button the coat. Instead, fold one side well over the other and the front will wrinkle less.

> A good way to pack slacks for travel is to roll them neatly

around a long cardboard mailing tube, starting with waistband. Takes little room, and avoids fold creases.

> Hangers will sometimes slip off the rod in garment-bag–type luggage, and clothes land in a heap on the bottom. A heavy cord or wire twisted around all the hooks will keep them in place.

> To carry several hats, put them in a plastic bag, blow it up with air, and tie the bag tightly. The air forms a cushion and prevents the hats from being crushed.

> Use sheets of aluminum foil as layer dividers in suitcases. Then use again during trip to wrap wet and soiled items.

> A valuable gadget for travel is a plastic vegetable bag, to be used to hold soiled clothes, damp toilet articles, etc.

> My wife swears by her several sets of plastic shirt bags. Three large envelopes are attached together and hold sweaters, underwear, stockings, and lots more. They are never unpacked, just lifted from suitcase to bureau drawer, and are wonderful time-savers.

> Heavy things should be packed in the bottom of the bag. But don't forget that's the part of the case that it stands on—not the bottom as you're packing it.

> Never sit on a suitcase to make it close. That can spring the locks. Pack less instead.

> If there's still room in suitcase after packing, fill void with crumpled papers to keep clothes from sliding around.

> Before going on a trip, put out everything you'd like to take. Then put about half of it back. Everyone takes too much.

> Try not to jam luggage; it can press wrinkles into clothes.

> If packing the night before leaving, leave the bag open. The air will keep things from wrinkling.

> When packing, stuff socks or stockings into shoes; they will be out of the way and will serve as shoe trees.

> Small travel clocks, jewelry and other small fragile items

will travel best if packed into extra shoes, cushioned with socks and/or extra paper handkerchiefs.

> If luggage has tie tapes or straps on the inside, put a fold of tissue paper under each knot or buckle. Then you can pull the tapes taut without wrinkling clothes.

> There's a lightweight collapsible kit bag on the market that can be folded flat in luggage and filled with soiled laundry and acquisitions while you're traveling.

> If you have valuables with you, check them at the hotel desk. A locked suitcase is a tip-off there's something of value inside—and it's easy for a crook to take the whole case.

☐ SEASICKNESS: Try ginger ale with lemon juice for seasickness.

> Honey mixed with salt is recommended by experts as a cure.

> If you suffer from motion sickness, avoid reading in trains or planes.

> Many people find the old smelling salts a great remedy for the woozy feeling of motion sickness when traveling.

> It's said that eating candy is a good antidote to seasickness, or motion sickness in a car.

> If you tip your hotel maid, try to hand it to her rather than leaving it in the room when you depart. That way, *she* will be sure to get it!

☐ TOILETRIES: Even though a toilet kit is plastic-lined, fold a paper towel to fit the bottom. It absorbs the moisture from damp toiletries.

> Coat the inside of a metal soap container for use while traveling with colorless nail polish to prevent rust and tarnish.

> Busy light-luggage travelers rely on hand laundering to keep down wardrobe needs. As a box of detergent or soap flakes is unhandy to pack, make travel packages. Cut 7-inch squares of Saran Wrap and pour on a mound of washing pow-

der. Vary size for different amounts of laundry. Gather ends of wrapping and fasten with clear cellophane tape.

> If carrying liquids or lotions in plastic squeeze bottles, compress the sides a bit as the tops are put on. This creates a suction and makes them leakproof.

☐ UNPACKING: Unpack clothes and give them a good shake before hanging them up. That will help revive the shape.

> Unless unpacked clothes are badly mussed, go ahead and wear them. Most wrinkles will come out in the first half hour in the air.

> When clothes are mussed on arrival, hang in a closet; put a dampened terry towel over a hanger inside and close the door. The moisture will take out wrinkles.

☐ AND A LOT OF OTHER THINGS: Ear stoppers are a blessing for travelers to large cities, where construction often goes on at all hours.

> Ear stoppers are a blessing for travelers to large cities, where construction often goes on at all hours.

> A back saver: All hotel luggage racks are too low. Save stooping by putting an empty dresser drawer on rack, then the suitcase. Or put case on dresser top before packing.

> Never put a razor in a toilet kit without first removing the blade. It can cause much damage.

> Oft-used identification and credit cards can be kept from getting dog-eared if coated with clear nail polish.

> Keep passport number, and place of issue, on a handy slip of paper. You will not have to dig for passport every time information is needed. Better still, memorize the details.

> The handiest gadget to put in luggage is a small roll of cellophane tape, which has dozens of uses during any trip, among them making stamps stick to postcards and letters.

> There are few things handier than a small flashlight when you're traveling.

> If taking an electric razor abroad, take along a transformer plug to reduce the continental current to our 110 or 120 voltage. And be sure the plug is adaptable to various types of outlets.

PART TWO

KITCHEN SNOOPING— QUICK COOKING HINTS

APPETIZERS

☐ A S P A R A G U S : Asparagus tips wrapped in prosciutto (ham) and tied with pimento are delicious.

☐ A V O C A D O : Add mashed avocado to onion-soup mix, flavor with lemon juice, and use as a dip.

> Blend mashed avocado with lemon juice, salt, oregano and Tabasco for a dip.

☐ C A R R O T S : Marinate carrot and celery stalks in dill pickle juice to go with cocktails.

☐ C E L E R Y : Stuff small wedges of celery with anchovy fillets mixed with cream cheese.

> Top blue cheese, inserted into celery stalks, with sweet pickles.

> Stuff celery with bits of chopped nuts mixed in with cottage cheese.

> Try stuffing celery stalks with pimento cheese, or with peanut butter and pimento cheese.

> Wet celery stalks will hold salt.

> Celery can be kept for a week or longer if first rolled in brown paper, then in a towel and kept in a dark, cool place.

> For crisp celery, immerse it in ice-cold water, with several ice cubes, for a few minutes before serving.

☐ C H E E S E : Worcestershire sauce mixed with mustard and added to cheddar cheese makes a fine bar snack.

> Serve canapés of cheddar cheese mixed with finely chopped pimento, green olives and walnuts.

> Add crisp bacon and chopped almonds to a cheddar cheese spread.

> Add a small amount of caraway seeds to cream-style cottage cheese.

> Mix chopped onions with cottage cheese.

> Yogurt, cottage cheese, chopped parsley, a touch of mayonnaise and a package of onion soup all mix well together for a low-calorie cracker spread.

> Work minced red onion or chopped nuts together with minced anchovies into cream cheese.

> Mix blue cheese and cream cheese, then add chopped onions and crushed garlic.

> Combine bacon bits with cream cheese and some horseradish.

> Mix grated onion and a dash of Tabasco sauce with cream cheese and serve as a spread.

> Blend together: a 3-ounce wedge of Roquefort cheese, 2 tablespoons of chili sauce and 1 teaspoon of capers.

> Mix chopped stuffed olives with chopped Roquefort cheese.

> Mix just a bit of cognac or sherry into cheese spread.

> Mash and blend Camembert cheese with minced garlic and a generous amount of dry sherry. Spread on triangles of brown bread and toast until cheese is golden brown.

☐ CUCUMBER / PICKLE : Add thinly sliced cucumbers and sweet onions to yogurt.

> Try cucumber slices topped with sour cream and red caviar.

☐ EGGS : Add some soy sauce to chopped eggs.

> Mash hard-boiled eggs and anchovies to a paste.

> Add a little Roquefort cheese to stuffed eggs.

□ L I V E R W U R S T / K N O C K W U R S T / S A U - S A G E S : Mix sour cream and chopped onions with mashed liverwurst.

> Put chutney on slices of knockwurst, sprinkle with Parmesan cheese and put under broiler.

> Broil Vienna sausages in half a slice of buttered bread (closed with a toothpick) for a cocktail snack.

□ F R U I T : Dip dates in yogurt.

> Place cheese slices between two wedges of apple.

□ M E A T B A L L S / G R O U N D M E A T : Prepare, in advance, marble-sized balls of ground meat formed around small blue cheese chunks, and freeze. When needed, broil and serve on picks.

> Add a jigger of sherry to the sauce for meatball hors d'oeuvres.

□ L I V E R : Combine small cans of liver pâté with deviled ham.

□ M U S H R O O M S : Sauté finely chopped onions and mushrooms, add a dash of sour cream, and mash up with hard-boiled eggs.

> Drain canned mushrooms and add French dressing. Chill well, drain, and serve on toothpicks.

□ O L I V E S : Take large ripe olives from the can; put in a jar, juice and all; add slivers of garlic and a "float" of olive oil. The garlic adds flavor; the oil preserves the glossy black look.

> Drain a can of pitted ripe olives, roll them in a little olive oil and stuff with tiny sticks of sharp cheddar cheese or carrot.

> Replace the juice in a bottle of olives with plain water—removes the excess salt.

☐ R A D I S H E S : To make accordion slices in radishes, make narrow slices (not all the way through) and chill in cold water. The slices will curl in an accordion effect.

> Fill large, hollowed-out radishes with a cheese spread.

☐ S E A F O O D : Along with finely chopped egg and onion, garnish black caviar with a few dill seeds.

> Sprinkle lemon juice on caviar.

> Use red caviar mixed with sour cream as a dip for celery.

> Blend minced clams with cream cheese, clam juice, onion and Worcestershire sauce for a spread.

> Place sardines on toast and sprinkle with grated cheese, then broil.

> Make a spread of canned sardines chopped up fine with onions, celery, hard-boiled eggs, and a drop of vinegar.

> Try tart grapefruit juice on seafood cocktail instead of lemon juice.

> Mix minced onion with finely chopped watercress, chili sauce and mayonnaise.

> Flavor shrimp cocktail with oregano instead of with lemon.

> Serve cold shrimp on toast covered with cheese sauce.

> Dip shrimp in chilled sour cream.

> Mix horseradish with tuna fish.

> Add drained canned tuna to 3 cups of cream cheese or cheddar cheese dip; blend thoroughly. Serve as a dunk or spread on crackers and melba toast rounds.

> To tuna fish, or salmon, or both, add chopped pickle and mustard-mayonnaise to flavor. Sprinkle with wheat germ.

☐ **VEGETABLES**: Raw vegetables—carrots, radishes, celery, cauliflower, etc.,—dipped into sour cream or mayonnaise are among the best-liked and most healthful party snacks.

> Season sour cream with a little garlic powder, a dash of lemon juice and some anchovy paste. This is a good dip for chilled artichokes.

☐ **AND SOME OTHERS**: Blend tomato-soup mix with a pint of sour cream and chill for a dip to use with potato chips or crackers.

> When making popcorn, add a crushed clove of garlic to the cup of melted butter and pour over the corn.

> Mix mint jelly with plain table mustard to make a dip for sweet and sour spareribs.

> Make a cocktail sauce of catsup, lemon juice, horseradish and, for extra flavor, a dash of celery salt.

> Put peanut butter on small pieces of bread and top with small pieces of bacon. Place under flame to brown.

> French-fried onions dipped in cheese are a good pre-dinner snack.

BEVERAGES

☐ **COFFEE**: As a substitute for cream and sugar, use a spoonful of vanilla or coffee ice cream in a cup of steaming black coffee. Ice cream sweetens without diminishing the coffee flavor.

> Use chocolate milk in coffee, instead of regular milk or cream, for a mocha flavor, like dessert.

> Sprinkle grated nutmeg in a cup of coffee.

> Prepare *café au lait* by pouring equal amounts of dou-

ble-strength coffee and hot milk into serving cups at the same time.

> Dip sugar cubes in vodka before flavoring your demitasse with them.

> To a demitasse about ¾ full, add a dash of one of the following: white crème de menthe, Curaçao, anisette, Cointreau, cognac, bourbon or rum.

> Coffee or tea may be frozen in ice-cube trays and used at a minute's notice when iced coffee or tea is desired.

> Pour a jigger of brandy into iced coffee, add the juice of one orange, and top with whipped cream.

> Add a tablespoon of chocolate syrup to a glass of iced coffee.

> Always preheat a drip coffeepot before brewing coffee.

> Use 1 pound of regular-grind coffee and 2½ gallons of water to make 48 cups of coffee.

> Do not use less than ¾ of the capacity of a utensil. If less is desired, use a smaller appliance.

> Do not save time by using hot water instead of cold water when brewing coffee. Hot water can carry rust and other particles out of the water pipe which may affect the taste of the coffee.

> Make coffee with three times as much coffee as you usually do. When ready to serve, dilute it with boiling water to taste, thus easily storing fresh coffee until guests arrive.

> If brew is too weak, add just a little instant coffee to the pot. It will strengthen without changing the fresh flavor.

> Pour a little salt into coffee that has cooked too long to help take away the bitter taste.

> To keep leftover coffee fresh after brewing, put in refrigerator in a glass jar.

☐ HOT CHOCOLATE: Top hot chocolate with a marshmallow rolled in cinnamon.

> Put a teaspoon of instant coffee in hot chocolate.

> Before placing cocoa or hot chocolate on the fire, add a pinch of salt.

☐ J U I C E S : Instead of shaking frozen orange juice in container, try pouring it from one glass jar to another quickly. It aerates better than just shaking.

> Use a grinder when making lemonade. Put the whole lemon through and get far greater strength.

> Add cinnamon and lemon to grape juice.

> Add the juice of half a lemon and 3 drops of peppermint extract to a glass of grape juice.

> Use half apple juice and half milk for a thirst quencher.

> Keep stock of canned juices on hand in case of water shortage. They can also be used for cooking.

> Try a nonalcoholic cocktail of grated cucumber in tomato juice.

> A tomato-juice cocktail can be pepped up with the addition of Worcestershire sauce, horseradish, and a dash of Tabasco.

☐ T E A : Use either a china or an earthenware pot—metal has a tendency to change the flavor of tea.

> For extra-strong tea, add a pinch of baking soda.

> Add an orange peel to teapot a few minutes before serving tea.

> Add a piece of crystallized ginger or some sticks of peppermint to hot tea instead of sugar.

> A pound of loose tea should make 200 cups.

> See that a china pot is occasionally filled with a baking soda solution. Let it sit for a while before rinsing.

> Add fresh mint to a pitcher of iced tea.

> Try sweetening a glass of iced tea with a spoonful of grenadine. It also has less calories than sugar.

> Boil ginger root in water about 4 minutes, strain and pour over cracked ice for iced ginger tea.

BREAD

☐ BISCUITS: Before putting biscuits in the oven, brush them with slightly beaten egg yolk and sprinkle with sesame seeds.

> Add grated orange rind to biscuit dough. Split the biscuit while hot and spread with butter and orange marmalade, then put together again and serve piping hot.

> To make biscuits from a ready-bought mix extra good, use light cream instead of water for the liquid.

> Finely chopped chives in dough enhance the taste of biscuits served with a meat or poultry dish.

> Add a teaspoon of sugar to biscuit mix and use cream instead of milk; the result is an old-fashioned shortcake par excellence.

> Before baking canned, refrigerated biscuits, remove them from the can, place them on a cookie sheet and let them stand at room temperature for a short while. When baked, they will rise about twice as high. . . . For extra taste, dip them in melted butter before they go in the oven.

☐ BREAD: For sesame-seed bread, split loaves of French bread in half the long way; spread with garlic-flavored butter and sprinkle heavily with sesame seeds; heat in a 400-degree oven for 10 minutes and brown under broiler for 3 to 4 minutes.

> Toast slices of stale bread, rub with fresh garlic, and cut into small cubes; delicious with soup.

> Melted cheese on toast is good, but it's even better if the toast is first spread with deviled ham.

> Sprinkle bread with orange juice and oven-bake until crisp.

> Combine 1 can condensed tomato soup, ¼ cup milk and 1 cup shredded sharp cheddar cheese. Cook over low heat, stirring until cheese is melted, and pour over toast or toasted muffins.

> For the best cinnamon toast, sprinkle hot buttered toast with a mixture of 1 tablespoon of cocoa, 3 tablespoons of sugar and ½ teaspoon of cinnamon.

> A good method of making garlic bread is to first bake a loaf of bread 2 to 3 minutes. Slice and spread with garlic butter (now available in jars), then toast.

> Split a small loaf of French or Italian bread from end to end. Spread with garlic butter, heat in oven, and, if desired, sift some grated cheese on the buttered part.

> A great substitute for steamed Chinese bread is to cut the crust off white-bread slices and steam them for five minutes until soft and fluffy.

> In baking bread, be careful of two things: 1) Never try to bake too much at the same time. 2) Never place pans too close to oven wall. Heat must circulate freely on all sides of pan to give evenly baked results.

> To prevent a hard crust from forming when you're baking bread, put a small dish of water in the oven.

> Keep French or Italian bread in a plastic bag in the refrigerator. It will dry out in the bread box.

> Don't freeze white bread unless it is whole. Individual slices will get soggy when thawed out. But have rye bread sliced before freezing, as it will thaw out more quickly and stay fresh longer.

> Thaw frozen bread quickly by holding a hot steam iron about ½ inch above the cut slice.

> For croutons, mark ridges on bread with a knife blade before toasting. It will break easily into desired squares.

> When grinding stale bread, tie a paper bag at the outlet of the meat grinder to eliminate a big cleanup job.

☐ M U F F I N S :   For delicious muffins, add ½ envelope of onion mix to other ingredients before beating the mixture.

> Try grating Swiss or American cheese and sprinkling it on toasted English muffins.

> Split corn muffins, top with a sprinkling of molasses, add chopped nuts and broil.

> Ever try praline muffins? Top toasted English muffins with a topping that is a mixture of brown sugar, margarine and finely chopped nuts.

☐ R O L L S :   Slice fresh rolls, spread applesauce on halves and heat in oven. Delicious—and needing no butter or jam.

> A good way to warm rolls or biscuits is to place them in a paper bag which has been thoroughly wetted. Put in a hot oven and leave until the bag is dry. The rolls will be as nice and fresh as when they were first baked.

> Another way to warm and freshen rolls is to place 2 tablespoons of water in a skillet, insert a trivet or rack, and arrange rolls on top. Cover skillet and warm the rolls over low heat for 10 minutes.

CHEESE

☐ R E C I P E S :   Blend cottage cheese and sour cream, add to cold spinach and stir together.

> Add chopped anchovies to cottage cheese.

> Put leftover Welsh rabbit with some sardines on slices of buttered toast and cover with thinly shredded raw onion—then reheat.

> One quarter cup Roquefort cheese, crumbled and blended with ½ cup chopped pecans and ¼ cup butter, is marvelous when spread on toast squares.

> Cream cheese makes a fine topping for hot gingerbread if you whip with confectioner's sugar, grated lemon rind and a little lemon juice.

> Room-temperature blue cheese mixed with sour cream and served with fresh strawberries makes a fine dessert.

☐ CUTTING AND GRATING: Cheese can be sliced thinner with a dull knife than with a sharp one.

> Keep cheese from crumbling during cutting by heating the knife in boiling water.

> Rub a raw potato over surface of grater after grating cheese. Potato will push cheese residue through holes, making cleaning easier.

☐ OLD CHEESE: Hardened cheese can be softened by wrapping in a cloth that has been wrung out in cold, salted water, or in a mixture of water and vinegar. Cover cloth with aluminum foil and put in refrigerator.

> Swiss, Muenster, American and similar cheeses are still tasty and edible when dried out. Simply grate and use with spaghetti, soup or vegetables.

> Cheese that has become moldy should not be discarded. Put it in a covered container with a few lumps of sugar. The mold leaves the cheese and goes into the sugar. Eat the cheese and throw away the sugar.

☐ SPREADING: Cream cheese: Add a drop of milk to cold cream cheese spread and mix thoroughly to make it spread easier.

> Cottage cheese: Add a little skimmed milk to cottage cheese to give it a fluffy base for use in spreading.

☐ S E R V I N G :   Only unripened cheese tastes best chilled; all others require 1 hour at room temperature to bring out distinctive flavor.

> Serve cheese with bread and butter, not salty crackers, which take away from the flavor of the cheese.

> If cheese comes wrapped in foil or waxed paper, don't remove the wrapper; slice through it as you use the cheese.

> Serve Parmesan cheese when it is 3 or 4 years old. Best for Italian dishes.

☐ S T O R I N G :   Coat the cut side of cheese with butter and it will last indefinitely.

> Cheese will keep better if wrapped in foil, plastic bag or cloth that has been moistened with vinegar.

> Instead of being kept in a cool dry place, grated cheese will hold up much better and longer if it is refrigerated.

CONDIMENTS

☐ G A R L I C :   A toothpick stuck in a clove of garlic will make removing the clove easier after a dish of food has been cooked.

> Chop garlic up fine with a knife, put coarse salt on it and mash with the flat of a knife. That way you have the taste only without biting into pieces of garlic.

> The tight skin of garlic is easy to remove if you run hot water over the cloves first.

> Remove garlic from oil after it has been fried to a golden

brown; after that it lends a burned bitter taste to the dish being prepared.

> Make garlic butter by letting 1 clove of garlic stand 2 hours in ½ pound of softened butter. Remove clove before using.

> Garlic will hold up much better if kept in plastic bags.

> To avoid garlic breath, only use the juice and not the fibers, as this is what produces the offensive odor.

> Crush a clove of garlic in a few drops of oil and vinegar, then strain the liquid into your favorite salad dressing.

> Put garlic bud into press unpeeled and the residue will lift out easily; the cleanup of the press will be simple.

> If you add a touch of lemon juice to dishes calling for garlic, it will greatly cut down the garlic aftereffects.

> Try garlic wine vinegar. One teaspoon equals 1 small clove of garlic. (To be used in place of fresh garlic.)

☐ HERBS & SPICES: Spices that come in paper containers will lose strength, so store the contents in a jar with a screw top.

> Herbs used in a quickly cooked dish or sauce give more deliciousness if moistened with a little milk or cooking oil and allowed to stand for ½ hour before using.

> Mix mustard powder, vinegar and garlic powder for hot mustard.

> Keep your spices in a cool, dry place. If stored over the stove, they are liable to deteriorate.

☐ MARSHMALLOWS: Keep marshmallows from sticking to the fork while being toasted by first dipping tines in melted butter.

> To keep marshmallows soft and fresh, put them in a bread box till needed. They absorb moisture from bread.

☐ N U T S :   Chop nuts by placing in a cloth bag and rolling with rolling pin.

> Almonds should be grated, not ground. Otherwise, too much of the oil is expressed.

> To restore stale nuts to freshness, warm them for ten minutes in an oven preheated to 300 degrees.

> Make deviled almonds by sautéing them in butter, then rolling them in a mixture of salt and cayenne pepper.

> Make candied peanuts by coating the shelled nuts lightly with maple syrup and heating them for a few minutes over a low flame.

> Fried walnuts? Instead of butter, fry them in a mixture of ½ cup of honey and ¼ cup of peanut butter.

> Mix shelled walnuts in a mixture of sherry, brown sugar and corn syrup until the nuts are well coated; then roll them in sugar and allow to dry.

> To toast almonds, spread them out on a cookie sheet or in a jelly roll pan and brown lightly in a hot oven. Stir the nuts a few times so they will brown evenly.

> Before shelling Brazil nuts, put them in a saucepan, cover with cold water and let boil for three minutes; then let stand one minute in cold water.

To prevent nuts from sinking in batter, chop them as directed and then coat them with flour.

☐ O I L S   &   F A T S :   Strain frying fat after each use by pouring slightly cooled fat through cheesecloth or a filter.

> A lump of sugar added to a pint of olive oil will keep it from getting rancid.

> Refrigerate all vegetable oils, including real olive oil.

> Make your own olive oil: Soak four large unstuffed olives in a cup of salad oil and keep in a tightly covered jar in the refrigerator for a week.

> Pour off the olive oil you have used for cooking shortly

before the dish is done, and add a small amount of fresh olive oil. It may cost a bit more, but the food will be tastier and more digestible.

> Paper cups are best for storing fat that will be reused. As it is needed, the paper can be peeled away and the fat sliced off.

☐ SALT : If cutting down on salt, use more lemon—particularly on hamburger.

> Do not stint on salt, even if on a diet, during very hot weather. You need it to replace salt lost by perspiring.

> The proper function of salt is to develop and bring out the natural food flavors. Sprinkle a small amount in fruit juices; it decreases the sourness of the acids and increases the sweetness of the sugars.

> Do not overdo the salt when baking with yeast; too much salt will slow up the rising process.

> Do not salt the things you put in the freezer. They may become rancid.

☐ SUGAR (BROWN AND GRANULATED): To keep brown sugar soft and moist, place a cut apple or a slice of bread in the container and cover.

> Keep brown sugar in a large jar along with dried prunes. The prunes keep the sugar from turning hard and the sugar sweetens the prunes.

> Get lumps out of brown sugar by putting it in a jar covered with a dampened piece of cheesecloth. The lumps should disappear in a few days.

> Soften caked brown sugar by putting in double brown-paper bags and placing it in the oven for about an hour.

> To keep granulated sugar from lumping, put a couple of saltine crackers in your kitchen sugar container.

☐ AND A LOT OF OTHER THINGS: Cooking semantics: "Glaze" means to cover with aspic, thin sugar syrup, or melted fruit jelly; "glacé" is to coat with thin sugar syrup cooked to the crack stage.

> Butter your large serving platters with a pastry brush before placing your hot cooked meats or fish on them; the food won't stick and will be easier to serve.

> Cook a day ahead a recipe that includes many spices, herbs or onions. This way the flavors are permitted to "marry."

> If you freeze baked goods, remember to use only pure flavorings, as the imitations change flavor when frozen.

> Grind cranberries and oranges together with juice, rind and all, then mix with broken walnuts and a little sugar.

> When freezing moist foods, line the storage container with a plastic bag; then you can lift the food right out without waiting for defrosting.

> Always permit food to cool before straining.

> Mix one part of prepared horseradish with six parts of plum preserves for turkey, goose, roast beef or pork.

> To restore curdled mayonnaise, place 4 tablespoonfuls of cold, melted butter in a round-bottomed bowl and gradually work it into the mayonnaise. This will return it to its proper consistency.

DESSERTS

☐ BAKING TIPS: Keep cake from sticking to the pan by wrapping a towel dipped in hot water around it when it is removed from the oven.

> The seeds of the vanilla bean give off the most flavor, so be sure to slit the bean when you put it into a jar of sugar to make vanilla sugar for use in cakes, custards and puddings.

> Place waxed paper over dough before using rolling pin to keep the dough from sticking to the pin.

> Put crackers in a plastic bag, then roll to a desired fineness. They will pour from the bag into a container without scattering.

□ C A K E S : Spread honey over slices of pound cake, toast in the broiler for a few minutes, and serve with powdered sugar.

> Add a few sprinkles of sherry to batter when baking pound or sponge cakes.

> Try using orange juice instead of water in making a sponge cake.

> Streak a few teaspoons of instant coffee through plain cake batter for a "marbled" effect.

> Don't use flour for Swedish apple cake. Use bread crumbs rolled in sugar and cinnamon.

> When preparing pound cake mix, substitute pineapple juice for all the liquid required.

> Cake batter should only half fill the pan.

> When using bananas on a cake or pie, first dip them in fruit juice to prevent their turning brown.

> Test to see if a cake is baked by placing a wooden toothpick in the cake center; it is done if the toothpick comes out clean.

> Do not bake cakes with one pan directly below another. Stagger the filled cake pans on two racks.

> If your cake browns too quickly before it is thoroughly baked, place a pan of water on the top rack in your oven. . . . When you're baking small cakes, a dish of cold water placed on the bottom shelf of the oven will prevent burned edges.

> If batter becomes too stiff, add beaten egg a little at a time. Using milk for thinning will only result in a poor cake.

□ C H O C O L A T E : Try adding a teaspoonful of vinegar

to the baking soda next time you bake a chocolate cake—it will be fluffier and moist.

> To avoid white deposits on a chocolate cake, dust the pan with cocoa instead of flour.

> When a square of chocolate is called for and you have none, substitute 4 tablespoons of cocoa and ½ teaspoon of butter.

☐ TINS: When using new tins, first butter them and put in a moderate oven for 15 minutes to avoid burning the cake.

☐ FRESHENING: A circular cake will remain fresh much longer after cutting if slices of bread are pinned to both cut sides with toothpicks.

> Dip stale cake for just a moment in cold sweet milk, then heat it in a moderate oven.

> To keep fruitcake from drying out, pour a little bourbon or sherry over it.

☐ BREAKING, CRACKING, STICKING: Powdered sugar sprinkled liberally on waxed paper used to wrap iced cake will prevent frosting from sticking to the paper.

> If the cake sticks to pan, and could break, hold the pan over a low flame for about 5 to 8 seconds. The cake will come out intact and in perfect shape.

> Leave layer cake 10 minutes, loaves 20 minutes, and angel and sponge cakes one hour before removing from cake pan.

> Sprinkle a cake plate with powdered sugar to prevent cake from sticking.

☐ CUTTING: If cake is frosted, rinse knife in hot water before using to slice.

> When cutting a cake, cut the first slices from the center by cutting the cake in half. Push the halves together and the remainder will stay fresh and moist longer.

☐ CANDY: In warm weather, keep chocolate candy in the refrigerator, but wrap it in aluminum foil so it will not turn white.

> Popcorn will pop better if sprinkled with a little water before being placed in the popper.

> Toss fresh popcorn with grated Parmesan cheese and melted butter.

> To ensure smoothness when making candy, allow it to cool to lukewarm before beating. Never cool it in a draft.

> If candy comes out sugary, add a couple of tablespoons of corn syrup to any of the recipes.

☐ CHEESECAKE: Try adding a little melted chocolate and half a jigger of cognac to cheesecake batter.

> Allow cheesecake to remain in oven an hour after baking to prevent dropping.

> Make cheesecake with a ginger snap crumb crust and top with cold canned peach slices.

☐ CHOCOLATE FUDGE: In melting chocolate, it is best to use warm but not too hot water, as it could be scorched.

> When shaving chocolate, use a vegetable-paring knife for quick, easy results.

> If low on milk, use cold coffee when making fudge.

☐ COOKIES: If shaping wafer cookies into cone forms, and the wafers become too rigid to work with, reheat them in the oven and they'll soften.

> To plump raisins for cookies, put the washed raisins into a colander and place over boiling water. Let steam for five minutes, then cool.

> Remove soft or sticky cookies from the sheet by simply greasing the spatula.

> A few slices of bread in the cookie jar will keep soft cookies that way longer.

> Slices of apple or orange in the cookie jar help mellow and moisten cookies. Remove the fruit in a day or two. Keep the cookies covered tightly.

> Bake cookies lightly and remove from the oven when slightly undercooked. They will finish baking on the hot pans as they cool.

□ CUSTARDS: Vary rice-custard dessert with the addition of ripe bananas. Chill before serving.

> Mix crushed strawberries in vanilla custard and top with whipped cream.

> Substitute corn syrup for part of the sugar to prevent an icy consistency in a mousse or bombe. (One part corn syrup to 2 parts sugar is a good rule.)

> Custards made with undiluted evaporated milk usually have an interesting, slightly caramel flavor.

> A teaspoon of corn flour blended into the egg mixture before addition of sugar and milk prevents baked custard from becoming watery.

□ TOPPINGS FOR CAKES AND PIES: Cover white cake with chocolate-coated candy mints. When melted, spread.

> Boil a small potato, mash it and add powdered sugar and vanilla. Use almond as a flavoring, and the icing will taste like marzipan.

> Beat up a little fresh fruit juice with powdered sugar until smooth, then spread on cake.

> Try miniature marshmallows broiled till golden brown atop a pie.

> Add 1 package instant pudding to 1 pint whipped cream for a quick cake frosting.

> Crush peanut brittle fine, then fold into whipped cream and ice cake with mixture.

> Top a frozen éclair with Cherry Heering.

> When icing a cake, dip utensil into a container of boiling water occasionally. This will keep icing from drying out and will keep it smooth.

> Before frosting an angel food cake, spread a thin layer of softened butter over the top and sides. Frosting will spread more easily and the cake won't crumble into the icing.

> Dust cornstarch lightly on cake before icing. This prevents icing from running, and it will have a smoother appearance.

> Cakes with fillings or frosting made with eggs should be kept in refrigerator.

> Prevent cake filling from soaking into the cake by sprinkling the top of each layer with powdered sugar before frosting or filling.

> Cream whipped in advance will hold if 3 tablespoons of unsifted powdered sugar is added to each ½ pint of cream before whipping. Cream whipped this way can be put through a pastry tube.

> When baking marshmallows on top of a pie or cake, sprinkle sugar lightly over them to keep them from running over the rim of the pan.

> When cake icing gets too thin and there's no powdered sugar with which to thicken it, use powdered milk instead.

> Lemon juice beaten into white frosting that has become too hard or stiff will soften it.

> The secret of preparing delicious fruit cocktails is the lemon juice, brown sugar and cinnamon added to them.

> Sprinkle grapefruit half with a dash of cinnamon and broil for about 15 minutes.

> Dip grape clusters in egg white, then in granulated sugar, and chill.

☐ GELATIN DESSERTS: Add two tablespoons of grenadine to each serving of gelatin.

> Add Burgundy wine and a few dashes of lemon juice when mixing fruit gelatin.

> Put some sour cream between layers of gelatin.

> Add sour cherries and crushed pineapple to a package of lemon gelatin.

> Pour a little crème de menthe over gelatin before serving.

☐ GENERAL DESSERT TIPS: Try using sifted powdered sugar in place of granulated when making meringue.

> When packing candy and cookies for shipment, use a metal box lined with foil. Then place tissue paper and more foil between each two layers. This will prevent crumbling and breaking.

> You can easily achieve a beautiful glaze on baked fruits or sweet bread by drizzling honey over their tops while they're still warm from the oven.

> When making a flaming dessert, heat the spoon before pouring the rum or brandy into it. The hot liquor will immediately burn when lit.

> Homemade doughnuts never taste greasy if you add a few cloves to the fat they are fried in.

> Keep fruits, nuts and raisins from sinking to the bottom of cakes and puddings by heating them in the oven before adding to the batter; or they may be rolled in butter before being added.

☐ ICE CREAM & ICES: Flaming Mount Fujiyama: Place a bed of shredded coconut in a dessert dish. Add a cone-shaped scoop of vanilla ice cream, sprinkle with more coconut, and pour brandy over it. Light the brandy, which toasts the coconut for added flavor. (Ice cream resembles a mountain coming through the clouds, hence the name.)

> Lemon sherbet tastes even better when mixed with a little milk and whipped up in a blender.

> Form different flavors of ice cream into balls with a stainless steel scoop. Roll quickly in tinted coconut sprinkles or cake decorations and heap in a stainless steel bowl and pop into the freezer until serving time. Pass with smaller-size bowls filled with chocolate, berry and caramel sauces.

> Dip a large ball of vanilla ice cream in cherry liqueur and sprinkle with shredded coconut.

> Soak some grated coconut in green crème de menthe as a topping for ice cream.

> Maple syrup heated with rum and poured over vanilla ice cream makes a delectable combination.

> Try pistachio ice cream topped with raspberry preserves.

> Try pouring some hot coffee over vanilla ice cream. It imparts a mocha taste and melts too-hard ice cream.

> Top ice cream with peanut butter or blend four tablespoons of peanut butter with two squares of sweetened chocolate. Melt and then allow to freeze for a day. It tastes like peanut fudge.

> Marinate drained canned peach slices in orange liqueur and serve with vanilla ice cream.

> Simmer sliced canned peaches in maple syrup and pour over vanilla ice cream.

> Top ice cream with a blend of crushed bananas and raspberries.

> Make hot raisin sauce by mixing chopped raisins with butter, brown sugar and brandy. Stir and blend over a low flame; it is delicious over vanilla ice cream.

> Add a little Cointreau to chocolate syrup, then pour over vanilla ice cream.

> Combine applesauce, marshmallow cream and flaked coconut for a topping.

> Melt chocolate-coated peppermint wafers with a little water and pour over ice cream.

> Combine two tablespoons of dark rum with equal

amount of sweet butter, melt and use as a topping for vanilla
ice cream.

> Heat a 1-pound jar of orange marmalade in a chafing
dish, add a jigger of cognac, then flame and serve over vanilla
ice cream—much like Cherries Jubilee.

> Fold sour cream into your favorite fudge or caramel
sauce. Use on plain cake, fruit, gelatin, or ice cream.

> Grate nutmeg over homemade ice cream and add a cup
of sherry.

> Cook apricot preserves blended with orange juice for ice
cream topping.

☐ HOMEMADE ICE CREAM: Mix well: 1 pint
sour cream, 1 cup sugar, 1 package of defrosted frozen fruit;
put in an ice-cube tray and stir occasionally to prevent formation of ice particles.

> Take any ordinary custard mix and add three eggs, two
cups of cream and a cup of sugar. When this is blended, and
frozen for three hours, it makes a rich ice cream.

☐ APPLE PIE: Try sprinkling grated cheese and cinnamon over the apples.

> Add thin slices of banana to apple pie filling.

> Top apple pie with sweetened whipped cream with a
spoonful of apple juice over it.

> Try chilled sour cream on apple pie.

> Crumble Roquefort cheese over the top of a freshly
baked apple pie and slip back into oven for a minute.

☐ PIE CRUSTS: For sweet sugary crust, spread confectioner's sugar instead of flour on the pastry board.

> For a flaky upper crust on pies, brush the top crust lightly
with cold water before putting pie in oven.

> For a better crust, make it out of whole-wheat flour and
use butter or a vegetable shortening instead of lard.

> For thicker pie crust, use a glass baking dish instead of a metal pan.

> To get a flakier, tender crust, form the ingredients into a ball after blending and allow to rest for 15 minutes before rolling out.

☐ FRUIT PIES: When baking fruit pies that are inclined to be juicy, bake the shell for about five minutes prior to putting in the fruit. Prevents soggy lower crust.

> Try Swiss cheese over hot pineapple pie.

> Pour melted cheese over the crust of any fruit pie for a gourmet taste.

> Wheat germ sprinkled liberally on any fruit pie for the last ten minutes of baking will add a crust with a nutlike flavor.

> A half teaspoon of almond extract makes cherries or cherry pie taste great.

> For a pumpkin pie when there are no pumpkins, use cooked yellow squash.

> Make a deep-dish peach pie with one cup of mincemeat, and serve slightly warm with cream.

> Pour a wine glass of sherry and a wine glass of California brandy on holiday mince pie the night before serving.

> Use one tablespoon of honey for each egg white to make meringue for lemon pie.

☐ AND A LOT OF OTHER THINGS: Before cutting a pie, dip the knife in a glass of water, to prevent sticking.

> Soft pies will cut more easily with a knife coated with butter.

> Give an open-face pie a quick freezing before wrapping for longer storage in the freezer. It's easy to handle this way.

> Allow a baked pastry shell to cool thoroughly before adding a filling.

> Use a small amount of tapioca for thickening (in place of flour) in fruit pies.

> To keep lemon chiffon pie from falling, add a teaspoon of baking powder to the recipe.

> To make a perfect meringue for pies, beat whites of eggs until stiff, but not dry. Make certain all sugar granules are thoroughly dissolved.

> For fresh blueberry pie, scatter brushed cornflakes over the top as a thickening agent.

> Always heat milk to the boiling point before mixing with eggs for egg custard pie. This will guarantee a crisp undercrust.

> Use pinking shears, dipped in flour, to cut lattice strips for fruit pies.

☐ PUDDINGS: Add chilled slices of banana to chocolate pudding for a tasty dessert, or top with thin slices of banana and shredded coconut.

> Mix a dash of sweet wine with pudding and top with sprinkling of cinnamon. Cinnamon is always good on chocolate or vanilla pudding.

> Add crushed pineapple and chopped nuts to rice pudding.

> Mix crushed strawberries into rice pudding.

> Stir small pieces of raw apple into rice pudding.

> Use raisin bread for bread pudding.

> Put fresh grapefruit slices on rice pudding and sprinkle with a mixture of butter, brown sugar and roasted diced almonds; broil five minutes and serve hot.

> Fold a cup of applesauce into vanilla pudding and mix while still warm. Then chill.

> Bits of crumbled pecans in your rice pudding will add to its flavor.

> A mixture of rice and chocolate puddings makes a delicious dessert.

> For old-fashioned rice pudding, use a large proportion of milk and bake several hours, stirring occasionally during the first hour.

> Coffee rings or sugar rolls can be used as bread pudding. Put ring or rolls in a deep dish, cover with milk and beaten egg, and bake in 400-degree oven until brown.

> Use coconut juice instead of water for speedy rice pudding.

> To avoid tedious stirring when cooking a pudding mix, try heating the milk first and then adding the mix. Three or four stirs brings it to a boil and you don't waste time standing over a hot stove.

> Cover hot pudding with plastic wrap to prevent a skin from forming while it chills. Or cover with a light sprinkling of sugar immediately after the hot mixture has been poured into the cup or mold.

☐ WHIPPED CREAM: Put a jigger of good brandy in whipped cream as a topping for fruit desserts.

> Add a little instant coffee or cocoa powder to sweetened whipped cream.

> Try beating applesauce and cottage cheese as a substitute for whipped cream.

> Whipped cream can be delicately sweetened and flavored by addition of cream sherry or port.

> Use lemon extract instead of vanilla in whipped cream when making a topping for mince and pumpkin pie.

> If you have leftover whipped cream, beat a couple of tablespoons of it into morning pancakes as part of the liquid.

> For fast whipped cream, pour extra-cold heavy sweet cream into a refrigerated container (plastic, metal or glass) and cover top of container. Shake it like a cocktail mixer and cream will be whipped up in a matter of seconds.

> Adding a few drops of lemon juice while whipping cream will speed up the stiffening.

> Use confectioner's sugar instead of granulated sugar to sweeten whipped cream for a fluffier, longer-lasting topping.

> Cream may be whipped well ahead of serving time if corn syrup is used as a sweetener instead of sugar.

☐ QUICK DESSERTS: Here's a simple dessert: Remove crusts from bread slices, cut into finger lengths and fry in butter until brown. Sprinkle with sugar and serve over sweetened applesauce.

> Top orange wedges with brown sugar and rum.

> For a quick, last-minute dessert, add a couple of tablespoons of port wine to applesauce and heat.

> For a gourmet's dessert, combine strawberries with an equal part of pineapple cubes and steep in Cointreau. Chill and serve with macaroons.

> Wine, cheese and fruit are one of the oldest and best-loved desserts. Port is the perfect wine to go with fruit and cheese.

> Quarter apples and bake in grape juice; top with marshmallows. Serve with all types of fowl.

> Mix 2 cakes of cream cheese and 1 cup of sour cream till blended and then stir in a small quantity of lemon juice. Pour over strawberries and top with powdered sugar.

> Cut marshmallows into tiny pieces, pour hot coffee over them, add whipped cream and chopped nuts, and chill.

DIET FOODS

☐ DESSERTS: Top fruit gelatin with cottage cheese and a dash of yogurt.

> Ice cream made from buttermilk has half the calories of regular ice cream.

> Angel food and sponge cakes have the lowest number of calories; one-crust custard is the lowest pie in calories.

> Mix cottage cheese with applesauce.

> Add unsweetened grapefruit juice to dissolved gelatin and fat-free milk. Beat until thick and fluffy, then freeze.

> Try pouring any fruit juice into an ice-cube tray and freezing. Before the cubes harden, stick a toothpick in each to form an ice cream pop.

> Chocolate ice cream has the most calories of any, coffee the fewest.

> Try drained canned chunk pineapple with pieces of cubed raw carrot topped by a spoonful of yogurt.

> Try making cheesecake with yogurt instead of cheese. There are far fewer calories.

☐ TOPPINGS: Instead of whipped-cream topping, add sliced banana to egg white and beat in blender.

> Yogurt parfait: ribbon layers of yogurt and fruit preserves.

☐ EGGS: When scrambling eggs, pour a little olive oil in the pan instead of butter. Swish it around, then pour most back into the bottle. The eggs will not stick, and calories are negligible.

> Scramble eggs in the top half of a double boiler. No fat is used—no extra calories added; totals about 80 calories.

> An onion omelet can be made without frying with oil or butter. First let the onions simmer in water until juicy and soft. Then add eggs and scramble. Oil or butter is not necessary, as the moisture of the onions prevents sticking.

☐ FISH: Instead of using oil or butter, fry fish in water or in grapefruit juice (or your favorite fruit juice); the taste will be terrific.

> Try using melted cheese as a dip when eating broiled lobster.

□ POTATOES: Use yogurt or whipped cottage cheese instead of sour cream on baked potatoes; add chives.

> Use yogurt instead of butter or milk for mashing potatoes.

> A baked or boiled medium-sized potato provides only about 100 calories—about the same as a large apple or orange, or half a large grapefruit.

□ RICE AND PASTA: Order brown rice with Chinese food, not white or fried.

> Use plenty of water when cooking rice or any pasta, such as spaghetti. The starch in them is dissolved in the water, which is poured off.

□ SALAD AND DRESSING: Sprinkle lemon juice on salads (and on veal and baked potatoes).

> Try tuna-and-grapefruit salad.

> Substitute plain, unflavored yogurt for mayonnaise in salad dressing.

> Serve a slice of fruit gelatin on a layer of lettuce.

□ VEGETABLES: A carrot is only 20 calories—it's a good after-dinner munch when dipped in cottage cheese spread. Store carrot slices in a jar of water in the refrigerator.

> Slice a whole peeled cucumber and put slices of cheese between; eat like a sandwich.

> Green pepper strips make a good snack. A medium-sized pepper has only 16 calories.

> Scoop out a lightly boiled Bermuda onion and stuff with cottage cheese and pimento mixture.

□ GENERAL WEIGHT-WATCHING TIPS:

Sprinkle a few drops of vinegar on any food. It curbs the appetite.

> If iced coffee or tea is already chilled, dissolve a non-caloric sweetener tablet in ½ teaspoon of hot water before adding.

> You'll eat less if you eat slowly.

> Those 900-calorie food concentrates that dieters like must be kept cold after they are blended. So if you take lunch with you, carry it in a small thermos bottle.

> Have steaks well done, as this melts out most of the marbling—which is fat.

EGGS

☐ BOILED: Add a few drops of Tabasco to soft-boiled eggs.

> To hard-boil eggs properly, put them in a pan, cover with cold water, bring to a boil, then cover with a lid and let stand for 15 minutes.

> When boiling eggs in an aluminum pan, add a dash of vinegar and pan will not turn black.

> Never drop chilled eggs into boiling water. Let them heat up to room temperature so that they will not crack.

> Seal a broken eggshell if it cracks during cooking by adding a little vinegar to the cooking water.

> A cracked egg can be boiled if it is first wrapped in aluminum foil.

> To keep the yolk from breaking when you're slicing hard-boiled eggs, dip the knife in water.

> Plunge hard-cooked eggs into cold water before remov-

ing shell to prevent a dark ring from forming around the yolk. The shell will also slip off more easily.

> To prevent hard-boiled eggs from spoiling after peeling, place them in water to which a little soda has been added.

> Prevent eggs from cracking when they're boiled by letting them stand in very warm water for a few minutes before boiling them.

> After boiling eggs, crack each shell and put them in a pan of cold water to which salt has been added. The shells will then slip off easily.

> To soften eggs that have been boiled too long, put them in a basin of water for half a minute. This not only will soften the eggs but will improve their flavor.

☐ DEVILED: Scoop out the yolks of hard-boiled eggs; mash with sour cream, mustard and finely chopped sweet pickle and replace in hard-boiled whites.

> Mash American blue cheese into your favorite deviled-egg filling, spoon hot cream-of-mushroom soup over eggs and serve with toast.

> In preparing deviled eggs, mix a little anchovy paste in the egg-yolk filling.

> Try adding a dash of garlic salt.

> Add a few teaspoons of juice from a jar of olives.

☐ FRIED: Top fried eggs and bacon with some grated Parmesan cheese.

> Fry ham and eggs in garlic butter.

> Serve fried eggs with a sauce of browned butter, vinegar and capers.

> When frying salami and eggs, do not add butter, as enough grease melts from the meat.

> Soak matzohs in eggs, add garlic and salt and fry.

> When the whites of frying eggs are half set, baste the

yolk with butter from the skillet—and enhance with one tea-spoon of white wine and one teaspoon of chives.

> Fold flat fried eggs in half and serve with honey topping.

> Dice onions in oil and sauté on low flame. Then try sunny-side eggs right on top. Add pepper and parsley to onions.

> Try covered-skillet method for frying eggs. Lightly grease skillet, break eggs into it and cook covered for five minutes. Use lowest possible heat.

> Add a little ground black pepper on top and cover with the lid—after adding a few slices of mozzarella cheese.

> Fried eggs will not "pop" and will taste better if you add a little cornstarch to the hot grease before dropping in the eggs.

☐ O M E L E T S : Mix a little ginger root and add it to an omelet.

> Dice a boiled potato, spice with garlic and fry in a pan. Then pour egg mix for a "peasant omelet."

> Stir cooked zucchini and sautéed onion into omelet mix.

> Eggs taste delicious mixed with cream (one tablespoon per egg), minced onion and a small amount of chili sauce. Beat briskly, then cook slowly till the eggs are set.

> Sliced bananas or raisins make a good omelet filling.

> Serve an omelet made pancake style with applesauce. Cook the eggs, spread on applesauce, then fold the eggs like an apple turnover and heat.

> Oyster omelet: First cook oysters, and then add to scram-bled eggs and fry in heavy cream.

> Try using chili con carne as a stuffing.

> Add cooked peas, asparagus and mushrooms to omelet.

> Add ¼ cup each of drained Chinese bean sprouts and crisp bacon crumbs to every three eggs in the basic recipe.

> Just spread deviled ham on the cooked eggs before folding and turning the omelet.

> Add leftover canned string beans to fried bacon, then mix with eggs.

> Whip heavy cream and mushrooms in with the eggs. Heavy cream makes a thick omelet.

> "Hoppel-poppel"—an omelet with sliced frankfurters, mushrooms and onions.

> Add fried tomatoes before turning omelet.

> Add finely chopped peppers to omelet and sauté in tomato juice seasoned with salt and pepper.

> Add capers and anchovies just before eggs begin settling.

> Make an omelet with sliced chicken and top with grated cheese for a late-supper treat.

> Never make an omelet of more than four eggs. Make two omelets if necessary.

> Whole cranberry sauce mixed with chopped raw onion and horseradish makes a tangy filling or topping for an omelet.

> If you want to make the kind of fluffy omelets you get in restaurants, add a pinch of powdered sugar or cornstarch to the egg mix—keeps it from collapsing.

> Add a small amount of water to eggs instead of milk or cream. Water tends to make an omelet more tender (it retards coagulation of the yolks), while milk or cream tends to make it tougher. Also, be sure eggs are not cold; take them from the refrigerator at least ½ hour before using.

> Two tips for the fluffiest omelet: 1) Separate eggs, beat whites till fluffy, then fold into beaten yolks. 2) Pop finished omelet into a 350-degree oven for about 2 minutes and it will be fluffy as a French soufflé.

> The butter temperature is important. The eggs shouldn't be poured into the skillet until the butter bubbles and turns slightly brown.

☐ P O A C H E D :   Top poached eggs with grated cheese.

> Serve chilled poached eggs on hot toast with a slice of Nova Scotia salmon for Sunday brunch.

> Use fresh cooked artichoke hearts as the foundation of eggs Benedict instead of English muffins.

> Substitute sautéed oysters for the eggs in eggs Benedict recipe. Delicious oysters Benedict.

> Try spinach sauce instead of hollandaise on eggs Benedict. Add a tablespoon of flour to a can of spinach soup and stir constantly till thick.

> Instead of ham in eggs Benedict, place lobster chunks on toasted English muffins. Top with eggs and hollandaise.

> Poach eggs and put each on a circle of buttered toast. Then top with hot curry sauce.

> Try beer, meat stock, consommé, tomato juice, wine or any other smooth liquid for poaching.

> Use an ordinary pan without a poacher by adding two tablespoons of vinegar to the water before it is brought to a boil. With the flame low, break each egg into a saucer and slide into pan. Vinegar keeps the eggs whole. If you have no vinegar, a drop of lemon juice also does the job.

☐ S C R A M B L E D : Add one slice of diced American cheese to two eggs and scramble.

> Use sour cream as a garnish on scrambled eggs.

> Make greaseless, fluffy scrambled eggs by frying them in milk instead of butter or oil. Heavy cream is even better.

> Try cooked rice and crab meat flakes in scrambled eggs; flaked crab meat and sliced scallions also combine well.

> Flake freshly cooked smoked haddock into scrambled eggs.

> Add chunks or cubes of pineapple, lightly seasoned with basil, to eggs and top with melted cheese.

> Try whipping eggs with pineapple juice or a little tomato juice instead of milk.

> Try grating orange rind into eggs before scrambling.

> Stir in a tablespoon of sherry before cooking.

> Crumble crackers and chopped nuts into eggs before cooking.

> Try a dash of oregano, mustard or Tabasco.

> Beat two eggs, add a dash of milk and a tablespoon of grenadine.

> Add ½ cup kernel corn and fried onions to scrambled eggs.

> Mix tomatoes chopped with cream cheese bits into the eggs.

> Cut up ½ can of mushrooms, brown lightly in butter and add to egg mix.

> Sauté sliced mushrooms and thin strips of onions in butter and use as topping for scrambled eggs.

> Scrambled eggs on fried tomato slices with hot canned mushroom soup as a sauce turn a commonplace snack into an interesting and tasty dish.

> In making scrambled eggs for sandwiches, add a teaspoon of bread crumbs. It prevents eggs from being too moist and makes them easier to spread on bread.

> Prevent overcooking by removing the pan from the flame after one minute, but continue stirring until the eggs are the right consistency.

□ GENERAL TIPS:

> Dishes in which eggs have been served will wash more easily if a small amount of salt is added as they soak.

> When beating egg whites, be sure to use an enamel, stainless steel, glass or porcelain bowl. Never use aluminum, because eggs darken aluminum.

> Egg whites beat up quicker and higher if a tiny pinch of salt is added and they are allowed to stand until they are of room temperature before beating.

> Never wash eggs until it is time to cook them. Water tends to rinse away the protective covering that keeps air from penetrating.

> If short one egg in a recipe, substitute one teaspoon of cornstarch. It's an almost perfect replacement.

FISH

☐ B A K I N G : Cut head off fish only after baking. If cut before, the cut end dries and toughens. Leaving the head on during baking seals in flavor and juices and shortens cooking time.

> When baking fish, pour minestrone soup and grated cheese over it before placing in oven, and let it all simmer together until done.

> Add chopped cashew nuts or almonds to baked-fish stuffing.

☐ B R O I L I N G : Add finely diced celery to hot tomato bouillon, then pour over a broiled fish.

> The classic way to enhance broiled fish is to baste it with a white dinner wine.

> Broil fish in a liquid to keep it from drying.

> Slice tomatoes over fish before broiling.

> To keep fish intact while broiling, it is best not to try to turn it, but to brown only the top crust. It is also a good idea to broil it right in an ovenproof serving dish.

> Sprinkle grated cheddar cheese over broiled fish, or melt a slice of cheddar cheese over broiled halibut.

> Pour carrot juice over fish before broiling.

> Sauté bread crumbs in butter, add a sprinkling of oregano and spoon over fish before broiling.

> Place lemon slices on fish when broiling for less fishy taste.

> Add a touch of dill, salt and lemon juice to fish before broiling, and no seasoning will be needed when finished.

> Use olive oil as a sauce on fish before broiling.

> Broil grapes along with fish.

> Add thin slivers of preserved ginger to basting sauce.

☐ BUYING : Make sure scales adhere tightly to skin and are colorful and shiny; the gills should be red or pinkish, never gray.

> The eyes of fresh fish are bright, clear, full, transparent and somewhat protruding. The eyes of stale fish often are cloudy or pink and somewhat sunken.

> "Fishy" odor associated with fish develops only as fish is held. When bought, it should not be disagreeably strong.

☐ CLAMS : When you're buying clams live in the shell, if the shell is open it should close tightly when tapped. Discard any clams that remain open.

> Clams to be cooked whole should be small. Littleneck clams are ideal. The larger varieties tend to become rubbery when cooked.

> Clams will be much easier to open if boiling water is poured over them beforehand.

> For Italian-flavored steamed clams, add garlic, parsley and a bit of olive oil to the water.

☐ COD : Try codfish baked in vegetable soup.

> Douse codfish balls in freshly squeezed orange juice before putting them in the oven.

☐ FRYING: Dip any type fish in salted milk before frying for improved flavor.

> Wipe fish dry before frying, then add butter.

> When frying fish, drop 3 or 4 pieces of celery, about an inch long, into skillet. This will eliminate odor and does not affect taste.

> To get a fluffy crust on small fried fish, first dip them in milk and then roll in flour.

> When frying fish and shellfish, be sure to remove from pan as soon as it flakes easily with a fork.

☐ FILLETS: Top fillet of sole with a tablespoon of heavy cream and a sprinkling of grated Parmesan cheese before baking.

> Bake fillet of sole in tomato stock.

> Season fillet of sole by placing in grape juice for an hour prior to cooking.

> Poach a fillet of sole in apple brandy.

> Fry fillet of flounder in anchovy butter.

> Dip fillets in buttermilk and then in seasoned bread crumbs before frying.

> Cover fish fillets with cream of celery soup, top with bread crumbs and bake for 15 minutes.

> Make a sauce for fish fillet by blending a little minced onion with equal parts of blue cheese and sour cream.

> For a Southern-style dish, heat a mixture of catsup and chili sauce, seasoned with red peppers, and serve with fried fish fillets.

> Cover fish fillets with a mushroom sauce, top with buttered bread crumbs, and bake in a moderate oven until the fish are done.

> When preparing fish, cut fillets into serving pieces *before* cooking. It is easier to cut and saves cooking time.

> Fish fillets that must wait a day before being cooked should be rubbed with lemon juice and salt to prevent a fishy odor being absorbed by other food.

> Fillet of flounder a little too fishy? Soak in milk overnight; also improves the flavor of the fish.

☐ LOBSTER: Broiled: Add some minced clams with the natural clam juices, and let them simmer with the lobster.

> Boiled: Try dropping a bouillon cube in the pot in which lobster is boiling.

> Tails: When boiling lobster tails, add salt and a dash of lemon to the water to help remove any gritty particles.

> Slit lobster tails down center and stuff with bread crumbs before baking.

> Roll lobster tails in bread crumbs and deep fry for 2 minutes.

> Put a dash of celery salt into the water when boiling lobster tails.

> When you slit and broil a lobster, put the claws on the tail so the tail won't curl up.

> Eliminate the smell from boiling lobster by dripping vanilla extract into the water. It won't change the lobster taste.

> Steam a lobster before broiling and it will retain its juices.

> To get more flavor from a lobster, bake instead of broiling it. The intense heat of a broiler dries the meat.

> Precook frozen lobster tails in salted water about five minutes before broiling. But simmer—don't boil—the tails.

> Lobster tails remain fresh longer if the meat is taken from the shell and its outer membrane removed, then returned to the shell before refrigerating.

> Cooked lobsters should be used within 18 hours. An excellent cooking test is straightening out the tail of the lobster;

if the tail springs back quickly, the lobster was alive when put to cook.

> The red findings inside a lobster are the coral, found in the female. Good to eat if you like it; more useful, however, to color the mayonnaise that some like on the meat.

> Add garlic powder and onion powder to melted butter for lobster dipping.

> Add mayonnaise to melted butter when serving lobster. Serve the lobster in chunks in hot coconut milk that has been seasoned with salt and Tabasco.

> Add a half teaspoon of olive oil and a pinch of celery salt to the melted butter.

☐ O Y S T E R S :   Fried oysters gain more taste if mixed with a teaspoonful of celery salt before rolling and frying.

> Dip raw oysters in melted butter, roll in a mixture of half bread crumbs and half Parmesan cheese, and broil.

> Instead of drowning oysters in cocktail sauce, pour on a bit of wine vinegar and a sprinkling of freshly ground black pepper.

> Add a small can of button mushrooms or whole-kernel corn to oyster stew.

> P R E P A R A T I O N :   Frozen fish need not be thawed unless it is to be fried, breaded or stuffed.

> If using a hardwood plank for fish, place it in a cold oven so that it will heat while you're preheating the oven.

> Fish aren't slippery if fingers are first dipped in salt.

> Rub melted butter down the back of fish to be cooked and the bones can be easily removed after cooking.

> Turn off the cooking fire *sooner* than seems necessary. Fish continue cooking as long as they are warm, so time should be measured from the moment heat is applied until fish are on plate. Most seafood dinners are ruined because they are *over-cooked.*

> Never coat fish heavily with crumbs, cornmeal, or heavy batter; heavy coating masks the natural flavor.

> To prepare barbecue fish and prevent it from sticking to the grate, use a layer of aluminum foil.

> If fish is extremely oily, soak it in milk for an hour before baking.

> When preparing frozen raw shrimp, soak in lemon juice after they're completely thawed and let stand for 10 minutes.

☐ REFRIGERATION: Always refrigerate fish as quickly as possible after bringing it home. Never defrost frozen fish and then refreeze. If possible, defrost fish in a refrigerator before using it or, in an emergency, immerse in cold water.

> When keeping fish in the refrigerator, place crushed ice under the fish—it keeps it fresh and moist.

☐ SALMON: Before broiling salmon steak, coat it with curry mayonnaise.

> Salmon will turn white if thrown right into boiling water. Immerse it before boiling the water.

> Try cucumber slices with baked salmon steaks.

> When broiling salmon steaks, pour dry vermouth around them in the pan.

> Baste salmon with lemon juice and sprinkle lightly with brown sugar.

☐ SAUCES, GARNISHES: Mix white wine with cocktail sauce for seafood topping.

> Mix butter, paprika and lemon juice and melt until foamy.

> Add chopped chives and capers to mayonnaise.

> Try combining 1½ cups of sour cream with ½ cup of crumbled Roquefort cheese for shrimp-cocktail dressing.

> For a lobster sauce, mix a little garlic spread with butter.

> As a side dish for fish, try grilled bananas or bananas fried in butter.

> Use only tart fresh fruit when the recipe for fish or shell-fish calls for it—never sweetened canned fruits of any kind.

> Garnish fish with onion rings that have been marinated in French dressing.

> Pour melted butter on top of fried fish for a softer taste.

> Baste broiled fish with a mixture of chives and horse-radish.

> Make tartar sauce with mayonnaise, finely chopped pickles, chives and parsley.

> Baste fish with a combination of barbecue sauce with pineapple chunks.

☐ SAUTÉING: Sauté fish in bouillon; when done, sprinkle with Parmesan cheese.

> Sauté fish in butter to which dill, capers and tarragon have been added.

> When sautéing fish, use a large enough pan so that fish won't be crowded; otherwise, they will steam and not acquire a golden-brown color.

> Use a small amount of Chablis wine to sauté fresh sole, and add a dash of lemon sauce when serving.

> Sauté fish in sour cream and minced onions, then top with chopped shrimp.

☐ SCALLOPS: For a main dish, serve broiled scallops in pea soup.

> Dip scallops in wheat germ (healthiest of all foods, it is said) and fry to golden brown.

> Add a teaspoon of chili sauce to sour cream and serve with fried scallops.

☐ SHRIMP: Add a tablespoon of lemon juice or a few drops of vinegar to the water when boiling shrimp.

> Boil shrimp, place in pan and top with mushroom sauce, then fry all together.

> Include pieces of peaches and apple slices in shrimp Creole.

> Make shrimp curry with chopped apples, or add some applesauce to the curry before serving.

> Dip shrimp in honey and bread crumbs and then deep-fry.

> Mix fried shrimp and fried rice and sprinkle with crushed pineapple.

> Dip fried shrimp in heated applesauce.

> Try dipping shrimp in buttermilk before flouring, then dry.

> Mix the batter with a generous amount of egg. The eggs bring out the crispness of the breading and make it fluffy and light.

> Here's a fish dish prepared in a hurry: Heat some canned shrimp in white wine, add a teaspoon of curry and serve in a ring of Minute Rice.

> Shrimp and cucumber are a pleasant pair; serve them with a mayonnaise dressing.

> Mix cooked baby shrimp with creamed cauliflower.

> Wrap butterfly shrimp in mint leaves before cooking.

> Try butterfly shrimp with a cup of crushed pineapple mixed with a spoonful of tartar sauce.

> Try adding the white of finely chopped hard-boiled eggs to shrimp sauce.

> Dip each shrimp in a sauce of ⅓ each of lemon juice, red wine, and water.

> Use mayonnaise mixed with a sprinkling of dry mustard as a sauce for shrimp or crabmeat.

> Sauté shrimp in butter, add white wine, and allow to simmer for a few minutes.

> Sauté garlic and onions in oil and pour over a shrimp dish.

> One pound of fresh shrimp, when cooked and peeled, yields ½ pound.

> The size of shrimp does not affect their quality.

> Canned shrimp can lose their "canned taste." Just soak them in two tablespoons of vinegar and a teaspoonful of sherry for 15 minutes.

> A toothpick will clean shrimp quickly. Slip toothpick under fine black thread along the neck of the shrimp and lift it off in one piece. Using a knife often spoils the shape of the shellfish.

□ STEAMING: Steam a whole fish in the oven. Place the fish on a rack in a roasting pan; add hot water, but don't have it touch the fish. Cover pan and steam until fish flakes easily. Use moderate oven heat.

□ TUNA: Mix chopped onions and Roquefort cheese with tuna fish.

> Add grated lemon or lime peel to creamed tuna or salmon.

> Mix instant minced onions with tuna fish.

> Tuna Benedict: Place drained, canned tuna on a toasted English muffin, and serve with hollandaise sauce.

> Make a tuna fish omelet, including some chunks of celery in the mix.

> When mixing dressing for tuna, use a raw beaten egg with a drop of vinegar instead of mayonnaise.

> Cover tuna casserole with Chinese egg noodles or chopped peanuts instead of potato chips. Or add sautéed green peppers to tuna casserole. Or, mix Chinese noodles and chunks of pineapple in a tuna fish casserole.

□ AND SOME OTHER THINGS: Add fresh chopped dill to marinated herring.

> "Sauce" crab meat with jellied consommé.

> Serve flounder cooked and broken into small pieces as a regular seafood cocktail.

> Brush striped sea bass with a light coat of fresh clam juice before cooking.

> Serve grapefruit and orange slices with seafood.

> To get fish browned, sprinkle generously with paprika before cooking.

> Use crushed salted crackers instead of prepared crumbs for breading fish.

> Use butter generously when cooking fish. Butter brings out best flavor of all fish.

> You don't have the fish stock called for in a recipe? Substitute bottled clam juice.

> Place hot fish sticks over a bed of cheese slices.

> Add a few peppercorns to the water when poaching fish.

FRUIT

☐ APPLES: When making stewed apples, start cooking apples with boiling water, not cold water, and then the apples will not stick to the cooking utensil.

> Save time and waste in peeling apples: First cut them in half, then in quarters; cut out core; then peel.

> Brown apple wedges in butter, sprinkle with cinnamon and top with 1 cup dry white wine.

> Apples recommended for baking: Northern Spy, Rome Beauty, Tompkins King, Stayman Winesap, Jonathan, and Yellow Newton.

> Cover the pan in which apples are baking; the steam held in by the cover helps the fruit to cook fast and evenly.

> Try stuffed baked apples with honey, dates and figs.

> Cover apples with maple syrup before serving.

> A stick of peppermint candy tucked inside an apple before baking gives a new taste.

> Try a dash of sherry over a baked apple.

> Apples should be slit with a knife in three or four places before baking. The skins will then not wrinkle while in oven.

> Stir a little lemon juice and nutmeg into applesauce.

> Try adding a stick of whole cinnamon (about 2 inches long) when cooking half a dozen apples for applesauce. Sugar should be added to sauce after apples are cooked.

> Applesauce tinted a pale green makes an unusual summer treat. Just add a few drops of mint extract to each serving. Applesauce may also be flavored with fresh mint leaves.

> Serve applesauce with chopped candied ginger and nutmeg.

> Add grapefruit slices to applesauce after it has been cooked and chilled.

> Add a couple of tablespoons of port wine to applesauce and heat.

☐ B A N A N A S :   Bake bananas with brown sugar and a little lemon juice.

> Slice bananas and top with shredded coconut and chocolate sauce.

> Chill sliced bananas in grape juice.

> Before adding sliced bananas to fruit salad, sprinkle lemon juice over them to prevent discoloration.

> Pour champagne over sliced bananas.

> Cover 12 bananas (for 12 people) with 1 cup of beer,

½ cup of brown sugar and a 6-ounce can of concentrated orange juice. Bake and serve.

> Try wrapping bananas in bacon strips and broiling.

> Fry bananas till brown in chafing dish; sprinkle with brown sugar and cinnamon and add ¼ cup of rum (for each 3 bananas) and ignite.

> Cut bananas in short lengths to fit an egg slicer, and you'll have your bananas cut in uniform sections.

> Green bananas can be ripened quickly if put in a paper bag with a wad of wet paper toweling and left on the kitchen shelf.

> Keep ripe bananas for later use by peeling them and standing upright in a tightly capped Mason jar in refrigerator. This will keep them fresh for a week or so.

☐ STRAWBERRIES: Add a dash of salt, a dash of pepper and a dash or two of gin to fresh strawberries.

> Place layers of strawberries, sour cream and brown sugar in a bowl and refrigerate for a few hours. The brown sugar dissolves and makes a sauce. Fresh strawberries may also be sprinkled with brown sugar and sour cream just before serving.

> Pour orange juice over strawberries, then add two tablespoons of rum.

> Strawberries should not be washed, hulled, sliced or sweetened until a few hours before serving.

☐ GRAPEFRUIT: Sprinkle pineapple juice over grapefruit chunks.

> Stir together equal parts of honey and dark rum as a topping for grapefruit.

☐ ORANGES: Soak fresh orange slices in dry white wine spiced with cloves and cinnamon; chill and serve.

> Slice navel oranges and cook gently in simple syrup.

☐ L E M O N S : Before squeezing lemons and oranges, grate the rind and use as flavoring for cakes, puddings, pies, etc.

> Keep lemons for months by putting them into sterilized canning jars; cover with cold water, adjust rubber rings and screw covers down tightly. Not only will they stay fresh, but they will yield more juice than when first bought.

> When grating lemon or orange rind, be sure not to grate too deeply. The colored part of the rind gives the flavor, while the white part causes food to taste bitter.

> Before removing skins from grapefruit, lemons or oranges, pour boiling water over them and let stand 5–10 minutes. The white part will peel off with the skin, leaving fruit clean for salads.

☐ C O C O N U T : A hard-to-crack coconut can be softened by steaming in a cloth over boiling water.

> If unused shredded coconut has become dry and hard, place it in a large strainer and steam over a pan of boiling water. It will become moist and fresh in a few minutes.

☐ M E L O N : Cut a cantaloupe into balls and chunks, drizzle with orange juice, toss with flaked coconut and chill.

> Dip bite-sized squares of cantaloupe into lemon juice and then into brown sugar.

> Fill halves of cantaloupes with green grapes, raspberries, and banana slices. Top with cottage cheese.

> Let a few drops of brandy soak into a slice of honeydew, chill and serve.

> Sprinkle cinnamon lightly on chilled honeydew.

> Honeydew, cantaloupe, watermelon or any round melon tastes delicious if round incisions are made about the stem and half a pint of dry sherry is poured inside the melon. The melon should then be iced for a day.

> Soak cold melon with port wine.

> Buy only large watermelons, or pieces of same, because they have a much higher proportion of flesh to rind than smaller ones.

> A ripe melon should give off fragrance and when shaken should echo the sound of seeds rattling inside.

> When you cut a melon and find it's not ripe, wrap it in aluminum foil and leave at room temperature to ripen without discoloring.

> In choosing a cantaloupe, thick, close netting on the rind indicates best quality.

> The best watermelon to buy is the one with the green and white strips down the outer skin. It is the sweetest and ripest.

> Store melons on the refrigerator's top shelf. It's better for them and the other food.

> Chill melons in paper bags to prevent their odor from spreading throughout the refrigerator.

☐ MIXED FRUITS: Try canned cranberries and applesauce, well chilled, served with a slab of American cheese.

> Mix crushed pineapple with small amount of rum, then pour over peeled orange sections.

> Soak dried fruit overnight in cranberry sauce. There's no need for cooking or adding sugar.

> Chilled canned pineapple chunks are wonderfully refreshing when they are teamed with fresh grapefruit sections.

> Add a dash of raw honey and lemon juice to a fruit cup. (Honey may be heated beforehand in cold weather.)

> Spice canned fruit cocktail gently with a stick of cinnamon and whole cloves. Simmer fruits and spices together about five minutes and chill several hours.

> Top small portions of cream cheese with fruit salad.

> Top sliced fresh fruit with yogurt and honey.

> Cook sliced apples and peaches with a little cinnamon

and sugar. When done, let it cool off and then top with walnuts and whipped cream.

> Sprinkle tiny pieces of blue cheese on fresh fruit salad.

☐ P E A C H E S : Fill cavities of halved peaches with confectioner's sugar, ground almonds and a dash of rum and bake.

> Stew peaches with brown sugar, a dash of cinnamon and a little brandy. Slice them, pour red wine over and crumble a macaroon on top. For gourmets: Prick a peeled whole peach in several places, place in wineglass and pour champagne over. The peach will turn—and maybe your head will, too.

> Try fresh peaches with orange juice and ½ glass of sweet white wine poured over them.

> Broil or bake drained canned peaches and pears. Fill with red or green jelly, and serve on meat platter.

> Spoon jam or jelly over peach halves and broil for three minutes.

> Heat canned cling peach halves slightly. Fill center with a spoonful of apple butter and a sprinkling of cinnamon. Serve as accompaniment for pork chops, roast loin of pork or baked ham. Hot canned cling peaches and meat pair up perfectly.

> To simplify peeling peaches, dip them into boiling water for a minute or two, then put them immediately under cool running water. The skin will virtually slip off.

☐ P E A R S : Add orange juice and pear syrup to canned pears and bake with a sprinkling of coconut.

> When preparing fresh pear halves for baking, remove the stem and the seeds. Place in baking dish, fill cavities with currant jelly and pour over them red wine diluted by ⅓ with water and flavored with ¼ teaspoon of cinnamon.

> Cover baked pears with a coating of stiffly beaten and sweetened egg white and return to the oven until brown.

> Serve pears with provolone cheese.

> Serve prosciutto ham with sliced pears instead of melon.

> Put pear halves together with cream cheese mixture and top with chocolate sauce.

☐ P I N E A P P L E : Garnish sliced fresh pineapple with chopped mint.

> Mix avocado cubes with fresh pineapple chunks.

> Dip pineapple chunks first into honey and then into shredded coconut.

> Mix crushed pineapple and crushed cranberries and serve with Southern-fried chicken.

> Top chilled pineapple with sour cream.

> For a side-dish delight, grill pineapple slices, brushing with butter and sprinkling with brown sugar.

> The heavier of two pineapples of equal size will be sweeter and juicier.

☐ P R U N E S : Pour boiling water over prunes to make them plump, 1 quart of water to 1 pound of prunes. Add orange and lemon slices. Let rest 24 hours or more. Serve prunes and fruit slices in their own rich juice with a generous pouring of light cream.

> Plump prunes by pouring 2 cups of hot coffee over them. Allow to cool, add a little apricot brandy and let stand 24 hours. Serve with a dab of sour cream.

☐ R A I S I N S : Dried raisins will keep fresh for a long, long time if stored in a covered jar in refrigerator.

> Raisins stuck together separate easily when steamed briefly over boiling water.

> When chopping raisins, rub a little butter on either side of the chopping knife and the work is more easily done.

☐ O T H E R   T H I N G S   A B O U T   F R U I T : Mix a small pinch of baking soda with cream before pouring over acid berries or fruits to prevent curdling.

> If stewed fruits are souring, add a pinch of baking soda and reboil for 5 minutes.

> Cooked fruits will have better flavor and natural sweetness if served while hot.

> A pinch of salt added to very sour fruits while cooking will greatly reduce the quantity of sugar needed to sweeten them.

> Fruits tend to spoil more rapidly when wet, so the washing should be done shortly before serving.

> Wash all fruit rapidly. If it is allowed to stand in water, considerable amounts of sugar and vitamins C and B dissolve out and are lost.

MEATS

☐ B A C O N : Sprinkle Canadian bacon liberally with brown sugar, cover with milk and bake at least 30 minutes in a moderate oven. Add a dash of sherry just before the bacon is done.

> Place separated bacon slices on wire rack in shallow baking pan. Bake in a hot oven for about 10 minutes without turning.

> When selecting bacon, look for meat with the reddest lean and the whitest, firmest fat.

> To ensure dryness and crispness, keep turning the bacon in the pan—about 10 times—and then drain it on paper towels.

> To separate cold slices of bacon that are stuck together, put the quantity you want to cook in a skillet. As soon as it begins to heat, separate the strips.

> When frying bacon, save time by crisscrossing the slices and turning them all at once with a pancake turner; also saves time because more goes into the pan at once.

> The flavor and aroma of bacon fade after one week in the refrigerator.

☐ CORNED BEEF : Don't boil corned beef, simmer it.

> Add cabbage and potatoes about ½ hour before meat is finished cooking.

> Spice corned-beef hash by adding sharp cheddar cheese.

☐ BRISKET : Add cloves to boiled beef brisket.

> When boiling brisket of beef, add a sliced onion and a rib of celery with the leaves.

☐ STROGANOFF : Add ½ cup of sherry to each 2 pounds of sirloin for beef Stroganoff.

> You can simulate Stroganoff by browning chopped beef and adding sautéed sliced onions, mushrooms and sour cream.

> Make beef Stroganoff with cocktail-size hamburgers instead of slices of beef.

☐ SAUERBRATEN : Add a can of beer to Sauerbraten along with vinegar.

> The best Sauerbraten is made with prime eye-round steak marinated for four weeks in red wine.

☐ FRANKFURTERS : Slash frankfurters in half and insert slivers of Swiss cheese; broil until cheese melts.

> Melt American cheese atop grilled frankfurters.

> Cut franks into pieces, thread alternately on skewers with pineapple chunks and green pepper slices, brush with salad oil and grill over coals.

> Use diced apples and sauerkraut as a base for grilled franks.

> Slit frankfurters and fill crevices with well-seasoned cold mashed potatoes, then grill.

> For juicier hot dogs, steam them in beer.

> Add chunks of franks to green pepper and sautéed onions. Add tomatoes, with a little of their juice, and heat till the franks are cooked.

> Frankfurters retain flavor when boiled if dropped into boiling water and covered.

> To retain flavor and keep franks from bursting, cook with only enough water to cover the franks. Bring water to a boil, add the franks, remove the pan from heat, cover and let stand for about 8 minutes.

☐ H A M : A generous slice of Virginia ham topped with asparagus and hollandaise sauce makes a wonderful main course for either luncheon or dinner.

> To add flavor to honey-cured ham, garnish with maraschino cherries and white asparagus tips in a vinaigrette sauce. Serve cold, sliced very thin.

> Add a tablespoon of molasses to the water when boiling ham.

> Add cooked chunks of ham to a casserole and top with crushed pineapple.

> Mix diced ham and creamed peas; spoon over toast or patty shells.

> Fry a sliced banana with a slice of ham, turning both to brown evenly.

> Spread deviled ham and pickle relish on toast, top with slices of cheddar cheese and broil.

> Top muffin halves with ham, pineapple slices and grated cheese and broil.

> When reheating leftover ham slices, put in a shallow pan and pour in rosé wine.

> Ham too salty? Cook (or bake) as usual; about 1½ hours before it is done, drain all of the juices and pour a small bottle of ginger ale over the ham and continue to bake till done. Use same juice to make gravy.

> Cover ham steak with apricots and pour apricot juice over the meat before baking for one hour.

> Add orange juice to butter in pan when frying ham steak.

> When broiling ham steak, baste it with pineapple or orange juice to cut the grease and add flavor.

> Mix 1 cup of honey with ½ cup of sherry and glaze.

> Spread apple jelly over ham.

> Make a paste of brown sugar, dry mustard and wine to glaze ham.

> While grilling ham steak, baste with 1 cup pineapple juice, ½ cup brown sugar, ¼ cup vinegar and 2 teaspoons dry mustard.

> Brush melted butter blended with cinnamon and raisins over ham steak 10 minutes before serving.

> Virginia ham should be wrapped in heavy, clean coarse cloth or paraffin paper when not being used, and put in a cool place.

> For instant sugar-cured ham and bacon, add 2 tablespoons of New Orleans molasses to 1 cup of water in a shallow receptacle. Placed sliced ham or bacon in this solution and let stand for an hour or two. Drain and cook.

> Leave the rind on ham while cooking. It will cook faster and shrink less.

☐ HAMBURGER :   Mix hamburger with crumbled ginger snaps.

> Pretzels, finely ground, make an excellent filler for hamburgers or meat loaf.

> Fill center of each burger with 2 teaspoons crumbled Roquefort cheese and ½ teaspoon olive oil. After filling is sealed in, place under fire and broil.

> Add cheese-crecker crumbs to the chopped meat.

> Combine ground beef with grated cheddar cheese, minced garlic, white wine and salt and pepper to taste.

> Add 1 raw egg and 2 crumbled soda crackers to each 2 pounds of chopped meat.

> When fixing chopped steak, mix 4 slices of wet white bread and 1 egg with each 2 pounds of meat.

> Top hamburger with broiled pineapple and a fried banana cooked with rum sauce, instead of French fries.

> Chop up sliced canned pineapple and mix it in with the ground beef.

> Fry hamburgers in lemon juice.

> Crush a couple of slices of pear into chopped meat to make it moist and fluffy.

> Mix slivers of lemon rind and dill weed into hamburgers.

> Spread hamburgers with 2 tablespoons of butter and 1 tablespoon of prepared mustard.

> Add crushed garlic to chopped steak and pan-fry in olive oil.

> Try adding oregano, thyme, tarragon and fresh sliced mushrooms. Baste regularly with ½ cup of water and drippings in a moderate oven.

> Try a horseradish and sour cream sauce on hamburgers.

> For each 2 hamburgers mix in 1½ tablespoons of bourbon.

> Mix hamburger meat with port wine (1 jigger to 1 pound of meat), form into patties, top with blue cheese and broil.

> Organ meats such as liver, heart, etc., added to chopped steak make tastier hamburgers.

> Mix some ground Canadian bacon in with chopped meat before barbecuing.

> Add ½ cup of cream to each 2 pounds of chopped meat for hamburgers or meat loaf.

> Blend chives with sour cream and spoon over hot hamburgers.

> Before adding crumbs to chopped meat, soak first in milk.

> Try chopped peanuts or almonds mixed in with ground hamburger meat.

> Combine peanut butter with hamburgers and onions.

> Add crumbled walnuts and raisins to hamburgers.

> Marinate tomato slices in garlic oil; place on chopped steak or hamburger before broiling.

Mix a handful of dehydrated onion-soup flakes to ½ pound of chopped meat.

> Add a raw egg and fried onions to a pound of raw chopped meat.

> Mix 1 pound of ground beef with 1½ cups of chopped onions, 1½ cups of chopped celery, 1 teaspoon of salt, pepper (to taste), 1 can condensed tomato soup and 1½ teaspoons of barbecue sauce. Shape into patties and cook.

> Marinate chopped onions in garlic butter and place in meat before grilling.

> Mix chopped pimentos and celery into chopped meat before broiling.

> Simmer mushrooms in sherry until they darken slightly. Then top hamburgers with them in last few minutes of broiling.

> Combine canned cream of mushroom soup with a little milk, chopped olives and a dash of lemon juice for hamburger sauce.

> Instead of onion with hamburgers, try sliced radish.

> Weigh the meat and add about 25 percent of that weight in cold water from the tap. Makes hamburgers juicier and tastier.

> Use grated raw potato when mixing hamburgers. Stretches the portions and makes the meat very juicy.

> Stretch hamburgers for a crowd by adding ¾ cup of oats to 1½ pounds ground beef. Combine thoroughly with onion,

seasoning, 1 cup tomato juice; shape and chill until ready to use.

> Brush the surface of broiled hamburgers with butter to give a brown and crusty look.

> When storing hamburger meat in refrigerator, flatten it out to about ¼-inch thickness to keep it pink and fresh-looking. Putting it away in lump form cuts off the air supply and discolors the inside meat.

> To thaw frozen chopped meat quickly, heat in a double boiler with a smidgen of water and a bouillon cube.

> Sprinkle salt on bottom of pan before frying hamburgers to keep them from sticking to the pan.

> Ground beef stored in home freezer should be used within 2 or 3 months. Beef roasts and steak will hold their quality for 8 to 12 months.

☐ L A M B : Place chops in a glass of red wine that has a clove of garlic added to it before broiling.

> Crumble Roquefort cheese and sprinkle over loin lamb chops during last few minutes.

> Try shoulder lamb chops braised in orange juice.

> Sauté lamb chops in vinegar and brown sugar, then place orange slices on them before baking.

> Brush lamb chops with garlic-flavored salad oil before broiling.

> Try simmering lamb chops in a mixture of water and onion soup mix.

> Soak lamb chunks in burgundy wine for eight hours and use for shish kebab. . . . Or, marinate cubes of lamb in vinegar, oil, lemon, oregano and onions for three days prior to broiling.

> Marinate in lemon juice and ginger before broiling.

> Give ground lamb a new flavor by adding a little mint.

> For lamb-burgers, season ground lamb, shape into patties

and broil, brushing with hot barbecue sauce. Serve on toasted split rolls.

> Add tomato puree as part of the liquid when cooking lamb stew.

> Baste lamb from time to time as it is cooking with fruit juices. Avoids gamy or over-lamby taste.

> Mutton becomes extra tasty if a cup of black coffee is poured over it a few minutes before it is done.

> Add ½ cup of claret to lamb dishes before simmering.

> When making lamb dishes, remember that lemon juice goes well with lamb, and that the spices and herbs to use are thyme, mint and cumin.

> Lamb leftovers: Pour a can of tomato sauce into skillet, season lightly with marjoram and rosemary, and simmer slices of lamb in the sauce.

> When broiling lamb (chops, etc.), smear crushed garlic and tomato paste over meat before placing under broiler.

> Baste a leg of lamb with a good red wine.

> Before roasting a leg of lamb, cut slits in the meat and insert garlic slivers.

> Puncture the shank end with a sharp knife; insert garlic buds deeply. In upper leg of lamb, make six deep incisions widely scattered into deep surface fat (avoid cutting into lean meat), and insert into each gash a bud of garlic. Thread the skewer and set over a hot fire for 30 minutes and during that time baste with a cup of dry white vermouth.

> Peach halves filled with chutney make a delicious accompaniment to roast lamb.

> Squeeze a fresh lemon over lamb before roasting; cuts the fat.

> Eliminate the usual odor of a lamb roast by covering it with bacon strips before placing in the oven.

> Pour molasses over the meat while it is roasting.

> Baste lamb with French dressing (about ⅓ cup for a 4-pound leg of lamb). French dressing is also good as a gravy.

> Always serve lamb very hot or very cold, since the fat hardens quickly and becomes unappetizing.

> To rid lamb or mutton of its strong taste, remove all skin and fatty tissues before cooking.

☐ LIVER: Marinate calf's liver in lemon juice for 30 minutes before sautéing.

> Sauté liver in lemon and butter and sprinkle chili sauce over it before broiling.

> Marinate calves liver for a day in a liquid of sherry, bay leaf and garlic, then fry lightly in olive oil.

> Before placing liver under fire, smear with oil, crushed garlic and a little Burgundy wine.

> Dip slices of liver in beaten egg and seasoned bread crumbs before frying with onion.

> Put calves-liver slices in sizzling skillet and turn them immediately to seal in juices; then cook in regular way.

> Cover liver with milk and let stand for 20 minutes before frying. The leftover milk may be used in the gravy. The liver will be much milder in flavor, and cheaper liver can be enjoyed as much as the most expensive cuts.

> After lightly sautéing calves liver, add a little white vinegar and cook one more minute.

> Add bits of bacon and raw carrot to chopped liver.

> Cover liver with slices of beefsteak tomatoes topped with onion slices and bacon. Cook in moderate oven.

> One sure way to spot good liver is to look for traces of fat in it. If the fat is yellowish, the liver is tough; if the fat is snow-white, you are getting the best.

> If you can crush raw liver just by touching it with the tip of a finger, it is of an extra-good quality.

> Liver spoils quickly, so make sure it is perfectly fresh when purchased. It should be cooked immediately.

> Calves liver should not be exposed to high heat, and never overcooked; the moment it is, it becomes tough.

> When pan-broiling liver, salt up the pan before adding the meat; it prevents it from sticking.

☐ M E A T B A L L S : Place a small piece of blue cheese inside a meatball.

> Serve meatballs with a sauce of paprika and sour cream.

> Add peach quarters and heated peach syrup to a meatball dish.

> Try meatballs in a sauce made with Burgundy wine.

> Cut raw meatballs in half and spread both halves with sharp French mustard before frying.

> To make light meatballs, add a pinch of cornstarch to the meat, or add one teaspoon of baking powder to the meat mixture before cooking.

☐ M E A T   L O A F : Cook meat loaf in a piecrust; no sticking, and easy to cut.

> Add softened saltines (6 for each pound of meat) and 2 tablespoons of milk, top with can of beef-stock vegetable soup, and bake.

> Meat loaf has more nutrition if you use quick-cooking rolled oats instead of bread crumbs.

> Crumble blue cheese into meat loaf.

> Add chopped, pitted prunes or prune juice to meat loaf.

> Top meat loaf with whole-cranberry sauce, or applesauce, before baking.

> Put slices of pineapple in bottom of pan, fill with meat loaf mixture and bake. Turn upside down and serve. Try this in individual muffin tins also.

> Add raisins, or chopped coconut pieces, or chopped and drained canned apricots (with extra salt) to meat mixture.

> Broil slices of grapefruit atop meat loaf.

> Spread bread with Worcestershire sauce before adding to mixture.

> Sage is a good flavoring for meat loaf made from half ground beef and half ground pork.

> Strips of bacon placed lengthwise in bottom of pan prevents meat loaf from sticking.

> Add a half pound each of ground pork and veal to a pound of ground beef for an old-fashioned meat-loaf mixture.

> Bake meat loaf in black bean soup with a spoonful of cooking sherry.

> Add a package of onion-soup mix.

> Make meat loaf in a ring mold, filling the center with rice cooked in tomato juice, mashed potatoes or potato salad.

> Add a grated potato to meat loaf instead of cracker crumbs; makes it moist.

> Make a salad of leftover meat loaf by cutting it up and adding to uncooked green peppers and lettuce.

> Blend in a cup of finely chopped fresh spinach.

> Serve meat loaf on a bed of lettuce decorated with fresh vegetables.

> Try macaroni shells in meat loaf instead of bread crumbs.

> Marinate a meat loaf in dry sauterne before baking in the oven.

☐ P O R K : Broil pork chops in ½ cup of onion soup. Cook slowly and use a small flame in oven.

> Fry pork chops dipped in milk and egg, then in crumbled potato chips.

> Soak pork chops in sweet-and-pungent sauce and bread crumbs, then bake.

> Brush melted butter and pineapple juice on broiled pork chops a few minutes before serving.

> Dip pork chops in sherry or red wine before breading.

> When broiling pork chops, add a few drops of Worcestershire sauce to a little melted butter and brush over surface of meat. Repeat when meat is turned.

> Brush pork chops with a thin film of molasses before baking or broiling.

> When broiled pork chops are brown, spread small chunks of banana along top of chops.

> Place plain buttered noodles on top of pork chops before broiling. Top with a pony of sherry when serving.

> Spoon sour cream over pork chops before baking for 30 minutes.

> Pan-broil pork chops until golden brown on each side, using a small amount of juice from canned mandarin oranges. Remove from pan and place in baking dish. Add mandarin orange slices and juice and top with pineapple slices. Bake for about 30 minutes.

> Sprinkle Parmesan cheese over pork chops before broiling.

> Garnish pork chops with a mixture of horseradish and applesauce.

> Baste pork with orange marmalade and mustard sauce.

> Use heated crushed pineapple instead of gravy for fried pork.

> Dip slices of pork into a cinnamon and orange-juice mixture before frying.

> Add pineapple and tomatoes when cooking boneless pork; allow flavor to blend.

> Combine sliced pork with green peppers and cubed pineapple; simmer in sweet-and-sour sauce.

> Insert hot English mustard into slices of pork when basting with plum sauce while roasting.

> To make roast loin of pork moist, baste with orange juice.

> Baste roasting pork with pineapple juice and brown sugar. Serve in thin slices.

> Use whole cranberry sauce mixed with mandarin orange segments as a garnish for roast pork.

> Make a tasty crust on slow-baking pork roast by sprinkling it with caraway seeds 15 minutes before serving and turning heat up to high.

> Dip roast pork servings in applesauce and lemon juice before eating.

> Make applesauce at the same time as pork roast. Put apple, sugar and spices in a separate covered casserole. Baking improves flavor.

> Baste spareribs with orange juice. Or, top with sauerkraut and boil.

> For tenderloin, slice the meat crosswise, flatten the slices, then roll them in seasoned flour. Fry in butter, browning first, then cover pan to finish cooking.

> Broil pork chops and make sure they are well done. Meat should look white when a small slit is made near the bone.

> Always remove as much fat as possible before cooking shoulder of pork; cut into chunks of about 1 by 2 inches and cook.

> Test pork roast by simply jabbing it with a fork. If juice comes out, the roast is ready; if blood appears, keep on cooking it.

> For crisp spareribs, first bake in a moderate oven, then singe under the broiler for the last few minutes of cooking.

> Stack pork chops together and stand them on their sides, turning them as a unit once or twice until the fat on the outside is browned. Separate the chops and finish frying. The pan is well greased by them and the chops won't stick.

☐ ROAST BEEF AND POT ROAST: Shred leftover roast beef, scramble with eggs and top with tomato sauce.

> Add bits of celery and green pepper to roast 15 minutes before serving. It's better than a shakerful of seasoning.

> Sear beef in a very hot (500-degree) oven before continuing roasting at moderate (350-degree) heat.

> A fine sauce for roast beef is horseradish added to applesauce.

> Rub down a roast to be cooked in the oven with currant jelly and it will have the taste of being cooked over a wood fire.

> Coat pot roast with 1½ cups brown sugar, 2½ tablespoons vinegar, and 1 teaspoon dry mustard.

> Make pot roast in the usual way. Then put all vegetables and gravy into a blender. Let run till it is a thick, creamy brown sauce, and pour over meat slices.

> When cooking a Yankee pot roast, add a few slices of bacon; also include tomato sauce in the gravy.

> Add cooked seedless grapes to the gravy for pot roast.

> Freeze pot roast or braised meats with gravy.

> To prevent pot roast from becoming dry, pierce meat in several places and brush olive oil into holes till oil penetrates into meat fibers.

> To pick the best in beef, see that there's plenty of "marbling" (veins of fat); avoid beef with a wet look. Dark red is the best color, and the fat should be white or pink-tinged.

> When making pot roast, serve it the next day. It is tastier and softer when reheated.

> If cut of roast beef is too large for serving needed, roast it almost raw in the center but enough for plenty of outside cuts. Then refrigerate for a second cooking.

> Try warming a rib roast by placing the roast fat-side up in a shallow pan; allow the ribs to hold the meat off the bottom of the pan.

> Brush a roast or other meat that isn't as tender as it should be with one tablespoon of vinegar, then cook as usual.

> When a roast is put into the oven, set a small foil pan partly filled with flour beside it; when the flour has browned, it's ready for flavorful-brown-gravy making.

> Let roast beef stand at room temperature for 12 hours before putting it into the oven; your roast will be tender.

> It takes about 10 minutes per pound longer to roast rolled rib roast than regular rib roast, as the rib bone acts as a heat conductor.

> Put a lettuce leaf against cut side of leftover roast and it will stay moist and rare.

☐ S A U S A G E S : When frying sausages, add lemon juice to the pan. The citrus acid absorbs heavy grease.

> Sprinkle sausages and sauerkraut with brown sugar before baking.

> Pierce hot Italian sausages in several places and brown. Then place in a saucepan of English ale or white wine and simmer for 30 minutes.

> Before frying sausages, roll them in flour to keep them from bursting.

☐ S T E A K S : Quickly dip steaks in warm milk and grated cheese before charcoal broiling.

> Pour a cupful of diced cheddar cheese over a cooking sirloin steak and let it melt. Or, baste steak with a sauce of blue cheese mixed with a little oil and lemon juice.

> Dip steaks into coconut milk before broiling, to keep juices in.

> First rub steak with slices of raw pineapple and then add pineapple to the broiling.

> Top meat with canned peach slices when broiling, then pour a teaspoon of the peach juice over the meat.

> Dip thin slices of flank steak in a marinade of soy sauce, olive oil and thyme; broil an hour later.

> When serving steak, brush with a light coating of the

following: 1 tablespoon of chopped parsley and the juice of
½ lemon added to ½ cup of soft butter.

> Marinate steak in garlic olive oil 8 hours before broiling.

> Spread chive butter atop a grilling steak.

> Dip the sirloin in a sauce of equal parts of butter, garlic
and catsup, and then broil until very well done.

> To get a better flavor and crust on a steak, put a clove
of garlic in a little olive oil, mix in ½ teaspoon of paprika and
let it stand for 5 minutes. Then, brush the steak with the mix
prior to broiling.

> Chop capers together with meat for tartar steak.

> After pan-broiling steak, sprinkle it with fresh black
pepper and smear with butter sauce.

> Before broiling steak, brush with brandy and pepper.

> Spread a tablespoon of peach brandy on each side of
steak before broiling.

> Add red wine and onion juice to melted butter for a
steak sauce.

> After taking steak from a hot skillet, rinse out the skillet
with cognac, which is then poured over the steak as a sauce.

> Marinate steaks in beer for a few hours before broiling.

> As steaks broil, pour about ½ cup claret wine over each
side.

> Braise sirloin tips with onions, and simmer for 3 hours
with dark beer and a few prunes.

> Add onion rings to paper-thin slices of meat and pan fry
in oil.

> Sauté filet mignon or other steaks in tomato juice before
broiling.

> Thread cubes of beef sirloin and fresh mushroom caps
alternately on a skewer. Brush with garlic-flavored salad oil
and broil. This dish is called sirloin brochettes.

> Use a garlic press to squeeze a few teaspoons of onion juice onto broiling steak.

> Dip steaks in a pan containing a cup of heated milk flavored with garlic, then broil.

> Serve thin slices of fillet over gravy-soaked toast.

> Brush steaks with a light coating of New Orleans molasses before broiling.

> To store broiling steaks, lay them flat on clean wrapping paper, or waxed paper, Saran Wrap or aluminum foil. Wrap loosely. Keep in refrigerator and use within 3 to 5 days. Keep frozen steaks until ready to broil, or thaw in refrigerator.

> To keep steaks from shrinking on barbecue spit, remove them from refrigerator and leave at room temperature for one hour before barbecuing.

> When broiling steak, put 1 cup of water in bottom of pan to prevent grease from burning on pan and to eliminate smoke.

> Wipe steak with cold damp cloth before broiling.

> If you can't break the habit of using a fork to turn steak, remember to stick it in the fat, not the meat.

> Never season steak prior to cooking, as it tends to make the outside tough and prevent even distribution of heat through the meat.

> When pan-broiling steak, preheat the skillet until almost red hot, then sprinkle an even layer of salt over skillet bottom. The steak will brown quickly.

> Try baking a steak wrapped in aluminum foil; juices stay sealed in.

> If a steak catches fire in the griddle or broiler, douse it with baking soda to put out the flame. It can still be eaten after being rinsed with hot water.

> To cut shrinkage, pour liquid (chicken broth, wine, water) over steak three or four times while cooking.

> When stuffing flank steak, roll meat up from long side.

This way the fibers can be cut through when the meat is carved.

> Rare steak: cook at 140 degrees F. The result should be a browned exterior with a slice that is a rose-red color with a narrow layer of gray at the outer rim. Medium steak: cook at 160 degrees F. The result should be a browned exterior with a pink slice with a wider gray layer at edge. Well-done steak: cook at 170 degrees F. The result should be a grayish interior with brown exterior, and no pink visible.

> Steaks thinner than an inch should be pan-broiled or fried. A thicker steak should be broiled in the oven, 3 inches from the flame.

> For a medium-rare 2-inch-thick steak, place it about 4 inches from high heat and broil 20 minutes on each side. This is for a steak taken directly from the refrigerator, not for one at room temperature.

> Cook a steak without drying it out by having heat not so intense that the meat sizzles and pops during all the broiling. Never cut or stick a fork into meat to see if it is properly cooked. Here's a guide for the time required to cook to taste:

	RARE	MEDIUM	WELL
1″	5 minutes	6 minutes	8 minutes
1½″	9 minutes	10 minutes	13 minutes
2″	16 minutes	18 minutes	21 minutes

☐ S T E W : Chop a little leftover ham fine and add to a beef stew.

> Add sauerkraut to beef stew.

> Sprinkle stew with caraway seeds.

> Make old-fashioned beef stew by gently cooking, *not* boiling, meat for two hours. Then add vegetables and simmer the stew an extra half hour. Remove bay leaf and garlic.

> Beef-stew ingredients are tomatoes, carrots, Italian beans and macaroni.

> When making beef stew, don't add tomatoes until it is almost done.

> Add a glass of red Burgundy wine when stew is done, and let simmer for 10 minutes before serving.

> Sprinkle poppy seeds on the noodles in goulash.

> Add a jigger of Irish whiskey while cooking Irish stew.

> Add matzoh balls to Irish lamb stew.

> Add cabbage to a lamb stew. Cut it in wedges and place on top of meat and other vegetables about 10 minutes before stew is done. Cover stew kettle tight so the cabbage will cook tender-crisp in the steam.

> Add tomato puree to the stew to form part of the liquid.

> Seasoning is important. Add extra flavor by using tomato juice, catsup, chicken or beef broth or bouillon in place of water.

> To remove excess salt from stew or soup, add a peeled, quartered potato and boil for five or six minutes.

> When preparing stew for freezing, do not cook vegetables completely. They will finish cooking when the stew is thawed and reheated.

☐ VEAL : Squeeze fresh lemon juice over veal chops before broiling.

> Top veal chops with strips of Swiss cheese sprinkled with Parmesan cheese before broiling.

> After veal chops are dipped in beaten egg, bread them with barbecued potato chips, crushed like bread crumbs.

> Marinate veal chops in cold bouillon for one hour, then season and broil.

> Cook veal chops in liquid to prevent the meat from drying and to ensure its being tender and juicy.

> Serve tender brown slices of veal in a sauce of melted butter, lemon juice and butter-browned slivers of almonds.

> Press thinly sliced veal to extreme flatness, pound thin slice of ham into it and broil, adding rosemary and sage and pepper (no salt). Then pour white wine into pan.

> Wiener schnitzel should be fried in butter, and the pan should be sprinkled with paprika *before* the cutlet is dropped in.

> Fry veal cutlets the right way: Flatten out meat with a small hammer, then apply egg and breading, but—most important—fry only ½ a minute on each side. It should never be overdone, as it becomes tough.

> To tenderize veal, pour lemon juice over cutlet and let stand for ½ hour.

> Heat fresh tomato juice and pour over veal cutlets before broiling.

> Add a small amount of red wine to sautéed veal.

> Add 1 tablespoon of broth and 1 tablespoon of lemon juice to veal scallopini.

> Brush shoulder of veal with olive oil before roasting.

> Mix oregano and olive oil and pour on thin slices of veal before broiling.

> When making roast veal, do not use a rack in the pan. Line the bottom of the pan with cut-up celery stalks, lay the roast on top of celery and cover the roast with bacon strips.

> Since veal has very little fat, it requires long, slow cooking for best results.

> Before finishing cooking veal scallopini, top half of cutlet with prosciutto, the other half with cheese, and garnish with slice of tomato and mushroom cap.

> Fry very thin veal slices and top with fried eggs.

> Serve veal scallopini with green noodles.

☐ SWEETBREADS :   Serve on a bed of spinach.

> Serve calves sweetbreads topped with Virginia ham.

> Shake sweetbreads in bag filled with flour and bread crumbs before frying.

> Dip sweetbreads in a combination of buttered crumbs and Parmesan cheese, broil, and serve topped with mushrooms.

☐ HASH: For hash to be brown on the bottom, allow it to cook very slowly, without stirring, in melted butter.

> Fried hash can be turned into a real treat with the addition of chopped tomatoes, shallots and a little red wine. Canned hash works fine.

☐ TONGUE: When boiling smoked tongue with vinegar and bay leaves in the water, add a little sugar to it to bring out the flavor and kill the salty taste.

> Pour gingersnap sauce over tongue.

☐ MEAT PIE: Brush lower crust of meat pie with white of egg and gravy will not soak through.

☐ CHILI: The best kind of meat to use in preparing chili is not beef, as commonly supposed. Either chopped veal sweetbreads or veal tenderloin tips are to be used.

☐ KIDNEYS: Veal and beef kidneys should be parboiled and rinsed before cooking to remove their alkaline flavor, while lamb kidneys do not require this.

> When kidney stew is nearly cooked, add a pinch of flour and a full glass of champagne.

☐ TRIPE: Cut boiled tripe into small pieces, dip in a batter and fry in hot fat until crisp and golden brown.

☐ AND A LOT OF OTHER THINGS: When buying meat with bone, you'll find you need 1 pound for 2 good-sized servings. A pound of lean meat without bone will provide 4 servings.

> On buying meat: Center cuts are the best, because the muscles on that part of the animal do not get the wear and toughening of the shoulder and leg muscles.

> Adding a little vinegar or lemon juice to the water in which tough meat is cooked will make the meat much more tender and palatable.

> To retain all possible vitamins, meat should be roasted at moderate temperatures, or broiled or fried rapidly.

> When warming leftover meat, put in a heavy skillet and cover completely with lettuce leaves. Cover with tight lid and heat in moderate oven. Tastes as good as if it were just made.

> Cooking with red wine tends to bring out the meat's flavor, while white wine sweetens meat.

> Dry wine as a seasoning is considered unsurpassable by many. Okay, too, for nondrinkers, as the alcohol evaporates but the flavor stays.

> Canned meat will slide out of can easily if it is first put in hot water for a few minutes.

> The smaller the cut of meat, the sooner is should be used.

> Because ground meat and variety meats—especially liver, kidneys and sweetbreads—are extremely perishable, they should be used within 2 days of purchase. Cubed meat, such as stew meat, should be used within the same period of time.

> A frozen roast can be cooked in the same manner as a fresh roast.

> To hasten the thawing of frozen meat, place the meat in a plastic vegetable bag and secure the top with a rubber band. Place bag in pan of warm water and await results.

> Do not keep meat in freezer more than two weeks. The flavor can be frozen out.

> Cook meat as soon as it has been thawed—and never, under any conditions, should it be refrozen.

> When freezing cooked meat, combine it with a sauce or gravy to ensure a more airtight package to protect it.

> Meat should almost always be cut across the grain. One exception is mutton, which is carved at right angles to the rib bones.

> Ham and beef should be cut in very thin slices; lamb, mutton and pork, in fairly thick slices.

> If using a meat thermometer, be sure it is inserted so

that it rests in the thickest part of the meat, not against a bone or in fat.

> When pan-broiling meat, pour off fat as it accumulates; otherwise you will be pan-frying the meat. The frying pan may be lightly rubbed with fat before cooking if necessary.

POTATOES

☐ BAKED: Sprinkle grated cheese on top of potato and return it to the oven till golden brown.

> Top baked potatoes with cottage cheese mixed with minced onions.

> Add minced anchovies combined with butter and garlic salt to baked potato.

> Stir red caviar into sour cream and serve, instead of butter, with baked potato.

> Top baked potato with crumbled bacon in melted butter.

> Add crispy chopped bacon to sour cream and chives and mix inside of baked potato.

> Baked potatoes can be scooped out and mashed with buttermilk and chives, then restuffed in shells.

> Add minced onion to yogurt, then pour over baked potato.

> Top baked potatoes with onion dip made with sour cream, 1 tablespoon to each potato.

> Try sour cream and crushed pineapple as a topping for baked potatoes.

> Rub potato skin with a lemon rind before baking.

☐ BOILED: Cut potatoes into small marbles with a vegetable cutter before boiling. When done, roll them in melted butter and chopped parsley before serving.

> Sprinkle garlic powder and paprika on boiled potatoes.

> Pour cream of mushroom soup, sautéed onions and cooked peas over boiled potatoes.

> Pour sour cream and chopped dill over boiled potatoes.

> Boiling time will be hastened if two teaspoons of salt are added to the water.

> To get potatoes white and mealy, add a few drops of vinegar to the water.

> When boiling potatoes for several days' use, put an onion in with them and they won't turn black.

☐ FRIED: Sprinkle raw potatoes with salt or nutmeg before French-frying.

> Instead of catsup over fried potatoes, sprinkle with Italian dressing and Worcestershire sauce.

> Pan-fry sliced potatoes in butter and sprinkle with corn-flake crumbs plus grated Parmesan cheese.

> Cowboy-fried potatoes: Fry sliced potatoes and onions together (½ onion for each potato). When tender, break eggs (1 egg for each potato) over the mix. Stir lightly to break yolk; season; allow eggs to set, and serve.

> When browning potatoes, put 2 slices of bacon in pan, fry till well done, then chop into small particles and mix with potatoes.

> Add green pepper, cut julienne style, while frying potatoes.

> Sprinkle a little flour in pan when a brown crust is desired for fried potatoes or a crisp, dry hash.

> Brush cut potato strips with mixture of butter and anchovy paste before pan-frying.

> Try draining French-fried potatoes by putting them on several slices of bread. They come out crisp.

> To make French fries crisp, allow potatoes to stand in cold water for 30 minutes before cooking.

> Instead of slicing potatoes for French fries, scoop out

the potatoes with a melon scoop and deep-fry them to golden brown.

☐ H A S H E D B R O W N : Add melted butter flavored with mustard and pour over hashed potatoes.

> Put finely chopped green pepper and onion in frying pan along with bacon fat used to fry hashed brown potatoes.

> Add thin slices of frankfurter to hashed brown potatoes with onions.

☐ M A S H E D / W H I P P E D : Whip mashed potatoes with cream cheese to get fewer calories than with butter.

> Save the vitamins in the potato water by adding powdered milk and butter to the liquid and using it to mash the potatoes.

> Shape mashed potatoes into puff balls with an ice cream scoop. Brush all over with melted butter and Parmesan cheese mixture and broil.

> Add ½ cup shredded cheddar cheese to mashed potatoes, then beat mixture until the cheese melts and the potatoes are golden in color.

> Add well-beaten egg to three cups of mashed and seasoned potatoes; shape into patties. Top with butter and broil both sides until brown.

> Make mashed potatoes by whipping in a mixture of sauterne and melted butter. Sprinkle with grated Parmesan cheese and brown under broiler.

> Shape leftover mashed potatoes into patties and roll first in melted butter, then in crushed potato chips. Bake in a hot oven until well browned.

> Shape leftover mashed potatoes into a roll and freeze. When you want patties, slice the roll and pan-fry the slices in butter or bacon drippings.

> Add crisp crumbled bacon to mashed potatoes.

> Add a little rosemary or a dash of curry powder to mashed potatoes.

> Try adding shredded crystallized ginger to melted butter when whipping white or sweet potatoes.

> Mash potatoes and mix with buttered dry bread crumbs and lots of minced onions and use as a stuffing for roast chicken.

> Mix potatoes with string beans and sautéed onions; add a spoonful of sour cream, salt and pepper.

> Mash potatoes with carrots, top with grated cheese, bake in oven at 450 degrees for 15 minutes.

> Blend ½ cup of chopped pimentos into mashed potatoes and bake in a moderate oven for 15 minutes.

> If potatoes are too salty when cooked, add a little sugar.

> Use the water in which vegetables were cooked to mix with instant mashed potatoes.

☐ PANCAKES: After half-frying potato pancakes, place them on paper to absorb the oil, then bake in oven to make them crispy.

> Try apple butter instead of applesauce over potato pancake.

☐ SWEET POTATOES: Add apricots and apricot juice to baste potatoes.

> Add a touch of sherry to cooked sweet potatoes and sprinkle with powdered ginger.

> Flavor candied sweet potatoes with rum.

> Mash sweet potatoes with chopped pecans and plenty of butter.

> Stuff baked yams with diced turkey; top with cranberry sauce.

> Add brown sugar and crushed pineapple to browning sweet potatoes.

> Top pineapple rings with mounds of mashed sweet potatoes, and broil or bake until hot. Serve with ham or pork.

> Add raisins or chopped peanuts to mashed yams.

> Add sliced cooked Louisiana yams to chicken a la king.

> Fold cut pieces of cooked prunes into mashed yams. Serve with fresh ham or pork.

> Try whipping sweet potatoes with a little orange juice.

> Fill orange shells with mashed sweet potatoes, cranberry sauce or diced fresh fruit as accompaniment to roasts, broiled meats or poultry.

> Scoop out part of the sweet potato and replace with marshmallows; brown and serve. Or just top baked sweet potatoes with marshmallows.

> A 6-ounce sweet potato contains more than twice the amount of vitamin A needed daily.

> Add a slice of lemon to the pan in which you're cooking sweet potatoes to help retain flavor and color.

☐ AND SOME OTHER THINGS: Scalloped potatoes from leftover potato salad: Just put the salad in a baking dish, add a can of cream of mushroom soup, top with grated cheese and heat in a medium-hot oven.

> Potato knishes: Mix mashed potatoes with fried onions, salt and pepper. Put this mixture in white bread with the crust removed. Roll it up, dip in beaten egg, and fry in butter.

> Instead of bread crumbs for croquette-style dishes, try granules of instant potato.

> Cold potatoes cooked in bacon grease make the tastiest fries.

> Should potatoes finish cooking ahead of the rest of the meal, keep them from getting soggy by draining water from the pot and putting a folded tea towel on top. The towel will absorb moisture, yet keep the pan hot.

> When grating a potato, hold one end on a fork.

> Potatoes will stop sprouting roots when stored, etc., if apples are kept in the same container.

> When potatoes must be cut in advance of cooking, place them in a plastic bag in the refrigerator.

> Put potatoes into water only after it has started to boil.

> If you're planning to stuff potatoes, rub the skins with any cooking fat or oil before putting them in the oven. With the coating, the potato skins will stay crisp and make durable shells for stuffing.

> Mix Russian dressing with chives for a baked-potato topping.

> Serve baked potatoes with garlic and a dash of horseradish in butter sauce.

> Scoop out potato from jacket, mash with chopped chives and fried onions, put back, top with paprika and brown under broiler flame.

> Try a mushroom sauce atop a baked potato instead of butter.

> Potatoes can be baked in half the normal time if centers are removed with an apple corer.

> To hurry baked potatoes, place them on the oven rack and invert an iron utensil over them. This cuts baking time almost in half.

> Gash or prick baked potatoes as soon as they are soft inside to allow steam to escape; it prevents them from becoming soggy.

> A plain baked potato has only 90 calories.

> Bake a double quantity of potatoes; then slice the extras with skins on and fry for the next night's dinner.

POULTRY

☐ C H I C K E N : Pour a mixture of lemon juice with salt and pepper over chicken before baking.

> Baked chicken will come out softer if butter is spread over skin before baking.

> When baking chicken breasts, top with two spoons of wild rice, mushrooms and cream-of-mushroom soup; bake for one hour.

> Dip pieces of chicken in tomato sauce, sprinkle with cornflake crumbs and bake in moderate oven with no fat added.

> Boil chicken until nearly cooked. Place in casserole with slices of cheese, top with Italian sauce and bake for 15 minutes.

> Dip pieces of chicken in lemon juice, sprinkle with garlic salt and let stand overnight before broiling.

> Let chicken soak in Italian salad dressing for a few hours and then broil.

> Baste broiling chicken with a combination of soy sauce and lemon juice.

> Try basting broiling chicken with cooking sherry and orange juice.

> Use crushed ready-to-eat rice cereal as coating for chicken croquettes.

> Try coating frying chicken with buttermilk before dipping in flour.

> Try grated cheese in the breading for next batch of fried chicken.

> Before putting chicken into the pan to fry, first let it boil in water for about an hour. It will be much juicier.

> Coat chicken with wheat germ and pancake flour; fry in corn oil.

> Add a little baking powder to flour in which chicken is dredged. Helps fried chicken become real crisp.

> Dip the chicken pieces in orange juice, and add grated orange peel to the seasoned flour before frying.

> Chicken livers are tastier when sautéed in chicken fat.

> When cooking chicken livers, use a sharp-tined fork and perforate them all over. This will keep them from popping.

> Try white wine in sauce for chicken-liver dish.

> Spread honey over chicken before roasting; it will brown better.

> Boil jelly and wine and pour over roasted bird.

> When roasting chicken, baste frequently with pineapple juice.

> Rub bird with butter and place breast down in pan so butter and juice will run downward to moisten white meat during roasting.

> Stir a few banana slices into canned whole-cranberry sauce for roast chicken.

> Cook pineapple chunks with baked or broiled chicken.

> Try a glass of Burgundy in chicken gravy.

> Bake chicken with a full cup of sherry. First brown the chicken with onion and garlic, then add sherry and bake for an additional hour and a half.

> Pour a cup of white wine over roasted chicken and broil another minute.

> Substitute chicken broth for milk in medium white sauce and season with white pepper and nutmeg; add salt as needed. Serve as sauce with chicken croquettes.

> Thin liver paste with cream. Use it as a hot sauce over chicken breasts (with thin veal or hard-boiled eggs as well).

> Put a piece of ginger and some coconut flakes on broiled chicken.

> Baste a chicken with a mixture of orange juice and raw honey during last 30 minutes of roasting. Use drippings for gravy, adding a little orange juice to taste. The sauce ingredients are: ½ cup unstrained fresh juice, 1½ tablespoons honey, 1½ tablespoons salad oil.

> Sauce for chicken cacciatore is sauterne wine, oil and garlic plus peeled canned or fresh tomatoes.

> Add some rosemary and sage leaves to melted butter and use as a gravy for broiled chicken.

> Before cooking chicken, bring a pan of salt water to boil, then drop chicken in and allow to stand for five minutes. It will make chicken extra tender.

> Cored apples stuffed into chicken keep the meat moist and add a tart flavor.

> Fresh poultry should be wrapped loosely in waxed paper or foil, refrigerated immediately and used within three days.

> To test if chicken is cooked, move the drumstick gently up and down; bird is done if joint moves easily and twists off.

> Do not use a fork when cooking chicken. If skin is pierced, natural juices will escape.

> Boning a chicken is much easier if done while the bird is still slightly frozen.

> Keep leftover chicken or turkey from drying out by covering with a damp towel and then Saran Wrap, and refrigerating.

> When stuffing poultry, keep the filling in place by inserting the heel of a loaf of bread.

> Stewed chicken: Add a tablespoon of vinegar to water and refrain from adding salt until cooking is done. Meat will be more tender and will not fall away from the bone.

> Pour ¼ cup rum into small bowl; dip chicken into rum, then into bread crumbs before sautéing in melted butter.

> Add diced green pepper to a chicken dish.

> Cover chicken well with rosemary, seal it with fatback, place in a very hot oven for 20 minutes.

☐ D U C K : Glaze roast duck with honey and soy sauce, then bake with wine vinegar.

> To tenderize duck, boil in water with one tablespoon of vinegar for one hour before roasting.

> A tasty basting for duck is half orange juice and half port wine.

> Mix a glass of claret with the juice of two oranges and two cups of thick cream-of-chicken soup for a gravy for duck.

> Try adding a spoonful of cognac to orange sauce with duck.

> Stuff duck with grapes before roasting.

> When stuffing a duck, add pineapple bits to the filling and pour raw pineapple juice over duck; helps cut grease.

> Roast duck will be crisp and fat-free if a stalk of celery, an unpeeled apple and an unpeeled onion are put inside before cooking.

> Before roasting duck, put it under flame and let the fat run off. It is then ready for roasting and will be crisp and moist.

> Try the following additions to poultry stuffing:

> sliced peaches (for extra lightness);
> corn bread crumbs mixed with blueberries;
> apple juice instead of water;
> crushed apple or cored apples, for moistness;
> orange sections, a few pineapple tidbits and apple slices, for roast duckling;
> a cup of sliced dry apricots mixed with cup of parboiled rice—for duck or chicken.

> The following touches are delicious:

> toasted slivered almonds—an elegant addition to bread stuffing
> coarsely chopped cashew nuts in bread stuffing

☐ POULTRY STUFFINGS AND ADDITIONS:

> chopped liver with biscuit mix;
> mashed potatoes mixed with buttered dry bread crumbs and lots of minced onion;
> grated Parmesan cheese added to breading;

> mashed cooked yams in chicken stuffing;
> cooked rice, browned in butter with chopped cel-
    ery, onions, parsley, spices and stirred in large
    cup of bouillon, for turkey.

> A stuffing for chicken, turkey or roast suckling pig: Mix
1½ pounds of sauerkraut, 1 chopped onion, 2 chopped apples
and 4 small pork sausages, thinly sliced. Before stuffing,
moisten the inside with a liberal amount of brandy.

☐ TURKEY: Mix boneless turkey with raisins, rice,
onion and butter. Cook in casserole.

> Top smoked turkey with apricot sauce or pineapple and
bake.

> Baste turkey with a combination of orange juice and a
liqueur.

> Dip pieces of leftover turkey or chicken in tomato sauce
and bread crumbs and deep-fry in cooking oil.

> Add cheese to slices of turkey and melt by topping with
hot mushroom soup poured in spoonfuls.

> Don't stuff turkey until just before roasting; do not stuff
turkey and refreeze.

> Turkey that is stuffed will need a great deal longer to
cook, unless the stuffing is cooked before adding.

> Don't stuff too tightly or pack stuffing in too solidly, as
it swells during cooking.

> To hasten cooking time, cover bird with aluminum foil.

> Try toasting the bread before preparing it as stuffing.

> When considering what size bird to order, remember
that giblets and neck are included in weight of wrapped bird.
The rule is to allow 1 pound per serving when buying a turkey
less than 12 pounds, and ½ to ¾ pound per serving for one
over 12 pounds. If you count on about 1½ pounds of turkey
per person, you will have enough.

> Never thaw turkey at room temperature; thaw in refrig-
erator two or three days, leaving it in the plastic bag.

> A prestuffed turkey should be placed in the oven still frozen. It should not be kept longer than overnight without cooking.

> Season turkey the night before and cover with cheese-cloth or foil to let flavor soak in.

PASTA AND RICE

☐ M A C A R O N I : Use crumbled bacon as topping for macaroni and cheese.

> Mix cooked elbow macaroni with snappy cheese sauce; top with slices of tomato and add a layer of grated cheese. Broil until cheese melts and tomatoes are hot.

> Add a cup of mixed chopped ham and green pepper to macaroni casserole.

> Leftover macaroni can be baked in an onion, mushroom and gravy sauce in a casserole.

> Mix sautéed onions, mushrooms and tiny bits of beef into elbow macaroni.

☐ N O O D L E S : To cooked noodles add ground cooked ham and cream-of-mushroom sauce.

> Add sautéed green pepper and onions to cooked noodles. Mix in shredded cheese.

> Add poppy seeds to hot buttered noodles, mix thoroughly and serve at once.

> Sauté shredded onions and cabbage; when cooked, mix with wide noodles and butter and salt.

> Mix chopped prunes with cooked broad egg noodles and butter and bake in oven for ten minutes.

☐ P I Z Z A : Spread English muffins with canned tomato sauce. Top with chunks of canned, drained tuna and sprinkle with oregano. Top with slices of mozzarella cheese and broil until cheese bubbles.

☐ R I C E : Stir a little orange juice into rice while it is simmering on fire.

> Cook rice in beef broth made from bouillon cube or in onion soup instead of water.

> Pour unsweetened fruit juice into rice.

> Fry rice and tomatoes in butter.

> Add chopped scallions, chopped chicken and a little soy sauce to plain boiled rice.

> Drop a few pieces of onion in a pot in which you're boiling rice.

> Combine sautéed mushrooms and green pepper with cooked rice.

> Allow cooked rice to stand about 10 minutes, then add orange marmalade (2 tablespoons to 1 cup of quick-cooking rice).

> Add sautéed raisins and diced pimento to cooked rice.

> Soak raisins in orange juice and stir into hot cooked rice prior to serving.

> Add grated orange along with butter when seasoning freshly cooked rice.

> Sprinkle rice with cheese before serving. Or, pour Roquefort cheese dressing over rice.

> Mix an egg or two with leftover rice; fry and serve with meat course.

> A slice of dry bread placed on cooked and drained rice will absorb excess moisture and leave rice dry and fluffy.

> Keep spaghetti or rice from boiling over by adding two tablespoons of butter or margarine to boiling water.

> Reheat leftover rice by putting it in a sieve and setting it over boiling water.

> Rice will absorb 3 times its bulk in water—so for 2 cups of cooked rice, start with ⅔ cup of rice and 2 cups of water.

> For best steamed rice, after bringing to a boil, reduce heat to lowest point and cook for 20 minutes.

> Always keep cooking rice covered, or else flavor and texture are spoiled.

☐ S P A G H E T T I :   Store leftover spaghetti by placing in glass or stainless steel bowl completely covered with cold water. Keeps in refrigerator for 2 days.

> Reheat spaghetti by covering bottom of pan with layer of water and cooking sauce and all.

> Top leftover spaghetti with melted cheese and fry.

> A tablespoon of salt will flavor spaghetti when you're cooking portions for 3 or more.

> Keep cooked spaghetti, macaroni, or noodles from sticking together by tossing with butter or a few tablespoons of sauce as soon as it is drained. Then second servings will be as attractive as the first.

> Prevent sticking by greasing the pan lightly and making sure there is enough water in pan.

> Add small amount of chopped chicken liver, mixed with tomato sauce and pimento.

> Mix ham, bacon and green peppers minced very fine and simmered in olive oil; add to spaghetti and mix.

> Add sautéed broccoli and stir with ricotta cheese.

> Mix chili con carne with spaghetti in a casserole. Sprinkle top with grated cheese and bake for ½ hour.

> Drain and mince anchovies; add them to hot olive oil or melted butter and mix in.

> Mix the gravy from roast beef with olive oil and stewed tomatoes as spaghetti sauce.

> Mix a can of spaghetti (with tomato sauce) with a can of minced clams in their juice. Heat and serve.

> Serve spaghetti with a sauce made of melted Swiss Gru-yère and diced prosciutto, topped with tiny hot cocktail onions.

> Clam sauce: For 2 full portions, use 2 cups of clams, 2 tablespoons of flour-and-butter roux and—here is the secret—½ cup of dry white wine. Simmer slowly until it is reduced by about half, and serve over linguini. Better than spaghetti.

> Basil has an affinity with tomatoes and helps to give spaghetti good flavor. Add ¼ teaspoon to sauce.

> Freeze spaghetti sauce for 3 days before heating and using it.

> Cooking spaghetti sauce under 3 hours does not allow for a perfect blending in of ingredients. The flame under the saucepan should be adjusted to the heat that permits the sauce to bubble slowly but not boil.

> Always use the tiny plum tomatoes; they give the sauce finest flavor.

☐ HINTS FOR PASTA: When you're cooking any pasta, the water should be boiling and continue boiling throughout cooking. Do not cover, but stir occasionally.

> Homemade pasta will be lighter in texture if you add seltzer instead of tap water.

SALADS

☐ BEEF: Toss small chunks of rare roast beef with a dressing of mayonnaise, sour cream, blue cheese, salt, pepper, and a little olive oil. Serve on lettuce, or mix with chunks of lettuce and tomato.

☐ CABBAGE AND COLE SLAW: Try adding crushed pineapple or blue cheese to cole slaw.

> Use sour cream, lemon juice, sugar and salt for cole slaw dressing.

> Add chopped raisins or cooked raisins and thin slices of pineapple to cole slaw.

> Use green cabbage and purple cabbage for a half-and-half mixture.

> Don't throw away vinegar left over from sweet pickles. Pour over grated raw cabbage; marinate before serving.

> Add caraway seeds to cole slaw along with chopped fresh dates.

□ C H E E S E : Mix olives, chopped walnuts and crumbled crisp bacon into cottage cheese and serve in lettuce cups.

> Put small cubes of cheese (American is suggested) into mustard dressing and add chopped hard-boiled eggs and caraway seeds. Eat with picks. Actually, it is a cheese salad and can also be used with tomatoes, lettuce and onions.

□ C H I C K E N : Add sesame seeds and chopped almonds to chicken salad.

> Try adding ½ cup of toasted cashew nuts to chicken salad.

> Try adding diced pineapple and diced celery to chicken salad.

> Seedless grapes add texture and flavor to chicken and ham salads.

> Dice freshly peeled apples into chicken salad; garnish with raisins.

□ F R E N C H D R E S S I N G : Stir in a beaten egg, a dash of Tabasco and a tablespoon of melted butter to improve store-bought French dressing.

> Add a dash of white Bordeaux to French dressing and shake well.

> Add whole pimento-stuffed olives and a clove of garlic to French dressing and refrigerate.

> Make French dressing in the salad bowl: Put salt and pepper at bottom of bowl, add vinegar and stir well until salt and pepper are dissolved. Add oil, 3 parts to 1 of vinegar.

> Serve French dressing with artichoke hearts.

> Heat French dressing, add chopped hard-boiled egg and spices, pour over drained cooked spinach and toss well.

☐ MAYONNAISE: Try mixing 1 tablespoon of dry mustard, 2 tablespoons of cognac and 1 tablespoon of minced scallion into 1 cup of mayonnaise.

> Make Russian dressing by adding 2 tablespoons of chili sauce to 1 cup of mayonnaise.

> Thin Russian dressing with wine vinegar when serving endive-and-beet salad.

> To 1 cup mayonnaise add: 1 teaspoon of curry; or 1 tablespoon of chutney; or 2 tablespoons pickle juice (sweet or dill); or 1 tablespoon of horseradish.

> Blend mayonnaise with lemon juice and salt to taste for a salad topping.

> Stir sherry into mayonnaise for a salad extra.

> Mix mayonnaise, chopped onion, prepared mustard. Cover. Refrigerate for 1 hour. Pour over watercress.

> Substitute wine vinegar or lemon juice for plain vinegar when making mayonnaise in the blender.

> Heat mayonnaise with chopped onions and lemon juice. Serve warm over lettuce.

> Add a little honey to mayonnaise for fruit-salad dressing.

> Mash blue cheese with mayonnaise, then buttermilk and paprika. Add salt and pepper. Chill, tightly covered, to allow dressing to thicken slightly before serving.

> Add lemon juice and a small portion of chopped Roquefort cheese to Russian dressing.

☐ OIL AND VINEGAR: Add a little grated Parmesan cheese to an olive oil and vinegar dressing.

> A good basic oil-and-vinegar dressing calls for 2 cups wine vinegar, ¾ cup olive oil, 2 whole garlic cloves; shake well in jar and refrigerate before serving.

> Any salad oil in a tightly closed bottle will keep indefinitely at room temperature.

> Use 40 percent olive oil to 60 percent saturated vegetable oil for homemade dressing.

□ OTHER DRESSINGS: A half teaspoon of sugar gives more zest to a Roquefort salad dressing.

> Add a little salt and pepper to hard cider.

> Substitute grapefruit juice for half of the vinegar in dressing.

> Add finely chopped sweet pickles to salad dressing for additional spice and flavor.

> Mix 1 ounce honey, 3 ounces vinegar and the juice of 1 lime. Shake well.

> Add 2 or 3 teaspoons of honey to 1 cup of sour cream. Stir until smooth and add lemon juice.

> Serve cheese sauce on salad. Mix undiluted evaporated milk, salt, oregano, and grated American cheese in a saucepan and, when heated, pour over salad.

> Yogurt and crumbled blue cheese with a dash of Worcestershire, salt and pepper make a delicious salad dressing. Some Chablis may be added.

> Combine 2 tablespoons of instant minced onion with 1 cup sour cream, 1 tablespoon vinegar, 1 tablespoon sugar and a dash of salt. Chill and serve.

□ EGG: Use tartar sauce instead of plain mayonnaise in egg salad.

> Extend egg salad with cottage cheese.

> Mix some chopped green pepper and pimento into egg salad.

> Add a little mustard sauce, or a few dashes of hot mustard and diced scallions.

□ TUNA: Use a cup of shredded Swiss cheese in tuna salad.

> Add pieces of lobster and chicken to tuna salad.

> Put a little oil, a little vinegar, and chopped onion in tuna-fish salad.

> Mix diced avocado with tuna.

> Add small can of chunky pineapple to tuna salad.

> Add chopped almonds or grated raw apple to tuna.

> Mix chopped cucumber and anchovy into the salad.

☐ SHRIMP: Crumble American blue cheese into shrimp salad and serve in avocado halves for a light supper.

> Dress the salad with French dressing instead of mayonnaise.

☐ GENERAL HINTS FOR FISH: Mix raisins with salmon and place on bed of lettuce and tomatoes.

> Salmon, cod, haddock and halibut are fish that flake easily after cooking, so they may be used in fish salads.

> Chop lobster and hard-boiled eggs and mix with mayonnaise. Chill and serve with a salad.

> Use vinegar instead of lemon juice on fish salads. Vinegar cuts down the odor more effectively and tastes good.

☐ FRUIT AND GELATIN: Add finely diced figs to fruit salad.

> Marinate avocado overnight in French dressing made with lime juice.

> Put a drop or two of honey in fruit salad.

> Serve cranberry sauce as a topping for salad of orange slices on a bed of lettuce.

> Alternate slices of avocado with slices of orange and paper-thin red onion rings. Garnish with sprigs of watercress or other greens.

> Dilute mayonnaise with small amount of orange and grapefruit juices and serve with salad.

> Serve oranges and pineapple on lettuce with French dressing; top with coconut flakes.

> Instead of using water for making gelatin salads, try using fruit juices.

> Give a tang to gelatin salads by adding a 7-ounce bottle of ginger ale to boiling water.

> Try fresh pineapple chunks with cubes of jellied cranberry.

> Store leftover vegetables in covered containers and add to gelatin for salad.

> Add orange juice to fruit salad and allow to soak for a while in refrigerator.

> Use coffee cups to mold gelatin salads. Handle helps in turning the gelatin out.

□ M A C A R O N I :   Give macaroni salad a rainbow look by adding green onion (scallions), diced sweet pickles, coarsely grated carrot, pimento strips and yellow mustard to the mayonnaise used for dressing.

□ P O T A T O :   To your next potato salad, add hard-boiled eggs, cucumbers, celery and tomatoes.

> Mix cold sliced potatoes with chopped parsley and then add to cream dressing.

> Poach frankfurters, just below the boiling point. Cut in penny-size slices and add to hot or cold potato salad.

> Try the following additions to potato salad:

> chopped cooked shrimp (to whipped potato salad);
> capers, raisins and celery seed;
> chopped walnuts and pimento;
> onions and celery chopped fine; plus dash of mustard;
> caraway seeds and a little onion salt

□ T O S S E D   G R E E N S :   Add small pieces of Swiss cheese and pimento to a green salad.

> Add raw cauliflower chopped very fine in a tossed green salad.

> Cut seedless grapes in halves and place in green salad.

> Crumble crisp bacon and cheddar cheese into green salad.

> Cold string beans are good in tossed green salad.

> Add match-sized strips of unpared red apple to a tossed salad.

> Pour fresh fruit juice over hearts of lettuce.

> Substitute fresh spinach and radish tops for lettuce in tossed salad.

> Leave tomatoes out of mixed green salad. They are too juicy, dilute the dressing and make the greens soggy. Have them as a side dish instead.

☐ VEGETABLES: Serve orange sections and asparagus stalks with French dressing.

> Add 1 tablespoon of mixed-pickle relish and 1 teaspoon of minced chives to cold cooked asparagus salad with French dressing.

> Combine slices of avocado with grapefruit sections.

> Serve a generous helping of sliced avocado and a side dish of blue cheese sauce to dip the slices into.

> Add diced cooked beets to a salad.

> Spoon chilled sliced beets over crisp greens; top with hard-boiled eggs and sour cream.

> Marinate cooked green beans in French dressing and add to salad.

> Add cooked string beans and French dressing to chopped-up celery and onions.

> Mix Italian onions, sliced tomatoes, cucumbers, oregano and oil to taste.

> Mix sliced cucumbers that have been steeped in salted ice water with sliced spring onions and serve with cream dressing.

> Add Spanish red peppers to spinach salad.

> Try a raw spinach salad, served with dressing of crisp crumbled bacon, bacon drippings and fresh lemon juice.

> Top spinach leaves with olive oil, vinegar and ham strips.

SANDWICHES

☐ C H E E S E : For toasted cheese sandwiches, spread mustard on bread slices first.

> Add slices of pineapple to a cheese sandwich before grilling.

> Butter the outside of the bread and grill in a heavy pan.

> Pour Welsh rabbit or melted cheese over a club sandwich and eat with knife and fork.

> Put sliced cucumbers with cottage cheese on pumpernickel.

> Spread heated asparagus over open grilled cheese sandwiches and top with sour cream.

☐ M E A T / P O U L T R Y : Spread rye bread with cream cheese mixed with caraway seeds and then add the meat. Serve with mixed pickles.

> Chop roast pork and mix it with crushed pineapple; wrap in a slice of bread and toast in the oven. (Just bend the bread in half and hold together with a toothpick.)

> For a different grilled ham sandwich, toast the bread slices on one side in the broiler. Top each untoasted side with generous slices of baked ham. Then cover the ham with crumbled American blue cheese. Sprinkle several drops of Worcestershire sauce on top of the cheese, and broil until the cheese begins to melt.

> Sprinkle grated orange rind on a sliced-chicken sandwich.

> Combine chopped turkey with coarsely cut olives and celery.

> Combine bacon with sliced cucumbers and mayonnaise.

☐ PREPARATION AND PRESERVATION: If bread is too fresh, chill it before using for sandwiches.

> Party sandwiches can be made to last longer and look more attractive if they are stacked back into loaf form, wrapped in a damp towel, and put into the refrigerator to chill for an hour.

> Use shears to cut the crusts from fresh bread; they do a neater job than a knife.

☐ SPREADS: Put a layer of jellied cranberry sauce between two slices of peanut-buttered bread.

> Add apple slices to peanut butter.

> Grill peanut butter between slices of bread (as you would cheese).

> Youngsters will flip for sandwiches made from a spread of peanut butter, seedless raisins and marmalade.

> Mash 6 boneless sardines to each hard-boiled egg and moisten the mix with a little butter.

> Combine cream cheese, milk and lemon juice and blend until smooth. Add onions and pepper and spread on bread.

> Grate or grind American cheese; then mix with chili sauce, butter, dry mustard, scraped onion, a dash of cayenne for a sandwich spread or cracker topping.

> Mix cream cheese, anchovy paste and dry vermouth to a melty smoothness.

> Combine tuna fish, cheese and minced onion; spread on bread and broil.

> Mash up sardines with Roquefort cheese and diced green peppers.

> Rinse a can of shrimp, and, after draining with cold

water, chop and mix with coarsely grated cucumber and mayonnaise. Flavor it with onion.

☐ "DIFFERENT" SANDWICHES: Slice and peel an apple and make a "sandwich" by spreading cream cheese with strawberry jam and/or chopped nuts between two apple slices

> Cut crisp rolls lengthwise and butter the cut sides; add a layer of cole slaw and one of fried oysters.

> Spread egg salad on bread slices, top with bacon strips and broil.

SAUCES, GRAVIES
AND GARNISHES

☐ FOR BEEF: Add a pinch of horseradish to pot roast or roast beef gravy.

> Just add mushrooms, a little sour cream and a dash of wine for pot roast.

> Chop garlic and blend with vinegar and oil; serve over broiled steak or chopped steak.

> Melt cheese and olives over a thick slice of roast beef.

> Thin horseradish with cream if it is to be served with boiled or roast beef, with applesauce if to be served with ham.

> Leftover coffee adds richness to ham, beef or pork gravies. Use about 1½ cups to 3 to 4 cups of gravy.

> Add barbecue sauce and water and mix lightly to spark meat gravy.

> Stir a sprinkling of dried dill into gravy.

> Add a teaspoon of prepared mustard to liquid just before removing from stove.

> Sauté onions, then add canned mushrooms with juice, milk, salt and pepper, and simmer.

> Use thinly whipped potatoes in place of flour to thicken gravies.

> Add a little orange juice and a few pinches of sugar to gravy.

> To separate extra fat from meat drippings, pour in a tall cup, set in cold water and, when cooled, scoop the top off.

> A few drops of vinegar in sauce or gravy will prevent curdling.

> Mix flour and water for gravies by beating the mixture with an egg beater. Use a blender to whip up larger quantities.

> Mix 1 cup of herb-flavored bread crumbs to 2 cups of gravy to thicken.

☐ FOR STEAK: Put a clove of garlic in olive oil, mix in ½ teaspoon of paprika, let set for 5 minutes. Brush steak with sauce before broiling.

> Combine 2 pats of butter, a touch of red wine and a drop of vinegar. Then pour sauce over steak while cooking.

☐ FOR CHICKEN: Add sautéed onions, mushrooms and sour cream to chicken soup and when good and hot, use as dressing over broiled chicken.

> Add chopped walnuts to beef or chicken gravy.

> Snip fresh dates into pieces, heat in melted apple-mint jelly and serve over baked ham or chicken.

☐ FOR HAM: Grilled ham, combine equal amounts of catsup, vinegar and water with ½ teaspoon celery seed and ½ teaspoon of dry mustard. Baste ham slices.

> For ham steak, mix 1 teaspoon mustard, 2 tablespoons brown sugar and ½ cup of peanut butter and use as glaze.

☐ RELISHES: Mix 2 tablespoons dry mustard or horse-radish with 1½ cups mayonnaise, 1 tablespoon of sugar and 1 teaspoon of lemon juice.

> Add diced orange, minced red onion and green pepper to sour cream for a relish.

☐ S A U C E S : Combine sautéed mushrooms with hollandaise sauce for a unique taste.

> Heat 1 can of condensed tomato soup (as is), stir frequently, then serve on hamburgers, pork chops, seafood, omelets or broiled cheese sandwiches.

> Butter sauce: Melt ¼ pound of butter over low heat; add lemon juice, salt, pepper and a dash of garlic powder. Save remaining sauce and refrigerate—remelt for later use.

> Improve cheese sauce by adding a small amount of condensed tomato soup.

> To remove oil from spaghetti sauce, stir in the juice from ½ lemon and 1 tablespoon of granulated sugar.

> Cook rhubarb with orange rind and serve chilled over cold meats.

> Add garlic and butter to tomato sauce, then pour on broiled beef cubes.

> If hollandaise sauce separates, remove it from heat right away, add an ice cube and beat.

> When cooking sauces, prevent sticking in pot by using asbestos pad to cover flame.

> Keep white sauce covered until serving to prevent film.

> Use a little Madeira to rinse skillet in which mushrooms were cooked and use as sauce.

> Use only unsalted butter in sauces.

☐ F O R   V E G E T A B L E S   A N D   F I S H : Mix dry mustard with sour cream as a topping for cold asparagus tips.

> Heat a blend of 1 tablespoon of prepared mustard and lemon juice with ½ cup of French dressing for a vegetable topping.

> Mix sour cream with fresh chopped dill and pour it over a vegetable plate.

> Add a dash of A-1 sauce to 3 parts mayonnaise and 1 part catsup for seafood sauce.

> Make a green mayonnaise sauce by adding ½ cup each of finely chopped parsley, chives and watercress to 1½ cups mayonnaise. Blend well.

> Combine chili sauce, horseradish, lemon juice and mayonnaise for seafood sauce.

> Mix sour cream and mayonnaise, half and half, with a dash of lemon and cayenne pepper and salt and use as a sauce for asparagus, broccoli, and mild-flavored fish.

> Combine English dry mustard with mayonnaise for fish sauce.

> Use well-buttered split-pea soup as a sauce for whole peas. Makes a tasty side dish.

> For a seafood cocktail, combine 1½ cups of sour cream with ½ cup of Roquefort cheese.

> Add a teaspoon of grated cheese to hot butter for fish sauce.

> Make a shrimp sauce with Tabasco, horseradish and chili sauce.

> Mix together mayonnaise, chopped fresh dill and lemon juice as dressing for either fish or vegetables.

> Use yogurt instead of cream sauce when serving deviled crab.

☐ WINE SAUCES: Add a white dinner wine to dry mustard and let sit for a few minutes for a sauce for cold cuts or sandwiches.

> Decrease salt when cooking with wine.

> A sturdy wine sauce will flavor and tenderize less-expensive cuts of meat.

> A useful wine for cooking is sauterne.

> Drip white wine over cooking chicken.

> Mix white wine and clam juice (to taste) and add chopped parsley and minced onion for fish sauce.

SOUP

☐ BEAN: A little vinegar and soy sauce jazz up the flavor of bean soup.

> Just before serving black bean soup, stir in some sherry.

> When cooking black bean soup add a few slices of frankfurter, or add 2 tablespoons each of finely chopped onion and rice.

☐ LENTIL SOUP: Add chopped raw scallions to lentil soup; chopped cooked shrimp may also be added.

> Add a dash of lemon juice to lentil soup.

☐ CHICKEN: Instead of clams, use chunks of chicken for chicken chowder.

> Season chicken bouillon broth with pepper and garlic powder, then pour over mashed potatoes.

> Add a dash of red wine, crushed garlic and croutons to chicken soup.

> Add chopped scallions, nutmeg and grated Parmesan cheese to chicken rice soup.

> Mince fresh dill and add to steamy chicken broth.

> Serve chicken soup with noodles and matzoh balls.

☐ CONSOMMÉ: Serve jellied consommé with diced avocado and lemon wedges.

> Serve cold consommé with a tablespoon of sour cream.

> Put a teaspoon of burgundy wine into each cup or bowl before pouring consommé.

> Add a touch of sherry to a plain, clear soup for a warm, exotic flavor in cold weather.

☐ CLAM CHOWDER OR BISQUE: Add a touch of sauterne to each cup or bowl of clam chowder; or add a larger amount to New England clam chowder as it is cooking.

> Mix consommé with minced clams in natural clam juice.

> Add a teaspoon of whipped cream to clam broth; or cover clam or beef broth with a thick layer of whipped cream.

> Add a little cream-of-mushroom soup and a few dashes of Worcestershire sauce to Boston clam chowder.

> Dice 4 strips of bacon and add to chowder; don't let the mixture boil—just simmer for 20 minutes.

☐ CRAB MEAT SOUP: Sprinkle flaked crab meat or salmon into vegetable soup.

☐ GARNISHES: Top iced consommé madrilene with sour cream and chopped anchovies.

> Garnish soup with paper-thin slices of orange or lemon.

> Substitute marrow balls for matzoh balls in soup. Scrape the marrow from the inside of bones; mash; add well-beaten eggs, matzoh meal, salt, nutmeg, and parsley. Roll into balls and drop in hot soup.

> Add capers to cream soups.

> Add a pinch of minced chives to Vichyssoise, a pinch of curry to consommé or cream soups, and grated coconut to chicken-curry soups.

> Garnish soups with whipped cream, lightly salted and sprinkled with paprika. (Individual whipped-cream toppers, sweetened or salted, may be frozen.)

> Float a mass of cheddar cheese on a bowl of hot soup.

> Slice tomatoes or green pepper paper thin and float atop soup.

> Garnish cream-of-asparagus soup with grated cheese or orange rind; both bring out the flavor.

> Add sharp parsley, garlic and a leaf of celery to mine-strone soup.

> In a brown-paper bag, heat plain or cheese-flavored pop-corn in a 350-degree oven for 5 to 10 minutes. Use as a top-ping for cream-of-spinach soup or other bland cream soups.

☐ MONGOL : Make puree Mongol by combining 1 can each of condensed pea soup and condensed tomato soup; add 1 can of milk, 1 can of water and a dash of curry powder.

> To a can of condensed pea soup, add an 8-ounce can of tomato sauce, ½ cup of Moselle wine, and ½ cup of water. Heat and serve.

☐ MUSHROOM: Cook frozen chopped spinach; then add canned mushroom soup and let simmer a few minutes.

> Add cooked broccoli, minced onions and a dash of nut-meg to mushroom soup.

☐ ONION: Mix 1 can each of condensed onion soup and condensed cream-of-chicken soup; add 1½ cans of water and top with grated cheese.

> Add grated cheese to onion soup while the soup is cook-ing.

> Spread liver sausage on rounds of toast, place in soup bowls and add hot onion soup.

☐ PEA: Cook pea soup with bits of ham and onion and celery chopped up very finely.

> Add slices of frankfurter, crumbled bacon and a little tomato soup to pea soup.

☐ POTATO: Stir in 1½ cups of grated sharp cheese shortly before serving creamy potato soup.

> Used diced frozen potatoes and onions for soup.

> Mix in blender 1 can of madrilene, 1 can of creamed potato soup and 1 cup of milk. Chill well.

☐ T O M A T O : Add ½ jigger of brandy to hot tomato soup.

> Add thinly sliced onion rings or a cupful of cooked diced broccoli to tomato soup.

> Add sautéed onions to tomato soup, or bits of chicken and rice.

> To stop curdling of homemade tomato soup, beat in a pinch of baking soda.

> Before combining milk with hot tomato soup, see that the milk is also hot.

> Add finely chopped dill to tomato soup, or use finely diced celery as a topping.

☐ C E L E R Y : Add a cup of cubed American cheese to celery soup.

> Add cooked broad egg noodles, sautéed broccoli and grated Parmesan cheese to celery soup.

☐ M I X E D V E G E T A B L E : Mix cooked string beans, peas and carrots into corn soup to make a vegetable soup.

> Toss a variety of vegetables into a kettle with bouillon and tomato soup; simmer gently for 15 minutes.

> If meat or a meat bone is not available as a base, glaze an onion in chicken fat.

> Dice some sausage and add it to canned minestrone or turkey-vegetable soup.

☐ U N U S U A L S O U P S : Add a tablespoon of plain yogurt to a bowl of steaming hot, clear soup.

> Imitate the famed Spanish gazpacho soup by chilling canned tomato soup and serving with bowls of croutons, chopped cucumber, chopped onion, etc., as garnishes.

> A dash of Worcestershire sauce in Vichyssoise gives it a new tang.

> Canned cream soups plus diced leftover chicken or turkey will make a tasty "a la king" or Tetrazzini in no time.

> Combine tomato soup, pea soup and bouillon and add a few dashes of sherry and a can of fresh crab flakes.

> Substitute 1 can of meat stock (or 2 bouillon cubes dissolved in 1 cup of water) for 1 cup of milk in cream soups.

> Use a turkey carcass to make a broth by cooking it in a small amount of water with a celery stalk, a carrot, a sliced onion, a bay leaf and peppercorns.

> Add sherry to cheese-flavored soups, and sliced bits of roast beef to any soups.

VEGETABLES

☐ A S P A R A G U S :   Serve melted butter, lemon juice and crushed garlic over asparagus.

> Try adding chopped green pepper to melted butter sauce when serving asparagus.

> Pan fry bacon until partly cooked, wrap around drained hot asparagus, cover with thick cheese sauce and broil.

> Try salted whipped cream and pimento strips as a dressing for asparagus.

> Top cold asparagus with a dressing of sour cream and chives.

> Always open cans of whole asparagus spears from the bottom so that the tips will not break as you ease the spears out.

> Peel top layers near the tough ends of asparagus with a shredder before boiling. The whole stalk can be eaten.

> Trim 1 inch from butt end of asparagus, soak in cold water for 10 minutes and store in refrigerator wrapped in a plastic bag until ready to use. Cook in boiling water, covered, for about 15 minutes.

> Cook asparagus standing up. Use the coffee percolator without the inside piece. Stand the spears upright, or tie them in a bunch, and place in percolator with ½ inch of salted water. The tips will not be overcooked, and the base of all the spears will be tender and edible.

☐ LIMA BEANS: Add cheddar cheese and milk to cooked lima beans, then serve when cheese and milk are blended together.

> Combine cooked lima beans with ½ cup sour cream, ¼ cup chopped green pepper and 2 beaten eggs; bake in a well-buttered casserole for ½ hour.

> Cover lima beans with a sauce of olive oil, lime juice and dill.

☐ BAKED BEANS: Try the following additions to baked beans:

> ⅓ cup sherry, 1 teaspoon instant coffee and a dash of dry mustard;
> dry mustard and small pieces of sautéed onion;
> chopped onions and diced frankfurters, to canned beans;
> 3 or 4 tablespoons of mustard sauce before baking;
> a few slices of pineapple, a teaspoon of molasses and brown sugar;
> yellow cheese and bacon curls, over canned baked beans before heating;
> horseradish and chopped onions.

> Add a carrot and a pinch of nutmeg or ginger (no salt) to water in which navy beans are boiled. Helps flavor and digestibility.

> After lentils are soaked, they will be double in bulk.

☐ BEETS: Bake beets in orange shells. Garnish with

juice from orange with two teaspoons of sugar and melted butter.

> Beets can be pan-fried, as potatoes can.

> Top cooked beets with a little vinegar and sour cream.

> Hollow out small or medium-sized cooked beets and fill with drained bottled grated horseradish mixed with a little sour cream. Serve with cold beer.

> Always use small, young beets. Cook with skins on and a little of the stem remaining—retains flavor. They usually take about 40 minutes, in salted water, to cook. Drain and cover with cold water. Reheat after removing skins.

☐ BROCCOLI: Try a sprinkling of crab meat atop broccoli.

> Simmer cooked broccoli in olive oil with anchovies.

> Top broccoli with 2 tablespoons of lemon juice stirred with a dash of paprika into ½ cup of mayonnaise.

> Top broccoli with a poached egg.

> Serve tuna in cheese sauce over broccoli (or asparagus).

☐ BRUSSELS SPROUTS: Pour a cup of sour cream with one sautéed chopped onion over cooked brussels sprouts.

> Top cold cooked brussels sprouts with French dressing.

☐ CABBAGE: Sprinkle toasted sesame seeds over creamed green cabbage.

> Before boiling cabbage, soak in pan of salt water to remove any hidden insects.

> Sauté shredded cabbage in seasoned butter.

> Just before the cabbage is done cooking, stir in chunks of cream cheese until melted.

> Cook shredded red cabbage with grated onion in equal

parts of water and vinegar, seasoned with sugar, salt and pepper.

> To retain fine color of red cabbage, add lemon juice or a tart apple.

> Add a cut-up small stalk of celery when cooking cabbage and there will be no odor. . . . Or, add ½ glass of milk and ½ slice of bread to vegetable while cooking. . . . Or, drop 2 English walnuts (uncracked) into the pot. . . . Presoaking cabbage in cold, salted water for 20 minutes also helps cut odor. . . . A pinch of baking soda in the cooking water will cut down odor while also helping to retain the color of green cabbage.

☐ C A R R O T S : Cut carrots into strips and cook until tender. Dip into beaten eggs and bread crumbs and fry in butter.

> Glaze carrots with orange marmalade.

> To keep carrots crisp, add a little sugar to the cooking water—1 teaspoon of sugar to each 3 cups of water.

> Season cooked carrots with a little sugar or honey, grated orange rind and orange juice.

> Peel and julienne young carrots. Braise slowly in butter until tender. Add ¼ teaspoon salt and 1 cup sour cream. Stir gently and serve topped with chopped chives.

> Boil fresh carrots with chopped onion and top with sour cream.

> Top sweet carrots with a hint of brown sugar and chopped peanuts.

> Boil carrots in ½ water and ½ pineapple juice.

> Mix peas and carrots thoroughly with melted cheese.

> Slice carrots thin, lengthwise, and drop in ice water, and they will curl.

> To retain color and add extra sweetness to carrots, whether boiled whole or sliced, let the water cook completely away, then add a little butter and cook for about a minute

longer, turning the carrots in the butter. Watch constantly to keep them from burning.

☐ CAULIFLOWER: Mix raisins with either raw or cooked cauliflower.

> Heat a can of condensed cheddar cheese soup with ¼ cup of milk and pour over cauliflower.

> Cover raw cauliflower with sliced American cheese, butter, and tomato sauce; bake in casserole for 20 minutes.

☐ COMBINATION DISHES: Marinate cooked or canned vegetables in Italian or clear French dressing for several hours, drain and serve.

> Sauté together onions and zucchini; sprinkle thyme and grated Parmesan cheese over them.

> Steam onions and peas; mix in hot cream sauce flavored with cloves.

> Sauté cooked peas and mushrooms in butter; season with grated American cheese.

> For deep-fried vegetables, such as celery or artichokes, add Parmesan cheese to beaten egg in which vegetables are turned before frying.

> Sauté thinly sliced carrot and onion together.

> Cream potatoes with a small amount of diced leftover cooked ham.

> Try dipping tomatoes, eggplant and such in leftover waffle batter; sauté lightly.

> Add parboiled small white onions, diced carrots and turnips to shoulder of lamb that is roasting.

> Sauté onions and serve with string beans.

> Mix mayonnaise with chopped green peppers, onions and a dash of vinegar. Serve with fish.

> Stir sliced pimento-stuffed olives into creamed onions.

☐ C O R N : With frozen or canned corn kernels, mix chopped onion, a can of condensed mushroom soup, sour cream and a little curry; cover with Swiss or American cheese and bake. (Great the next day!)

> Add small pieces of chicken to kernel corn.

> Make succotash with corn, wax beans and green beans plus the usual lima beans.

> Wrap strips of bacon around freshly boiled corn and place in broiler for a few minutes.

> Wrap a slice of bacon around corn fritters before frying.

> Stir sliced pimento-stuffed olives into buttered whole-kernel corn just before serving. Adds color and flavor.

> Roast corn on the cob by first boiling the corn for 15 minutes and then placing in frying pan with sizzling butter for 5 minutes, rolling it gently.

> Drain canned whole corn and heat with canned stewed tomatoes. Goes well with hamburgers.

> Corn on the cob butters best and easiest with a dab of butter on a crust of bread.

> When cooking corn on the cob, use tightly covered pot and put in only 2 inches of cold water and 2 tablespoons sugar. Don't add salt, as it draws the milk from corn.

☐ C U C U M B E R S : Soak cucumbers in beet juice for a salad garnish. In about 30 minutes the meat will turn pink, but the seeds will remain green.

> Cut cucumbers into small bits and stir-fry in garlic butter; add to baked potatoes.

> Always peel cucumbers, no matter how clean they appear. The skins have probably been waxed.

☐ E G G P L A N T : Spread thinly sliced eggplant on both sides with mayonnaise and then quickly broil.

> Fry eggplant until brown on each side and serve with grated Romano cheese.

> To boiled cubed eggplant, add cooked shell noodles and let simmer for a few minutes with oil and garlic; then top with grated cheese.

> Add vinegar, oil, bay leaf and garlic to cold cooked eggplant.

☐ STORAGE / FROZEN VEGETABLES: Peas and lima beans should be stored in the pod and corn in the husk to preserve full food value and prevent shriveling.

> Do not freeze lettuce, celery, raw tomatoes or carrots. They lose crispness when frozen.

> Green vegetables will keep for a longer time if kept continuously in the refrigerator. Do not leave them at room temperature for any period of time.

> Store onions in refrigerator. This prevents their sprouting, and a chilled onion won't make you cry as you cut it.

> Keep sliced eggplant in the refrigerator for two hours before frying, and it will not absorb too much oil.

> After cutting vegetables, store them in water until ready to cook. This maintains their original fresh color to give a brighter appearance when served.

> The tops of carrots, beets, turnips and parsnips should be cut off before the vegetables are stored. The tops draw the moisture and food value from the roots, leaving them wilted and limp.

> If you like kale, remember that kale flavor is improved by freezing.

☐ MUSHROOMS: Add a little lemon juice when sautéing mushrooms.

> Brown mushrooms in olive oil, and allow to marinate overnight in French dressing plus garlic.

> Place 6 mushrooms in aluminum foil, butter season with tarragon, fold foil and broil 8 minutes.

> Dip mushroom caps in a mixture of lemon juice and butter before broiling with steak.

> Cook mushrooms in onion soup.

> Fresh mushrooms require no peeling. Just wipe with damp cloth.

> Keep mushrooms white while cooking by dipping them in boiling water for just a few seconds. (Or squeeze ½ lemon over them when frying.)

> Soak mushrooms in cold water until soft; gently squeeze them dry. Makes them easier to clean and much tastier.

☐ O N I O N S : Soak soda crackers in water, then squeeze water from them. Add sautéed onions, pepper and salt, and stir in a couple of eggs. Let whole mixture bake for about 30 minutes.

> Remove centers of boiled onions. Chop centers and add diced cooked beef, moistening with mushroom sauce. Fill onions with mixture and bake.

> Place large raw onions, in their skins, in a baking tin and bake in moderate oven for 2 hours. Serve with butter and salt.

> French-fry onion rings in deep fat after soaking them for 30 minutes in buttermilk. Salvage the buttermilk, because it makes a delicious onion soup.

> For another way to make French-fried onion rings, soak thin slices in milk for an hour, then dip in flour and beaten egg and fry.

> Add a few drops of mustard to oil in which the onions are French-fried.

> Pan-fry scallions instead of the usual onions as an ac-companiment to liver. Cut scallions in short lengths, add green peppers and celery strips and sauté in butter until vege-tables are tender.

> When frying onions, pour a little cream over them before flouring. Gives them a tasty crust.

> Onions will brown faster if fried with paprika.

> Fry onions and add a few slices of bacon. Drain fat when bacon is crisp, and continue frying the onions.

> Old-fashioned sautéed onions may be cooked with steak, and they can also be fried in 1 part olive oil to 2 parts butter.

> Sauté onions in butter and add seasoning and vermouth; steam until golden.

> Heat cooked dried apricot halves with sautéed onion rings and serve with broiled chicken.

> Impale a piece of bread on the end of knife while peeling; it absorbs onion fumes.

> Instead of cold water, place onions in hot water before peeling. This not only reduces the irritating odor but also loosens the outer skins so that they peel off.

> When peeling an onion, slice off both ends. Then cut through the skin down one side of the onion and it will come off in one piece.

> Don't peel onions that are to be boiled. The skin helps keep flavor and food value from dissolving into water. After boiling, the skin is easily removed.

> One teaspoon onion powder equals ⅓ medium white onion.

> One teaspoon onion salt equals ⅐ medium onion. (When using this amount in recipe, decrease other salt called for by ½ teaspoon.)

> A secret ingredient in cooking is a vegetable called a shallot, a cross between an onion and garlic. It enhances gravies, meats, fish, etc.

> One tablespoon of instant minced onion is equivalent in flavor and seasoning to a medium-sized raw onion. Use this pleasant seasoner to give full onion flavor to meat dishes, vegetables, soups and salads.

> When using raw onions in a salad, cut them up the day before and put them in the refrigerator. Most of the sharpness will be gone and the salad will be much smoother.

> To cut extra-thin slices of onion which will hold together, simply leave the skin on the onion while cutting. The skin will then peel off easily without disturbing onion rings.

> The cooking onion is best when of average size. The large thin-skinned Bermudas, or onions from Idaho, are ideal for salads and for topping hamburgers.

> Ream a hole through the center of onion with a skewer before cooking and it will remain whole.

> If only half an onion is needed in cooking, save the root half—it will last longer.

☐ PARSLEY: Parsley will chop finer and be fresher-tasting if a little salt is added to leaves.

> Keep parsley fresh and pungent in a refrigerator by washing and storing in a tightly covered jar.

> Parsley washed in hot water keeps flavor better and is easier to chop than if washed in cold water.

> Use every sprig in a bunch of parsley. It's nature's own antidote for onion breath.

☐ PEAS: Pour melted American or Swiss cheese over peas and dot with chopped onion.

> Add crumbled blue cheese and a little celery seed to melted butter and pour over hot peas.

> For a side dish, stir a little mint jelly into cooked green peas.

> Instead of using sugar to sweeten peas, cook them with a few empty pea pods.

☐ SAUERKRAUT: Give flavor by slicing half a green apple into sauerkraut and adding a tablespoon of brown sugar.

> Add a pinch of caraway seeds and ¼ teaspoon of mus-

tard. (Caraway seeds act as an antacid.) A couple of teaspoons of caraway is about right for a 1-pound can of sauerkraut.

> Add a little red or white wine to skillet or oven-cooked sauerkraut.

☐ SPINACH : For extra-creamy creamed spinach, blend in cream cheese.

> Top cooked spinach with ground sesame seeds, soy sauce and oil.

> Combine chopped scallions and boiled rice with spinach.

> Mince some onions very fine and sauté in pan until done. Remove from fire and mix with creamed spinach; allow to simmer for a while.

> Top creamed spinach with sour cream and sliced hard-boiled eggs.

> Make creamed spinach and add bacon strips and pieces of garlic.

> Mix chopped spinach with sweet potatoes. Makes a tempting vegetable for kiddies.

> Add 1 undiluted can of cream-of-mushroom soup to spinach in last minutes of cooking.

> Mix creamed spinach thoroughly with whipped potatoes.

> Clean sandy spinach by soaking it in water with a little vinegar. It may also be soaked in salt water to clean.

> Cook fresh spinach without additional water. Just the water clinging to leaves after washing is sufficient.

☐ SQUASH : Top mashed squash with marshmallows and heat in the manner of candied yams.

> Top cubed squash with pineapple bits.

> Cook diced squash with a bit of brown sugar.

> Add white raisins to mashed hot squash; sprinkle with grated lemon peel.

> Salt zucchini 15 minutes before frying.

> Boil zucchini with onions, oil and garlic. Simmer for 15 minutes.

> Squash tastes great if the seeds and string portions are removed and the inside stuffed with cut-up strips of bacon. Place in baking dish and cook in hot oven.

> After it has been salted, simmer squash in as little water as possible for about 5 minutes.

> Slice zucchini in thin strips, toss in flour and deep-fry for shoestring zucchini.

☐ STRING BEANS: Add shredded orange rind to string beans as they are cooking.

> Add chopped pepper and canned pimento to buttered beans.

> Combine green beans with mushrooms sautéed in butter.

> For a nutlike flavor, crumble a few cheese crackers and stir into hot buttered string beans before serving.

> Add bacon strips, 1 teaspoon of sugar and ½ teaspoon of vinegar to beans while cooking.

> Mix sour cream with beef broth and pour over cooked green beans.

☐ TOMATOES: Try a touch of sugar instead of salt on sliced tomatoes.

> Stuff tomatoes with cheddar cheese and bake.

> Top tomatoes with grated cheddar cheese and black pepper.

> Brush tomatoes with French dressing before broiling them.

> Dust bread crumbs atop tomato halves brushed with butter; broil until brown.

> Slice a tomato, add some garlic butter and bake for 10 minutes.

> Stuff tomatoes with cheddar cheese, chips of crisp bacon and some of the tomato pulp. Top with more bacon and cheese; pop into the broiler.

> Frying tomatoes: First dip the slices (about ½ inch thick) in flour seasoned with salt, pepper and paprika.

> Cover broiled tomatoes with hollandaise sauce.

> To peel tomatoes the easy way, dip each one in boiling water for 1 minute, then in cold water; the skins will slip off without the use of a paring knife.

> When peeling tomatoes for crisp spring salad, plunge them into boiling water in a strainer. That way you can remove them without burning fingers or bruising tomatoes.

> Thicken stewed tomatoes, or a tomato sauce, with cornstarch instead of flour.

> Tomatoes stewed in sugared water have the flavor intensified and acid taste modified.

☐ WASHING: Do not soak fresh vegetables or salad greens in water for any great length of time. Soaking dissolves the minerals and reduces the vitamin content.

> Wash vegetables such as asparagus and broccoli in warm water first. It helps relax the head and loosen the sand.

☐ AND A LOT OF OTHER THINGS: Serve cooked celery with heated crushed pineapple.

> Pour vinaigrette sauce over cooked celery and serve.

> When endives are cooked, a dash of lemon and a pinch of sugar are double assets. The lemon keeps the endives white; the sugar guards against a too-bitter taste.

> Sauté escarole in olive oil and sprinkle with almond slivers.

> Relish: cut raw white turnips into thin slivers and sprinkle with salt and a tablespoon of olive oil.

> Parsnips: Heat pared, sliced cooked parsnips with brown sugar, butter, grated orange rind and a little orange juice.

> When boiling vegetables, use 1 teaspoon of salt for each quart of water.

> Canned vegetables are greatly improved when cooked in their own liquid, to which a pinch of marjoram or savory is added, then strained and heated in butter sauce.

> Mix a couple of tablespoons of mayonnaise into cooked vegetables just before serving.

> Use sour cream as a garnish for cooked fresh vegetables.

> Wilted greens can be restored to freshness by wrapping in paper towels dampened with cold water. Pop them into refrigerator until needed.

> Use a large, smooth tile as a chopping block for vegetables. It's easy to wipe clean, with no leftover smells.

> Preserve the look of vegetables by testing doneness with a toothpick rather than with a knife or fork.

> If vegetables are started to cook in cold water, considerable ascorbic acid may be destroyed before water begins to boil. Always add vegetables after the water is boiling.

> Salt added to green vegetables is more than a matter of taste. It preserves the natural color and flavor.

> When buying artichokes, look for bright green heads, firm base and tight leaves. Try to select ones without black or brown blemishes.

> When cooking green vegetables, lift the saucepan cover occasionally. It will help preserve the green color.

GENERAL INDEX

INDEX TO FOOD SECTION